Shared Cities Atlas

Shared Citi
Post-Social
Active Citiz
Central
Europe

Helena Doudová (ed.)
nai010 publishers

s Atlas.
t Cities and
nship in
Belgrade
Berlin
Bratislava
Budapest
Katowice
Prague
Warsaw

Shared Cities Atlas

Contents

It was in June 2016 that *Shared Cities: Creative Momentum* (SCCM) brought together eleven organizations from Belgrade, Berlin, Bratislava, Budapest, Katowice, Prague, and Warsaw, to create a space for architecture, art, urbanism and sharing, and to contribute to the transformation of urban life.

Since then, more than 300 activities have taken place across the Central European region: public discussions, street celebrations, festivals, exhibitions and artist residencies—with the goal to show urban citizens that their participation and actions not only matter, but that they are essential in the process of making cities a better place to live.

After four busy years, we are thrilled to present the *Shared Cities Atlas*. Showcasing our outcomes, it can be used as a toolkit of best practices developed in collaboration by eleven partners across the project's seven cities. The *Atlas* captures the trends of the sharing phenomenon in the Central European region through analysis of ideas as well as through infographics, and diagrams.

Finally, the *Shared Cities Atlas* presents an emerging generation of urban actors—a vibrant contemporary network active in today's Central European cities, reflecting the transitory situation rooted in the region's socialist past.

I hope you enjoy the journey through the Shared Cities as much as we did!

Johannes Ebert, Secretary General Goethe-Institut e.V.

The *Shared Cities Atlas* applies the new, global 'sharing paradigm' in architecture and public sphere to a site-specific situation in seven cities in Central Europe. The *Atlas* maps current practices of sharing and new fields of action in case studies, and contextualizes the phenomenon in research papers, data, and photography.

Ideas such as a 'right' to the city, common resources, urban commons—all of which are in vogue in contemporary architectural discourse—illustrate the paradigm shift towards a sharing perspective. Duncan McLaren and Julian Agyeman point out that in sharing cities the emphasis lies in the right to *remake* the cities as a form of urban social contract with a specific creative or critical agenda.[1] The *Atlas* presents creative forms of sharing driven by idealistic positions and collective actions—new approaches to sharing of spaces and architecture, experience and knowledge, data, or collective histories.

Thirty years after the Fall of the Berlin Wall, the region of Central Europe[2] still represents a blind spot on the map of Europe. The *Atlas* highlights the historical shift, or the specific and shared historical condition of the socialist (now post-socialist) cities from former East Berlin to Belgrade that have faced a system transition over the past 30 years. The essays frame the subject in terms of socialist and post-socialist space (D. Crowley); identify the ambiguous physical transformation of iconic late-modern and brutalist architectures into 'iconic ruins' and formulate strategies for their renewal (M. Mitášová, M. Zervan); describe contemporary urban public spaces going through a thorny process of instability and neglect (I. Kucina); all in the face of a system transition from socialism to a newly established market economy. The various facets of urban landscapes have been captured in city-specific photography-essays by Olja Triaška Stefanović.

Action, as theorized by Hannah Arendt, is a condition of plurality inherent to humans; human activities define the public realm and common (shared) world itself. For Arendt, 'to live together in the world means essentially that a world of things is between those who have it in common, as a table is located between those who sit around it; the world, like every in-between, relates and separates men at the same time.'[3] The activist, engaged approach is the common denominator uniting the authors of the case studies in the *Atlas*—independent NGOs, experts in architecture and urban planning, collectives, and artists. They recognize the inherent inner tension in sharing, between proximity and collectivity, the need to divide, negotiate and act over a shared world. The negotiation process materialized in the physical setting of a table and a stage in case studies *Urban Hub – Plato, Foyer*[2], *360° Podium* and in further case studies dealing with urban furniture and public squares.

The extensive data collection from the seven cities by Medialab Katowice resulted in three types of data documentation and

1
For a specific definition of the 'sharing paradigm' and the variety of ways and categories of sharing 'things', 'services' and 'activities', of its tangible and intangible dimension see D. McLaren, J. Agyeman, *Sharing Cities. A Case for Truly Smart and Sustainable Cities* (Cambridge: MIT, 2015), 3, 7–8.

2
The term 'Central Europe' is used in the publication to designate the region including Germany, Czech Republic, Poland, Hungary, Slovakia usually called 'Central and Eastern Europe', 'East Central Europe' and 'South-East Europe' in case of Serbia. The umbrella term 'Central Europe' relates to the historical identification of the newly-established states after 1918, as well as the new geographical realities after the accession of the Central European states to the EU in 2004 (with the exception of Serbia).

3
Hannah Arendt, *The Human Condition* (Chicago: University of Chicago Press, 2nd edition 1998), 52.

visualization: data-trends, city profiles, and data-stories. The data-trends and city profiles are based on a data-matrix of population, economic, spatial, and urban data that strive to create an international inter-city comparison of the living conditions in these cities and abroad. The data-stories are data-driven investigations of specific aspects of urban life. *Shared Cities Atlas* pays tribute to Otto Neurath, a pioneer in data collection and visualization, to his 'Bildstatistik' method and the Isotype communication system, aiming to provide visual, statistical and spatial comparisons of global trends. The 'City as Interface' (P. Mörtenböck, H. Mooshammer), the sharing of data and information and the aspects of digital platforms and networks, along with the intertwined digital and physical urban realms are critical points of interest in the book.

Trends in Central Europ in Data

What do data have to say about the quality of life in Central Europe?

From Berlin to Belgrade, the *Shared Cities Atlas* research has collected dozens of charts and maps to show the basic statistics on the quality of life in Central European locations. Because the idea that data can objectively capture the character of different cities remains contested, the *Data Trends* deliberately avoid giving ready-made answers, and instead encourage readers to ask critical questions about demography, mobility, spatial development, economy or costs of living.

The process of searching and compiling data was not an obvious one, if only for the great diversity of the cities studied. For instance, Berlin is more affluent than any other city covered by the study, Belgrade is located outside the European Union, and Katowice is not a capital. In some cases, the collected data refers to cities; in others, to larger metropolitan regions. In addition, Amsterdam, Athens and London serve as useful benchmarks against which we measure some of the recent trends. Also, the research processed data from different time points.

The process of collecting data was extremely time-consuming, requiring the use of a considerable number of sources, e.g.: Eurostat, OECD databases, statistical yearbooks of individual cities, and the Numbeo online database. For the curious reader, a detailed list is provided at the end of the publication, complete with links to online content.

: Shared Cities

A.01

Population
(millions of inhab.)

Countries
2016 (Serbia)
2017 (other countries)

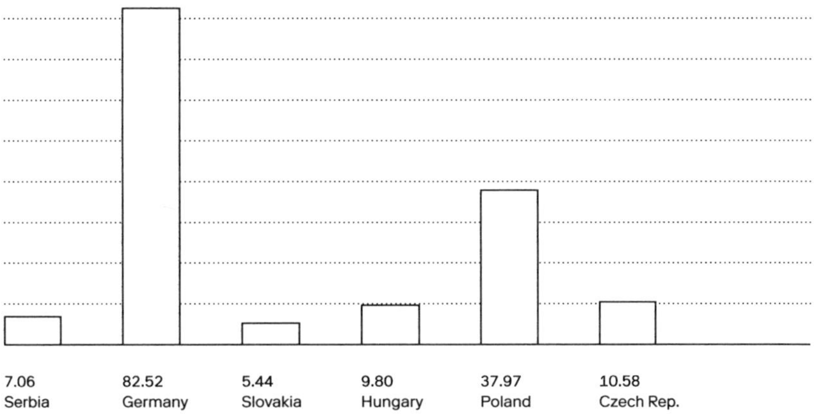

A.02

Population
(millions of inhab.)

Metropolitan regions
2016 (Belgrade)
2017 (other regions)

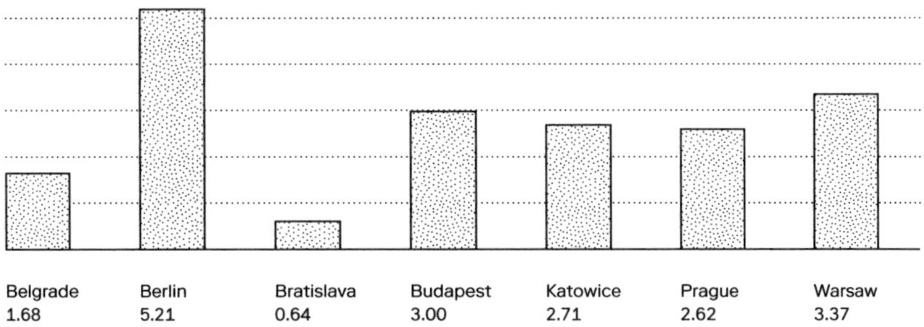

A.03

Population
(millions of inhab.)

Cities
2016

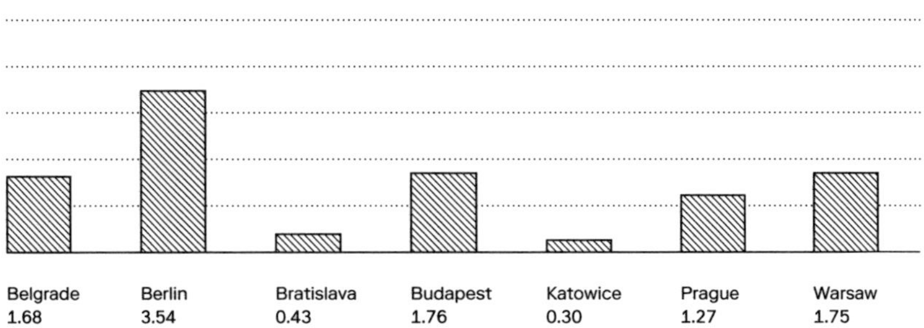

Situation

Netherlands
Berlin
Belgium
Germany
Luxembourg
Prague
Czech Republic
France
Austria
Switzerland
Liechtenstein
Slovenia
Italy
San Marino

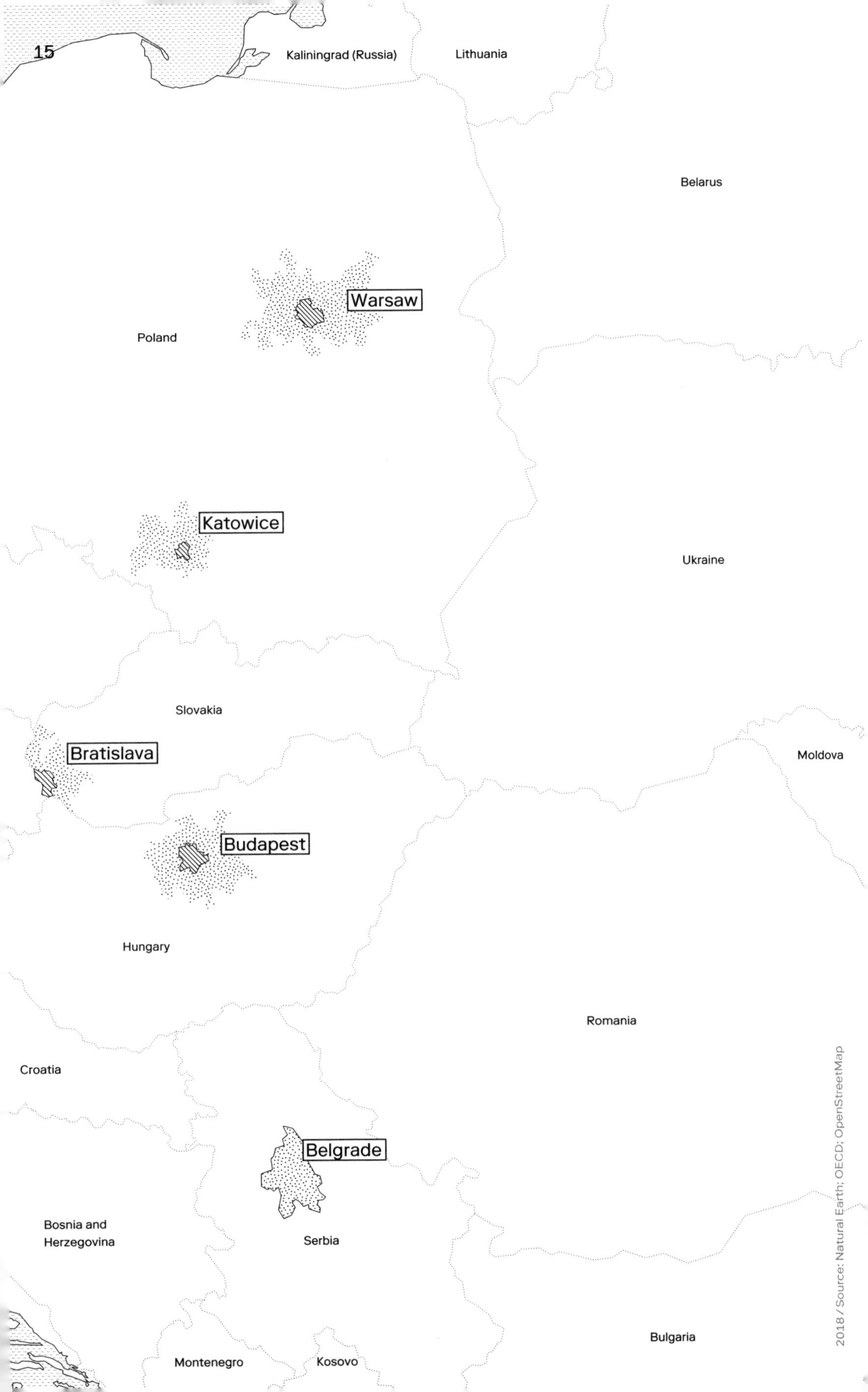

2018 / Source: Natural Earth; OECD; OpenStreetMap

Population and Society

B.01

Population
(millions of inhab.)

2016 (metropolitan regions)
2016 (Belgrade)
2017 (other cities)

City

Metropolitan region

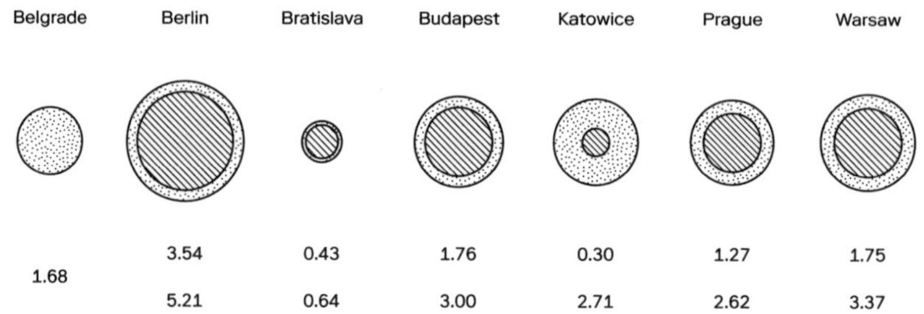

B.02

Population as a share
of national population
(per cent)

Metropolitan regions
2017

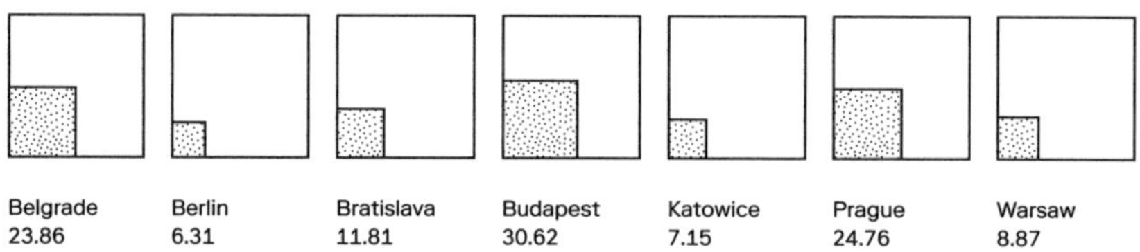

B.03

Population projection
(per cent of population)

Metropolitan regions
2016–2050

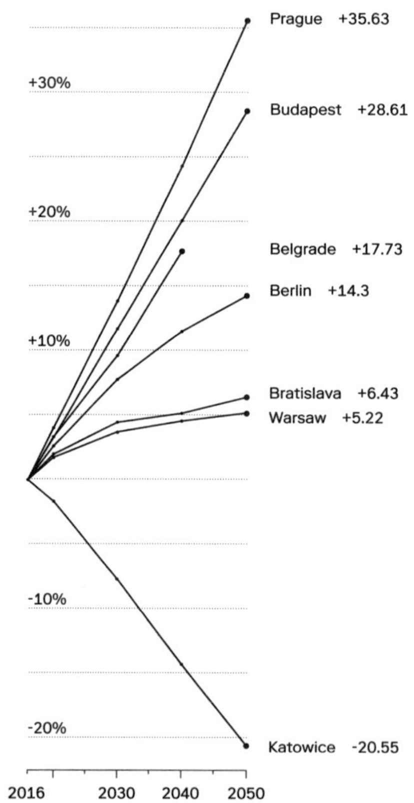

B.04

Population projection
(per cent of population)

Countries
2015–2050

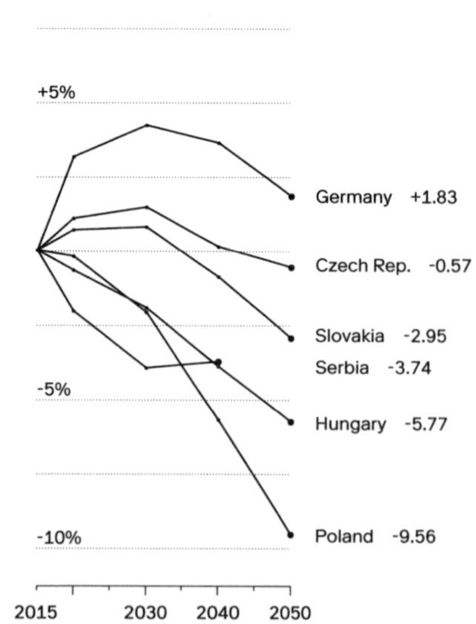

B.05

Old-age-dependency (Number of working age people [15–64]/one post-working age person [65+])

Metropolitan regions 2020–2050

The old-age-dependency ratio is traditionally viewed as an indication of the level of support available to seniors (those aged 65 or over) by the working age population (those aged 15 to 64), and as such is a useful barometer of our ageing populations.

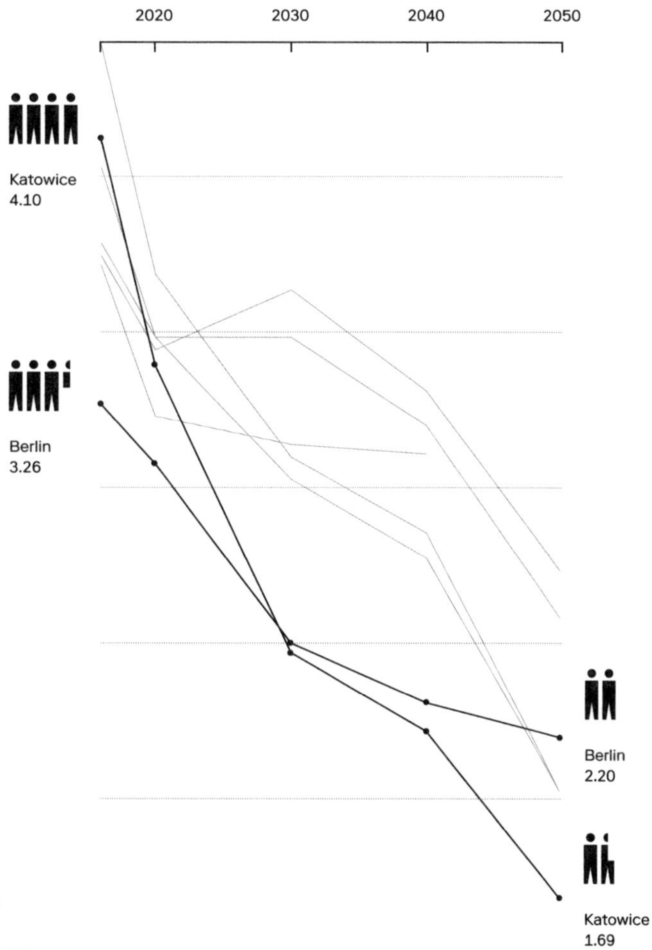

Belgrade
2016–2040 -0.60

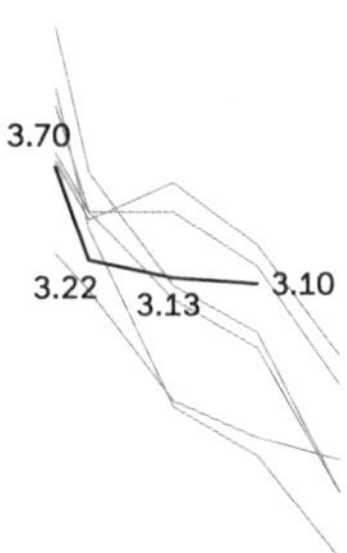

Berlin
2016–2050 -1.06

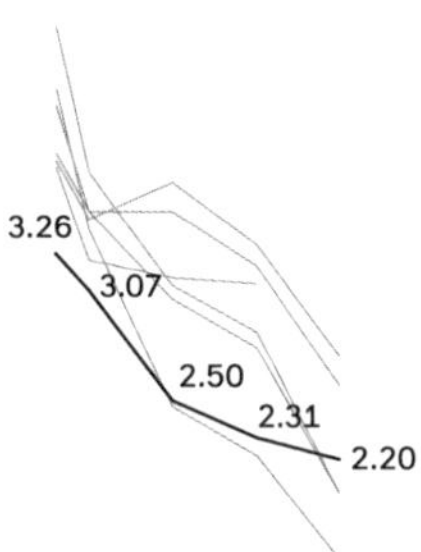

Bratislava
2016–2050 -2.38

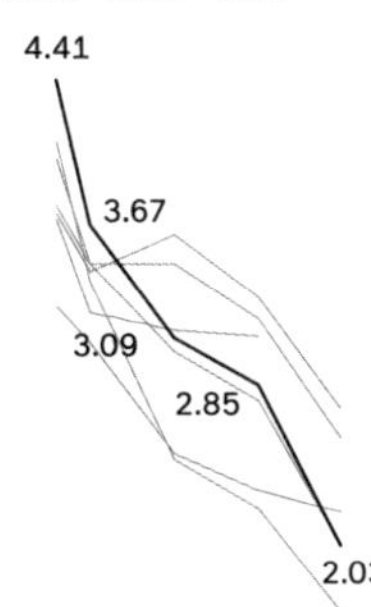

Budapest
2016–2050 -1.00

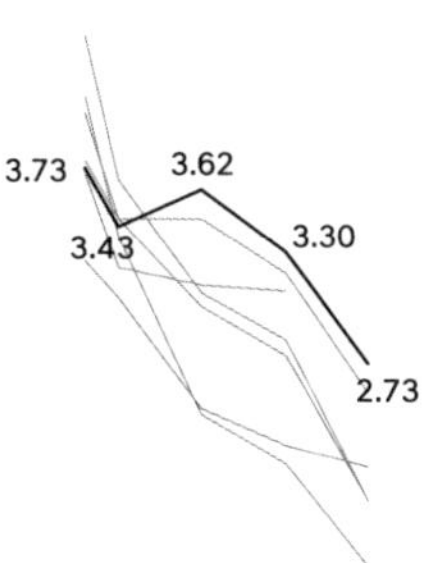

Katowice
2016–2050 -2.41

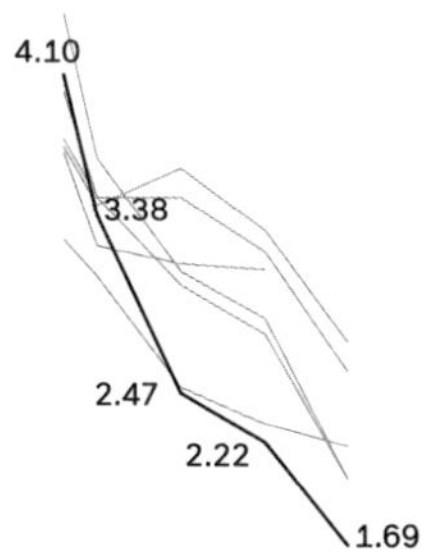

Prague
2016–2050 -1.19

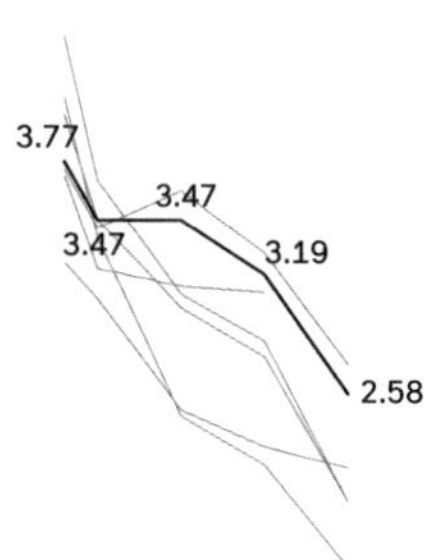

Warsaw
2016–2050 -1.98

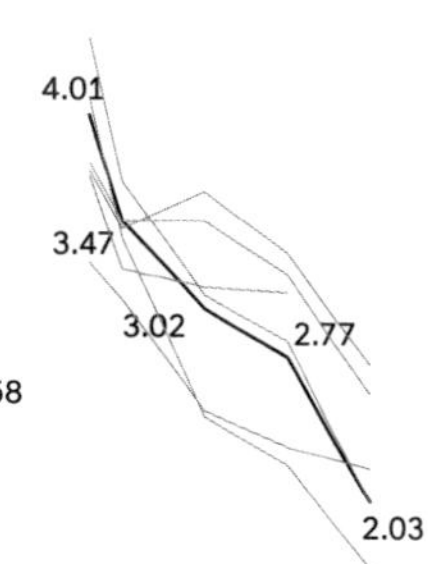

B.06

Population aged 65+ (per cent)

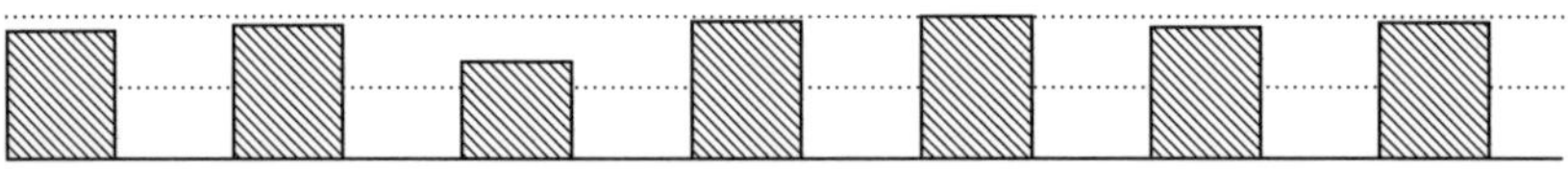

Cities 2016	Belgrade	Berlin	Bratislava	Budapest	Katowice	Prague	Warsaw
	18.28	19.06	13.97	19.59	20.39	18.75	19.47

B.07

Population aged 0–14 (per cent)

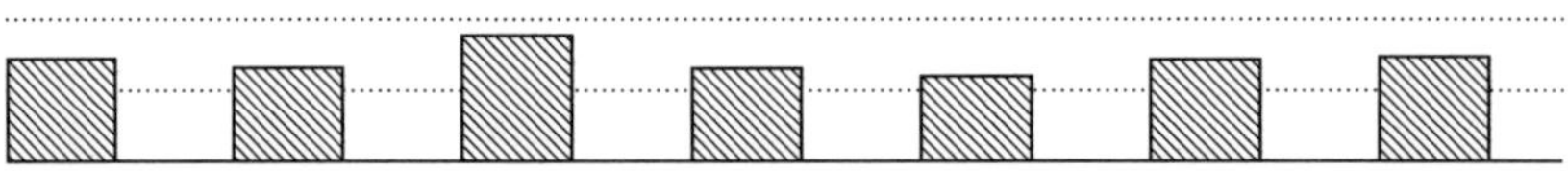

Cities 2016	Belgrade	Berlin	Bratislava	Budapest	Katowice	Prague	Warsaw
	14.81	13.60	18.08	13.49	12.37	14.70	15.10

B.08

Foreign-born population (per cent)

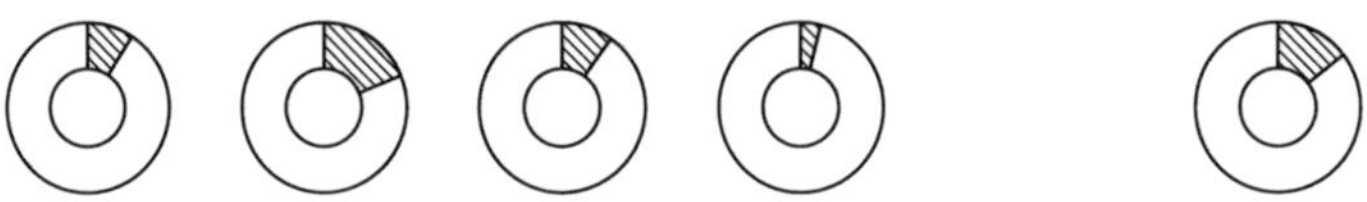

Cities 2016	Belgrade	Berlin	Bratislava	Budapest	Katowice	Prague	Warsaw
	9.3	19.1	10.1	4.1		14.5	

B.09

Local elections turnout (per cent)

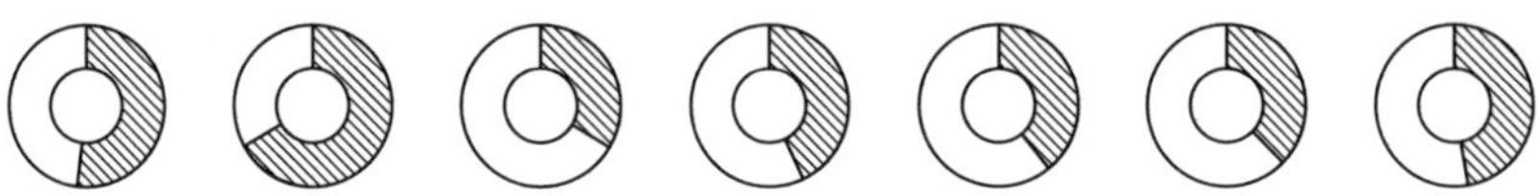

Cities 2016 (Belgrade, Berlin) 2014 (other cities)	Belgrade	Berlin	Bratislava	Budapest	Katowice	Prague	Warsaw
	52.02	66.9	33.79	43.1	39.27	37.72	47.24

B.10

Students

Cities
2017 (Katowice, Warsaw)
2016 (other cities)

	Belgrade	Berlin	Bratislava	Budapest	Katowice	Prague	Warsaw
(students/100 inhab.)	8.2	5.1	12.8	5.9	17.5	8.3	13.7
(total)	137,259	180,235	54,470	104,321	52,243	105,688	239,542

B.11

Graduates

Cities
2017 (Katowice, Warsaw)
2015 (Belgrade, Bratislava)
2016 (other cities)

	Belgrade	Berlin	Bratislava	Budapest	Katowice	Prague	Warsaw
(graduates/100 inhab.)	1.6	1.3	4.7	1.6	4.5	2.2	3.2
(total)	27,266	46,783	19,829	27,358	13,346	28,521	56,526

B.12

Museums

Cities
2017 (Katowice)
2015 (Berlin, Budapest)
2016 (other cities)

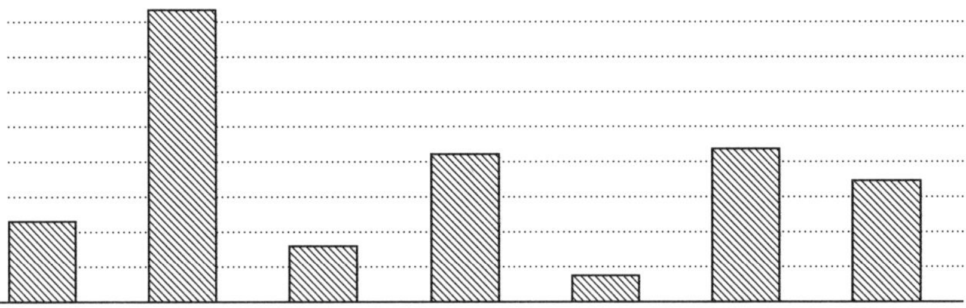

	Belgrade	Berlin	Bratislava	Budapest	Katowice	Prague	Warsaw
(number of museums)	47	167	33	85	16	88	70
(museums/100,000 inhab.)	2.8	4.7	7.7	4.8	5.4	6.9	4.0

■ = 1 museum

B.13

Theatres

Cities
2018 (Katowice)
2017 (Prague)
2015 (Budapest)
2016 (other cities)

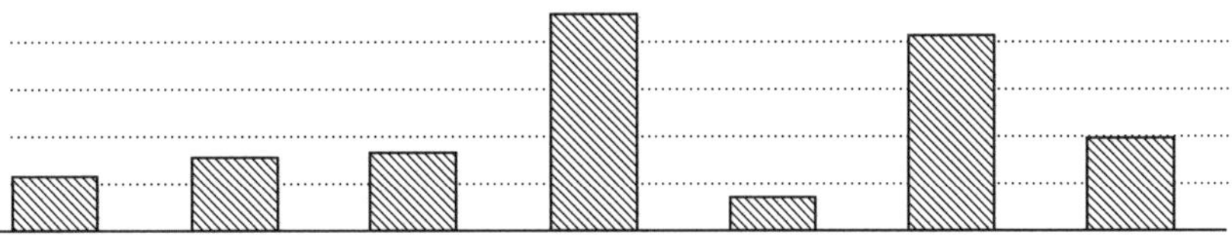

	Belgrade	Berlin	Bratislava	Budapest	Katowice	Prague	Warsaw
(number of theatres)	24	32	34	92	15	83	40
(theatres/100,000 inhab.)	1.4	0.9	8.0	5.2	5.0	6.5	2.3

■ = 1 theatre

B.14

Public libraries and book loans

Cities
2016

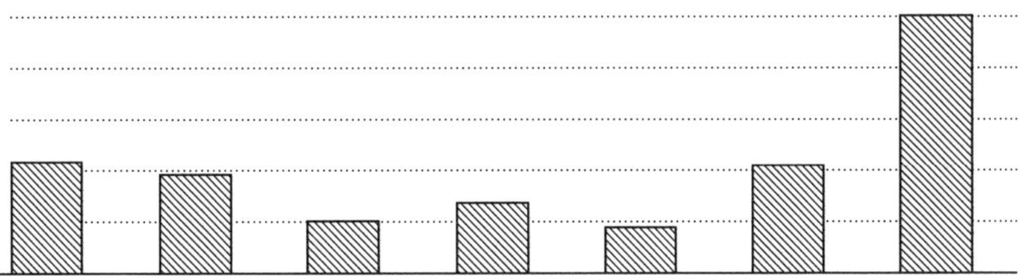

	Belgrade	Berlin	Bratislava	Budapest	Katowice	Prague	Warsaw
(number of public libraries)	88	78	42	56	37	85	201
(libraries/100,000 inhab.)	5.2	2.2	9.9	3.2	12.4	6.7	11.5
(book loans/inhab.)	1.2	5.9	4.0	2.1	4.5	5.6	3.5

■ = 1 library

■ = 1 book loan

Housing and Cost of L

C.01

Average household size (persons)

Cities
2011

Belgrade	Berlin	Bratislava	Budapest	Katowice	Prague	Warsaw
2.7	1.7	2.4	2.1	2.3	2.1	2.2

C.02

Proportion of 1-person households (per cent)

Cities
2011

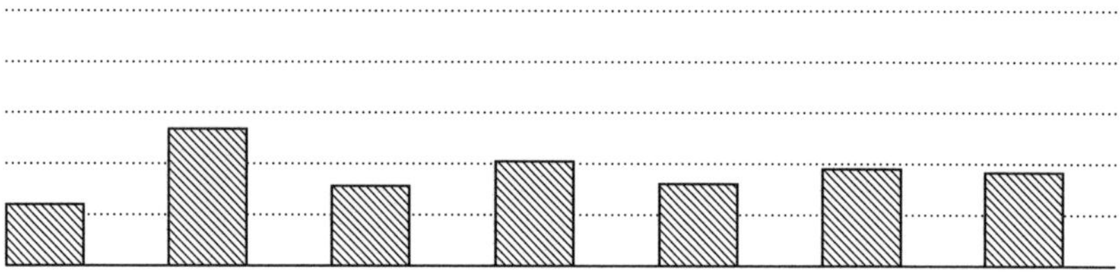

Belgrade	Berlin	Bratislava	Budapest	Katowice	Prague	Warsaw
24.6	53.9	31.8	41.4	32.7	38.5	37.1

C.03

Average area of living accommodation

Cities
2010 (Berlin)
2011 (other cities)

◆ = 5 m²

	Belgrade	Berlin	Bratislava	Budapest	Katowice	Prague	Warsaw
(m² per person)	24.48	45.00	26.10	34.55	26.60	22.08	29.40

C.04

Completed dwellings (number of dwellings)

Cities
2016

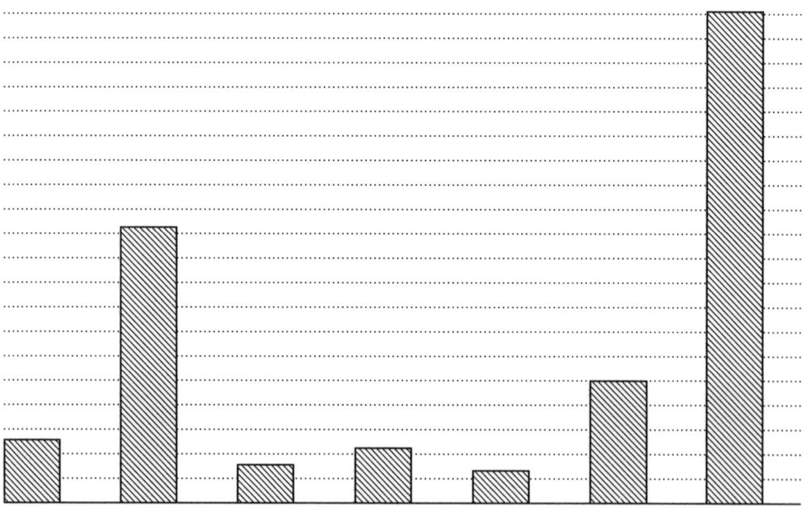

Belgrade	Berlin	Bratislava	Budapest	Katowice	Prague	Warsaw
3,167	13,659	1,952	2,777	1,675	6,092	20,119

ng

C.05

Housing costs

Cities
2018

■ = 500 €

	Belgrade	Berlin	Bratislava	Budapest	Katowice	Prague	Warsaw
Price/m² to buy apartment in city centre (EUR)	2,177.53	5,143.33	2,792.86	2,347.13	1,037.06	4,258.88	2,574.78

▨ = 100 €

	Belgrade	Berlin	Bratislava	Budapest	Katowice	Prague	Warsaw
Apartment rent (1 bedroom) in city centre (EUR)	314.90	795.64	581.75	421.18	317.35	640.86	541.98

▨ = 100 €

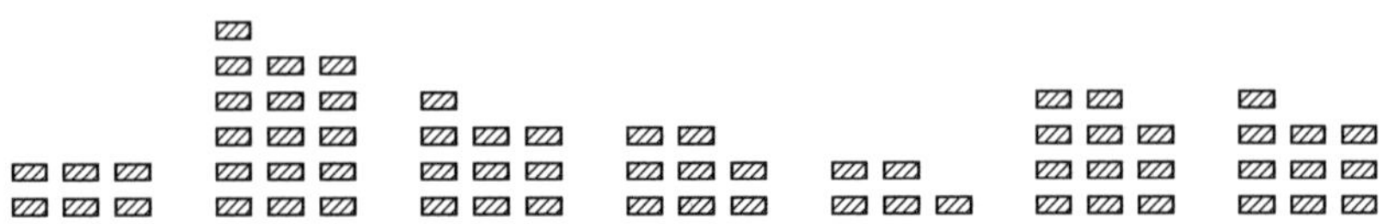

	Belgrade	Berlin	Bratislava	Budapest	Katowice	Prague	Warsaw
Apartment rent (3 bedrooms) in city centre (EUR)	600.25	1,560.96	1,031.67	766.46	491.88	1,116.20	958.62

C.06

Rent index

Cities
2018

The rent index is an estimation of housing rental rates in a city compared to New York City. A rent index of e.g. 80 means that rental rates are on average 20% cheaper than in NYC.

Belgrade	Berlin	Bratislava	Budapest	Katowice	Prague	Warsaw
12.55	33.32	23.55	17.95	12.75	25.89	22.67

C.07

Property price-to-income ratio

Cities
2018

The Property price-to-income ratio is the basic measure of housing purchase affordability (lower is better), which is calculated as the ratio of median house prices to median family disposable income.

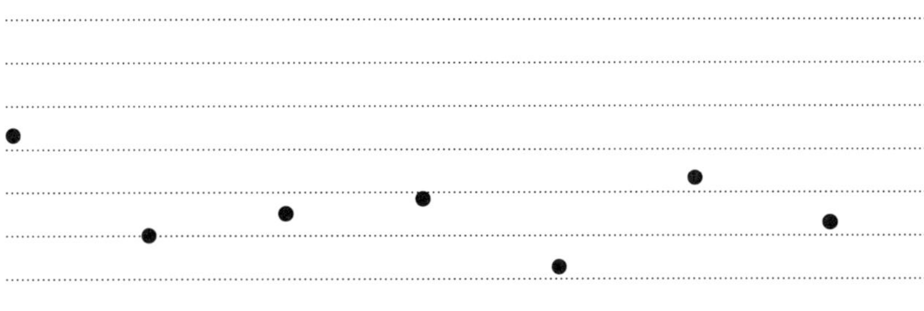

Belgrade	Berlin	Bratislava	Budapest	Katowice	Prague	Warsaw
21.71	10.12	12.62	14.32	6.45	16.74	11.58

C.08

Average monthly net salary

Cities 2018

▨ = 100 €

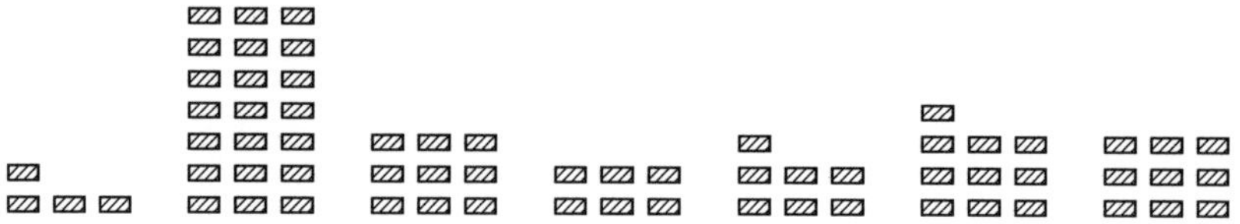

(EUR)	Belgrade	Berlin	Bratislava	Budapest	Katowice	Prague	Warsaw
	395.98	2,067.22	944.78	638.33	708.62	1,033.23	885.68

C.09

Local purchasing power index

Cities 2018

The local purchasing power index shows the relative purchasing power for goods and services in a given city for the average local wage. A local purchasing power of 40 means that averagely-waged residents can typically afford to buy 60% less goods and services than their counterparts in New York City.

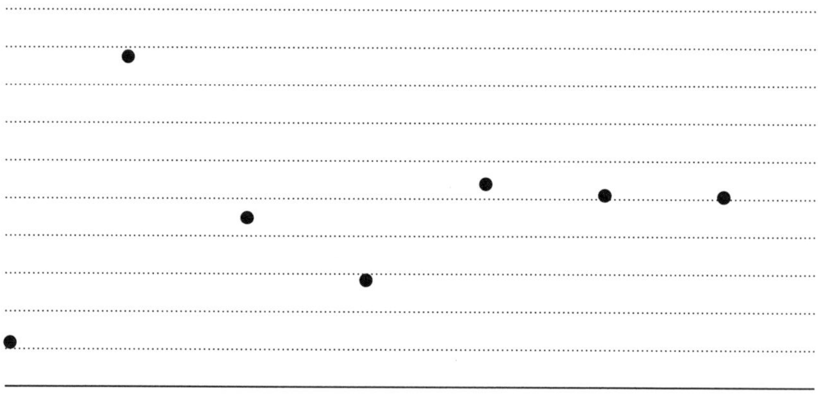

Belgrade	Berlin	Bratislava	Budapest	Katowice	Prague	Warsaw
41.75	117.58	74.94	58.40	84.00	81.09	80.67

C.10

Prices

Cities 2018

○ = 0.10 €; ● = 5 €; ⊘ = 0.50 €

	Belgrade	Berlin	Bratislava	Budapest	Katowice	Prague	Warsaw
1 min. of prepaid pay-as-you-go SIM plan (no discounts)	0.10	0.09	0.09	0.09	0.05	0.13	0.05
Internet (60 Mbps or more, unlimited data, cable/ADSL)	20.46	31.09	16.85	13.38	12.16	18.49	12.80
Three-course meal for two, mid-range restaurant	25.49	41.00	30.00	27.29	22.84	26.95	27.41
Domestic beer (0.5 liter draught)	1.53	3.50	1.75	1.51	1.54	1.35	2.17

C.11

Restaurant price index and groceries index

Cities
2018

The restaurant price index is a comparison of meal and drink prices in restaurants and cafés/bistros compared to New York City.
The groceries index is an estimation of grocery prices in a given city compared to New York City.

● Restaurant price index
○ Groceries index

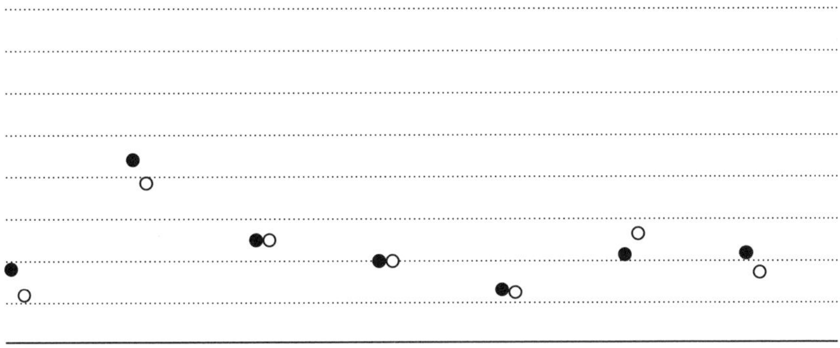

	Belgrade	Berlin	Bratislava	Budapest	Katowice	Prague	Warsaw
●	38.09	64.48	45.18	39.81	33.46	41.47	42.07
○	32.02	58.39	46.39	40.07	32.66	46.04	37.53

C.12

Cost of living index

Cities
2018

The cost of living index (excluding rent or mortgage) is a relative indicator of consumer goods prices, including groceries, restaurants, transportation and utilities.
A city with a cost of living index of 120 is estimated to be 20% more expensive than New York City.

● Cost of living index
○ Cost of living index + Rent index

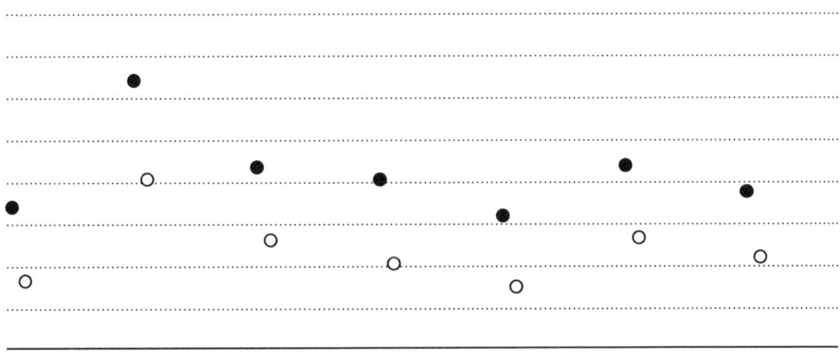

	Belgrade	Berlin	Bratislava	Budapest	Katowice	Prague	Warsaw
●	43.97	74.11	53.93	50.64	41.91	53.91	47.62
○	26.58	50.65	36.16	30.63	25.11	36.59	32.04

C.13

Quality of life index

Cities
2018

The quality of life index (higher is better) is an estimation of the overall quality of life by means of an empirical formula combining such factors as purchasing power, pollution, house price to income ratio, cost of living, safety, health care, commute time and climate.

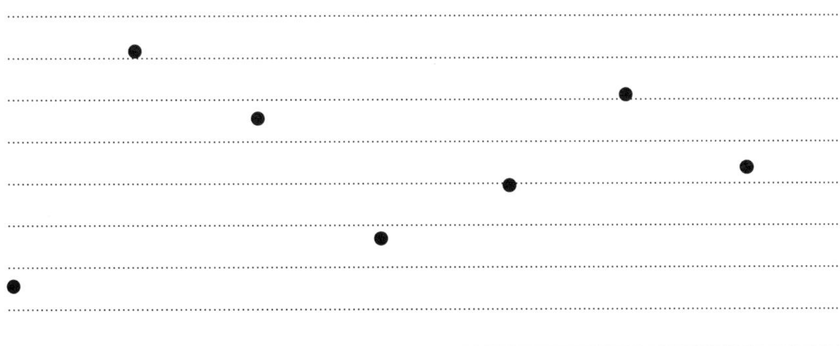

Belgrade	Berlin	Bratislava	Budapest	Katowice	Prague	Warsaw
115.50	171.94	155.67	126.85	141.24	161.09	143.67

Economy

D.01

GDP per capita (USD)

Metropolitan regions 2000–2012

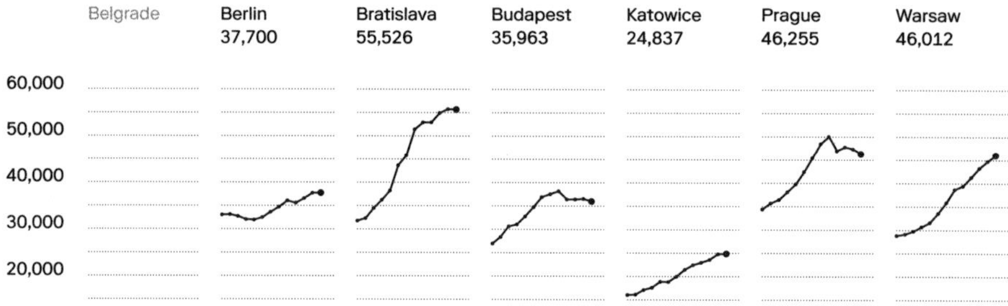

D.02

GDP as a share of national value (per cent)

Metropolitan regions 2009–2015 (Belgrade) 2000–2013 (Bratislava, Prague) 2000–2012 (other cities)

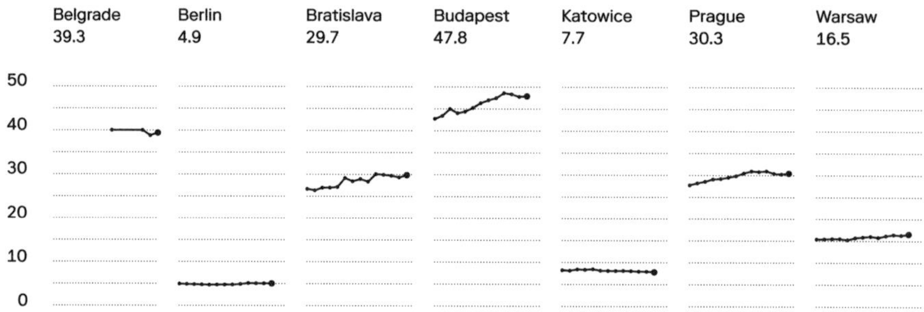

D.03

Patent applications in information and communications technology (applications/1 million inhab.)

Cities 2010–2012

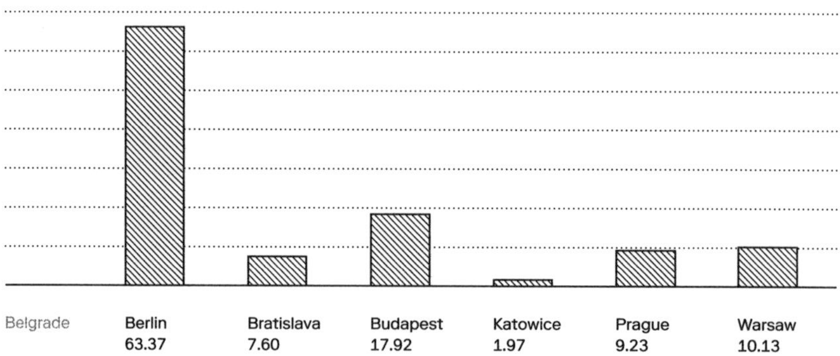

D.04

Community design applications (number/1 million inhab.)

Cities 2013–2015

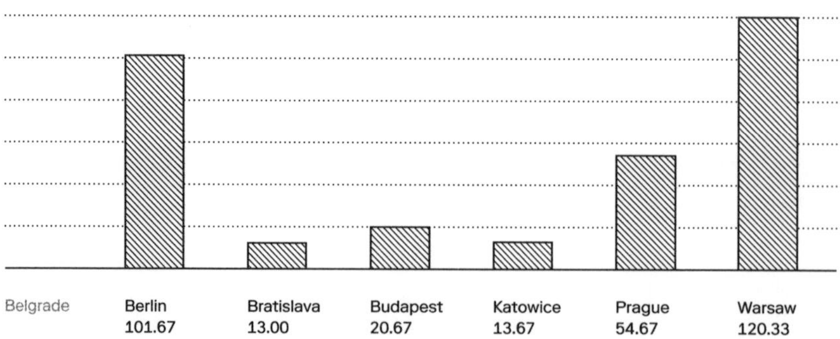

D.05

Employment structure
(per cent)

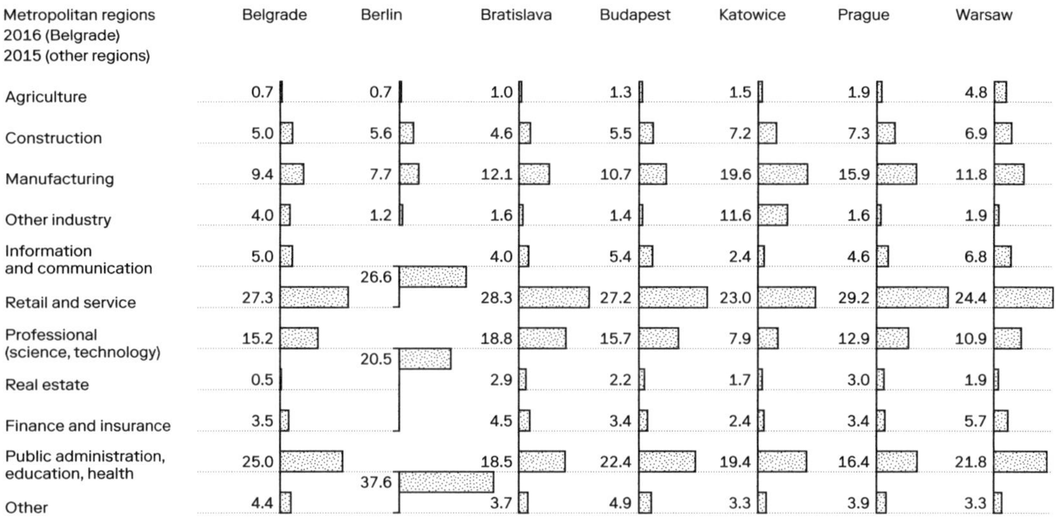

D.06

Unemployment
(per cent)

Cities
2016

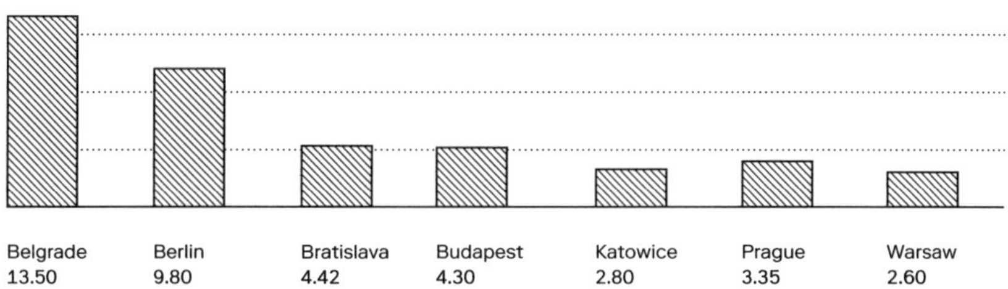

D.07

Tourism, overnight stays
(millions)

Cities
2016

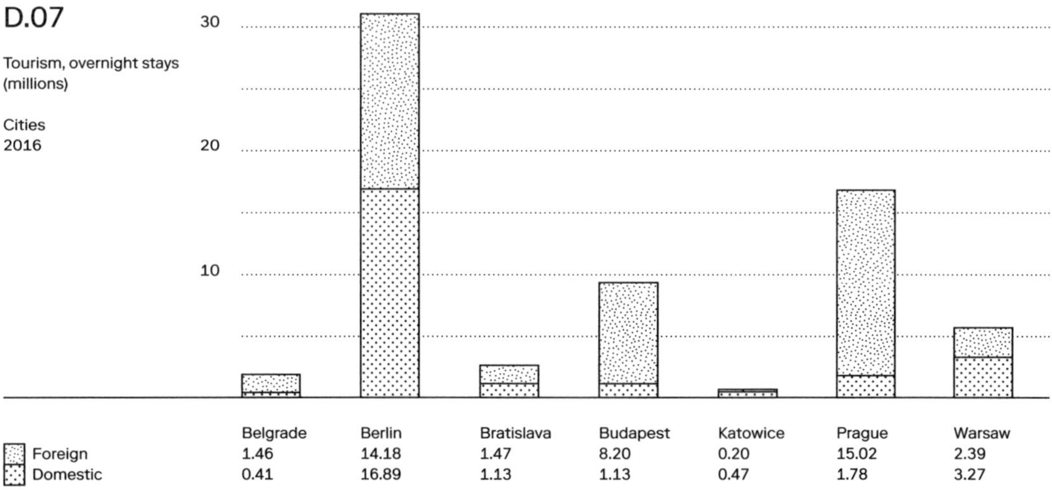

Mobility and Spatial De

E.01

Transport modal split (per cent)

Cities
2016 (Prague)
2014 (Budapest)
2013 (Berlin)
2015 (other cities)

The proportion of people using a particular mode of transport within the overall transport system of an urban area, and therefore an important component in developing sustainable transport within a city or region.

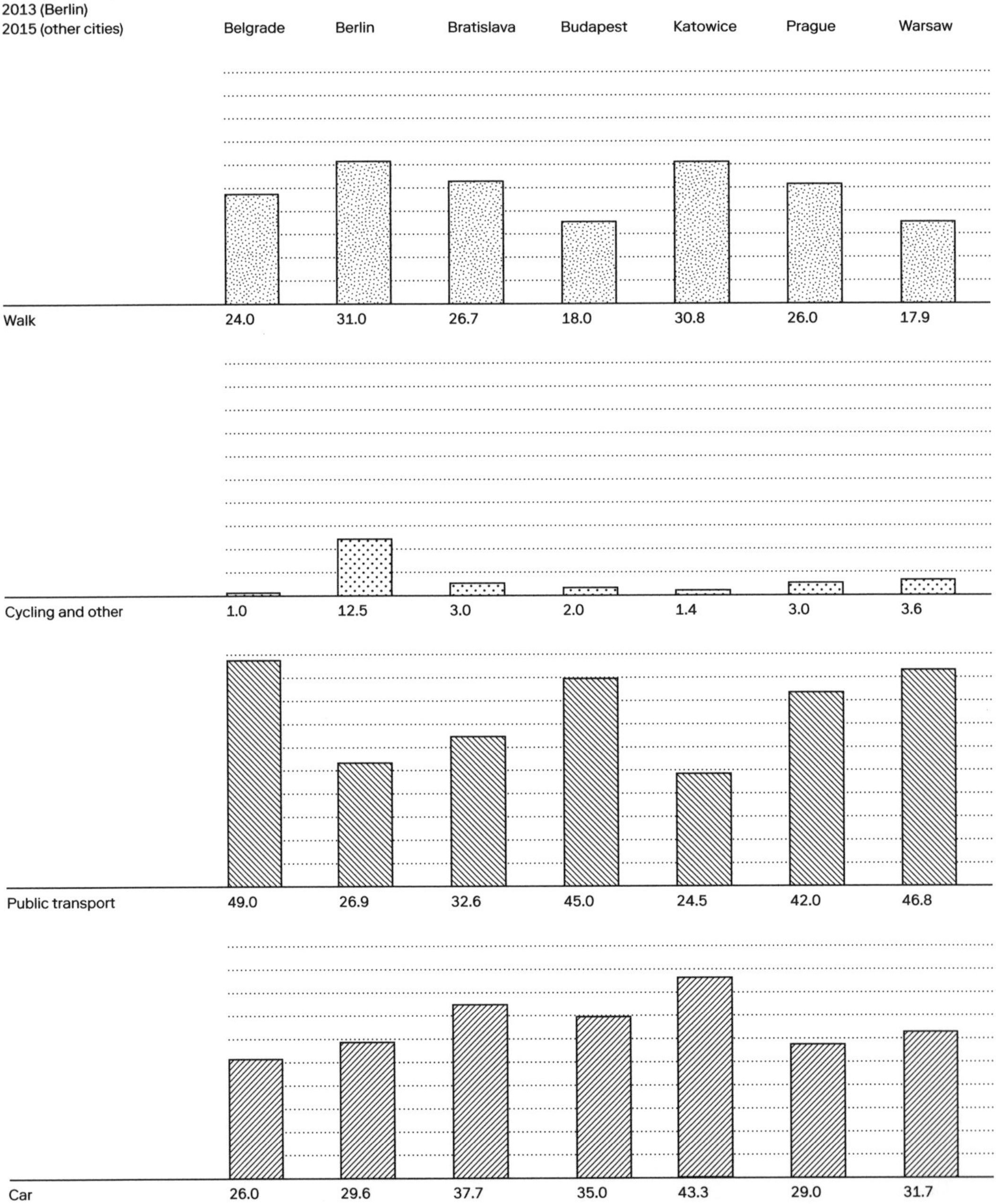

lopment

E.02

Bike roads

Cities
2018 (Katowice)
2017 (Bratislava, Budapest)
2016 (Prague, Warsaw)
2015 (Belgrade)
2012 (Berlin)

	Belgrade	Berlin	Bratislava	Budapest	Katowice	Prague	Warsaw
Bike roads (km)	83	986	110	129	75	472	493
Bike roads (km/100,000 inhab.)	4.9	27.9	25.8	7.3	25.2	37.1	28.1

E.03

Transport prices

Cities
2018

● = 5 €

	Belgrade	Berlin	Bratislava	Budapest	Katowice	Prague	Warsaw
Monthly pass – regular price (EUR)	27.19	81.00	27.00	28.80	27.64	21.18	25.13
One-way ticket on local transport (EUR) (⦸ = 0.50 €)	0.76	2.80	0.90	1.06	0.73	0.92	1.01
1 liter of gasoline (EUR) (⦸ = 0.50 €)	1.27	1.35	1.29	1.11	1.08	1.19	1.09

E.04

Registered passenger cars

Cities
2017 (Budapest)
2014 (Bratislava)
2016 (other cities)

■ = 20 cars

	Belgrade	Berlin	Bratislava	Budapest	Katowice	Prague	Warsaw
(cars/1,000 inhab.)	314	335	400	362	668	621	673

E.05

Urbanization degree (per cent of country surface area)

Countries 2016

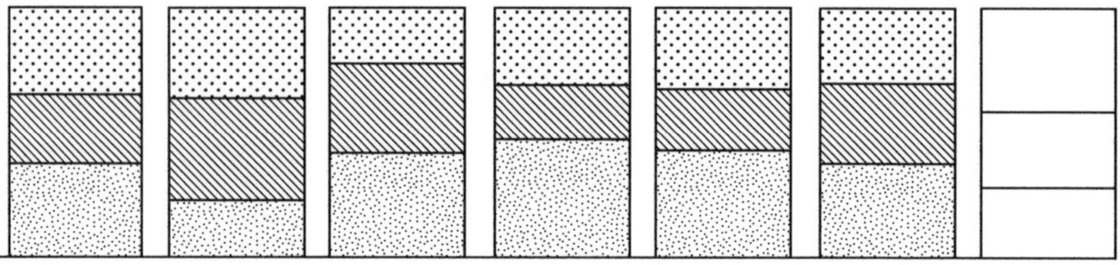

	Serbia	Germany	Slovakia	Hungary	Poland	Czech Rep.	European Union
Cities	34.8	36.1	22.6	30.9	32.6	30.2	41.2
Towns and suburbs	28.0	40.8	35.9	22.2	24.9	32.3	30.6
Rural areas	37.3	23.0	41.5	46.9	42.6	37.4	28.2

E.06

Distribution of population by dwelling type (per cent)

Countries 2016

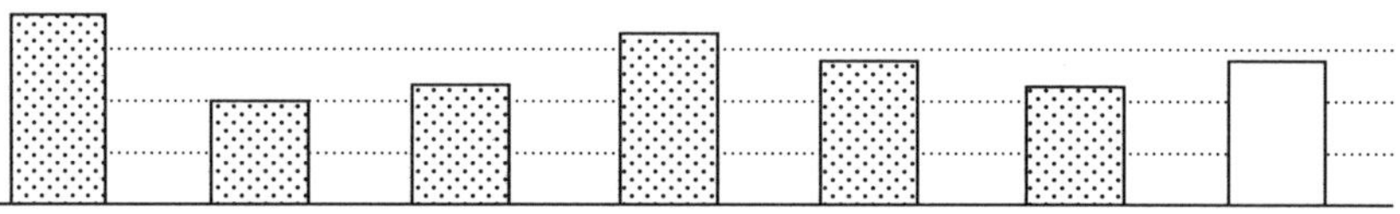

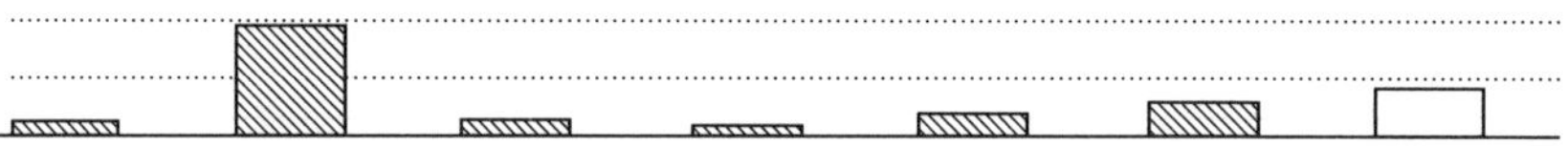

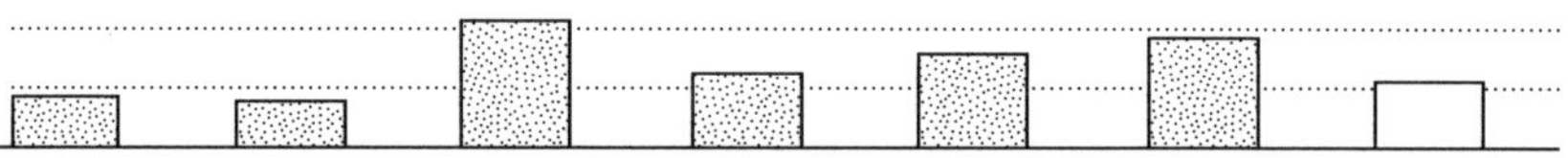

	Serbia	Germany	Slovakia	Hungary	Poland	Czech Rep.	European Union
House	75.3	41.6	48.0	68.1	57.4	47.4	57.5
Flat in building with less than 10 dwellings	6.1	40.2	6.7	4.7	9.0	13.0	18.0
Flat in building with 10+ dwellings	18.5	16.9	44.8	26.7	33.5	39.0	23.8

E.07

Sprawl index

Countries/ Metropolitan regions 2012

The sprawl index measures city growth (over the periods 2000–2006 and 2000–2012) in built-up areas against local population growth. The index is higher (lower) than zero when built-up area growth is greater (smaller) than population growth, leading to an increase (decrease) in city density.

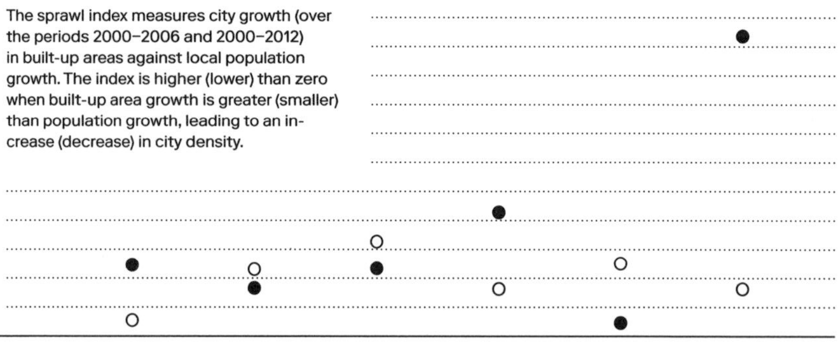

○ Countries
● Metropolitan regions

Serbia	Germany	Slovakia	Hungary	Poland	Czech Rep.	Poland
	2.7	11.5	16.3	8.1	12.5	8.1
Belgrade	Berlin	Bratislava	Budapest	Katowice	Prague	Warsaw
	12.3	8.3	11.7	21.4	2.3	51.8

E.08

Population density (inhab./km²)

Cities 2016

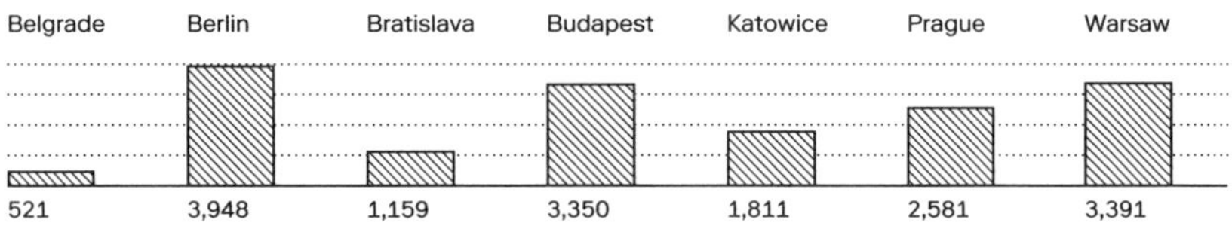

E.09

Population density (inhab./km²)

Metropolitan regions 2015

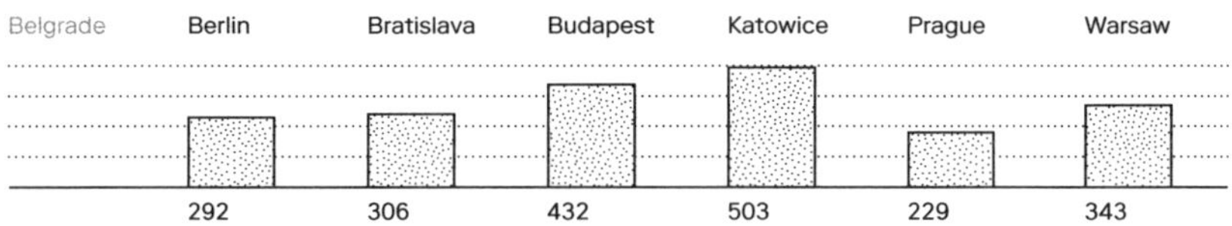

E.10

Urbanized area (km²)

Metropolitan regions 2012

E.11

Built-up area footprint

Centered on railway station 6×6 km

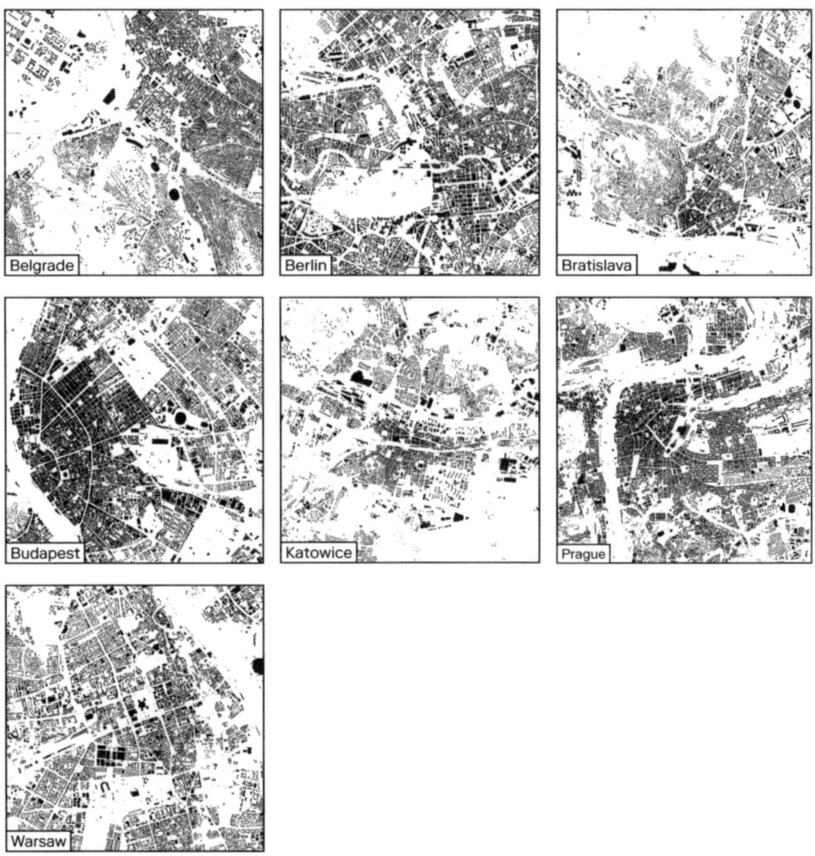

International Benchma

F.01

Population (millions of inhab.)

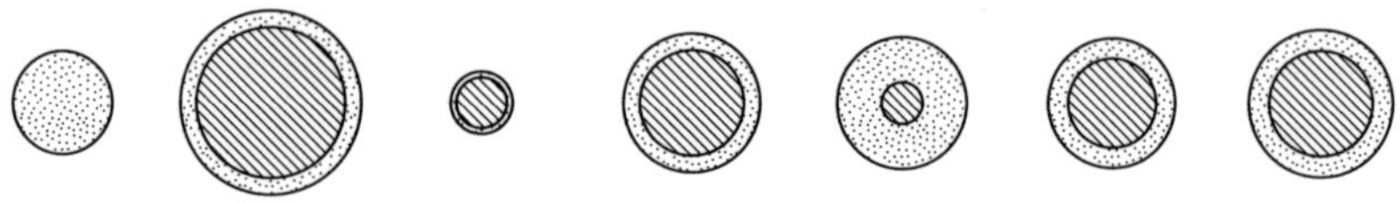

	Belgrade	Berlin	Bratislava	Budapest	Katowice	Prague	Warsaw
City	1.68	3.54	0.43	1.76	0.30	1.27	1.75
Metropolitan region		5.21	0.64	3.00	2.71	2.62	3.37

F.02

GDP per capita (USD)

Metropolitan regions 2000–2012

Belgrade	Berlin	Bratislava	Budapest	Katowice	Prague	Warsaw
	37,700	55,626	35,963	24,837	46,255	46,012

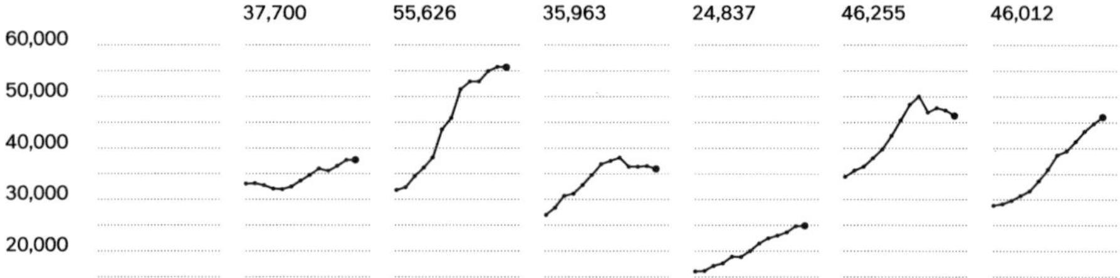

F.03

Average household size (persons)

Cities 2011

Belgrade	Berlin	Bratislava	Budapest	Katowice	Prague	Warsaw
2.7	1.7	2.4	2.1	2.3	2.1	2.2

F.04

Museums (number of museums)

Cities
2018 (Athens, Amsterdam, London)
2017 (Katowice)
2015 (Berlin, Budapest)
2016 (other cities)

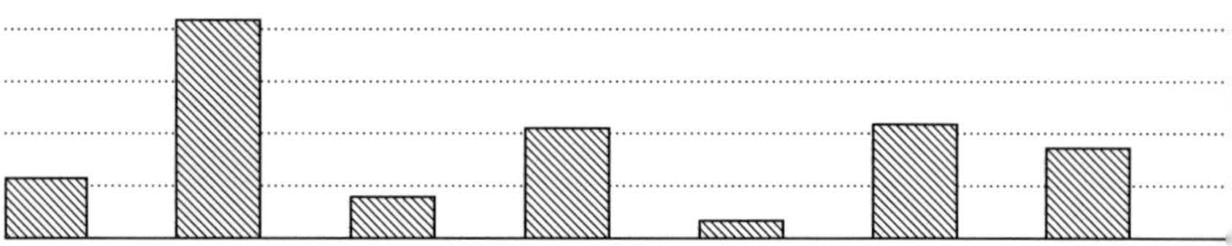

Belgrade	Berlin	Bratislava	Budapest	Katowice	Prague	Warsaw
47	167	33	85	16	88	70

F.05

Quality of life index

Cities 2019

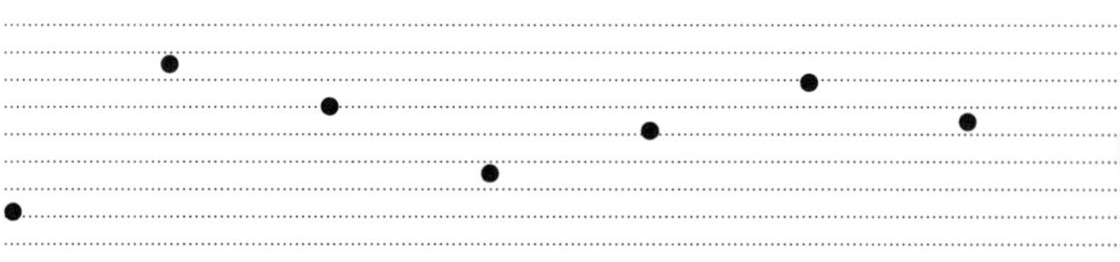

Belgrade	Berlin	Bratislava	Budapest	Katowice	Prague	Warsaw
112.08	166.17	149.54	125.67	141.24	159.4	144.29

ing

Amsterdam Athens London

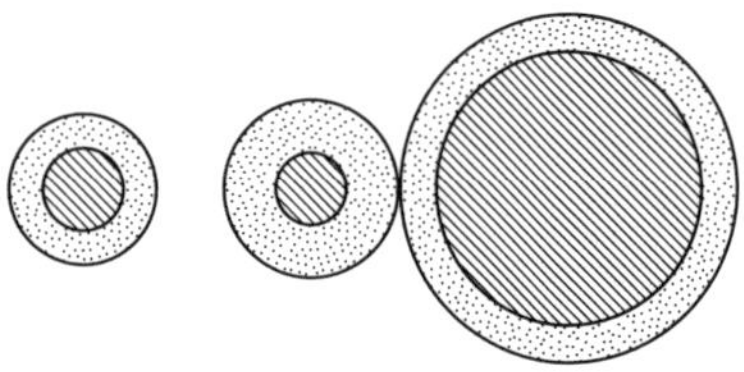

0.84 0.66 8.80

2.73 3.77 14.19

Cities
2011 (Athens)
2017 (Amsterdam, London)
2016 (other cities)

Metropolitan regions
2016 (Belgrade)
2017 (other cities)

Amsterdam
50,410

Athens
35,438

London
53,976

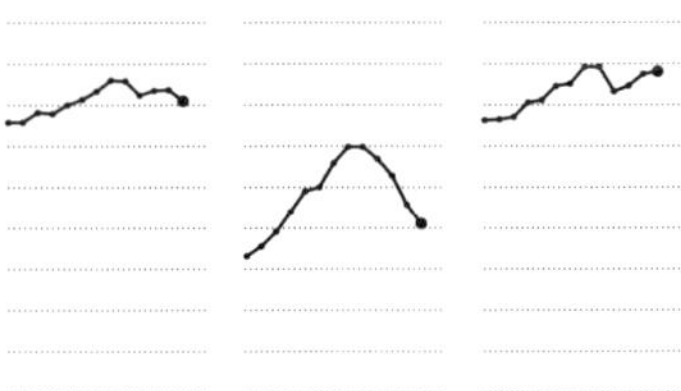

Amsterdam
1.8

Athens
2.2

London
1.6

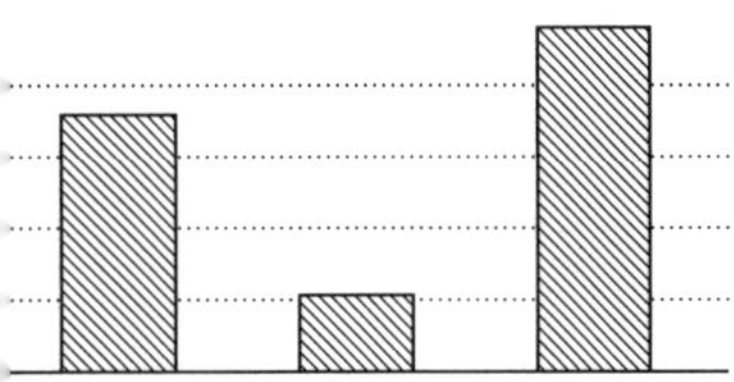

Amsterdam
144

Athens
44

London
192

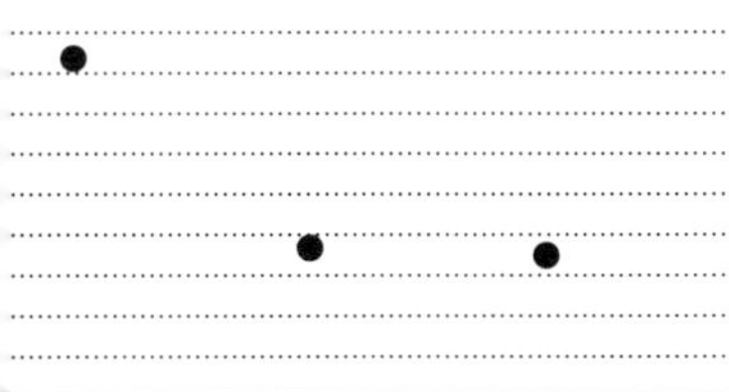

Amsterdam
173.79

Athens
126.54

London
124.50

The quality of life index (higher is better) is an estimation of the overall quality of life by means of an empirical formula combining such factors as purchasing power, pollution, house price to income ratio, cost of living, safety, health care, commute time and climate.

F.06

Average monthly net salary

Cities 2019

▨ = 100 €; ⦸ = 0.50 €

	Belgrade	Berlin	Bratislava	Budapest	Katowice	Prague	Warsaw
Average net salary (EUR)	387.86	2,103.44	970.08	723.24	712.39	1,080.09	942.20
One-way ticket on local transport (EUR)	0.76	2.80	0.90	1.09	0.74	0.94	1.02

F.07

Prices

Cities 2019

● = 5 €

	Belgrade	Berlin	Bratislava	Budapest	Katowice	Prague	Warsaw
Monthly transportation pass – regular price (EUR)	27.02	81.00	27.00	29.55	27.89	21.46	25.61
Meal, mid-range restaurant (EUR)	5.06	8.50	6.00	5.66	4.20	5.45	5.83
Cinema ticket, international release (EUR)	4.22	11.00	7.00	5.66	8.84	7.01	7.00

F.08

Housing costs

Cities 2019

▨ = 100 €; ▬ = 500 €

	Belgrade	Berlin	Bratislava	Budapest	Katowice	Prague	Warsaw
Apartment rent (one bedroom) in city centre (EUR)	328.75	872.42	572.89	465.71	317.47	700.33	556.02
Price/m² to buy apartment in city centre (EUR)	2,288.96	5,296.88	2,772.00	2,713.53	1,105.78	4,552.99	2,752.39

F.09

Property price-to-income ratio

Cities 2019

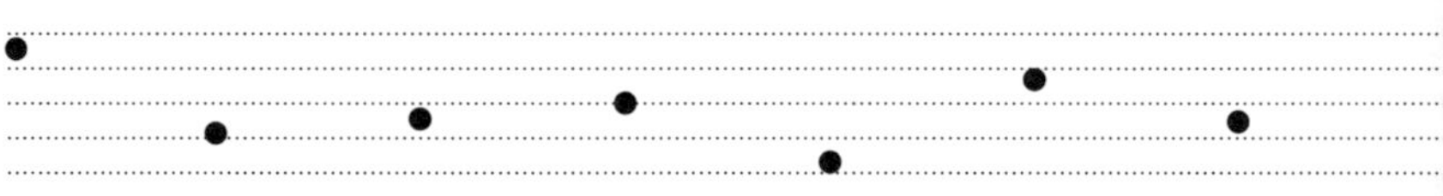

Belgrade	Berlin	Bratislava	Budapest	Katowice	Prague	Warsaw
22.31	10.61	12.43	14.86	6.45	17.58	12.09

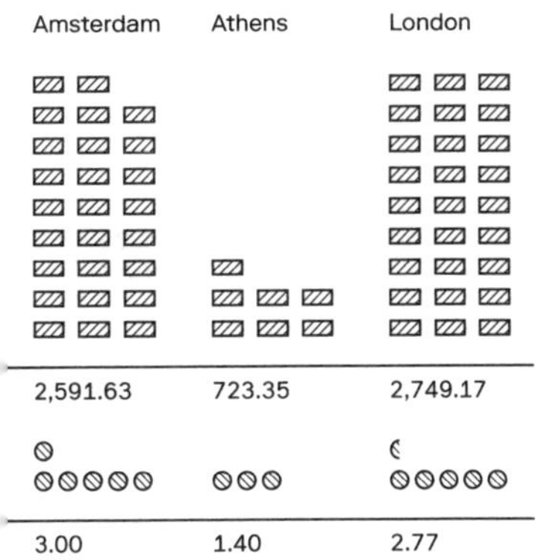

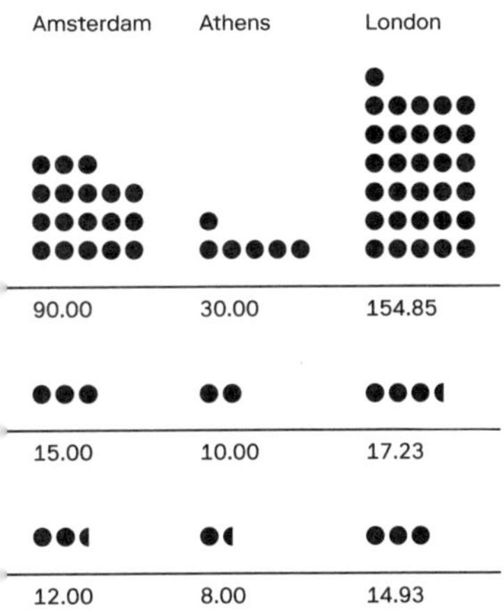

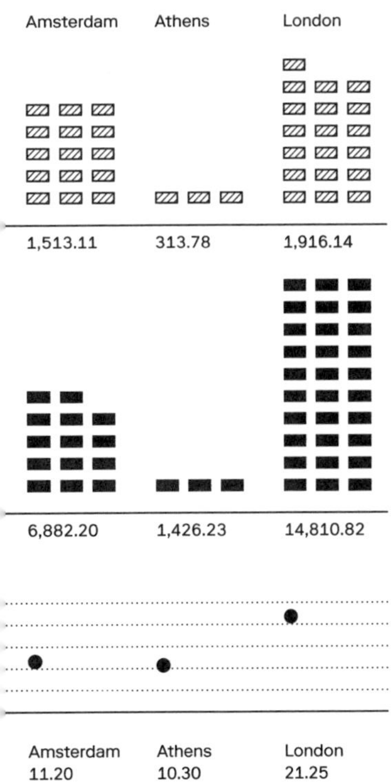

The Property price-to-income ratio is the basic measure of housing purchase affordability (lower is better), which is calculated as the ratio of median house prices to median family disposable income.

Sharing Arc
and Spaces

itecture

Bratislava

Prague

Space in Socialist and —Divided or Shared?

Living Collectively

The vision of a better life that stimulated the formation of the Soviet Union and the socialist states of the Eastern Bloc after 1945 promised many things. Among its many bold assurances was the motivating idea that space would be shared by all. Private ownership of space—whether in the form of buildings, streets, or country estates—would end and universal rights would be extended under the mindful watch of a benign state intent on its own disappearance (Engels' notion of the 'withering of the state'). In the aftermath of the October Revolution for instance, the 'bourgeois' conception of home—understood both socially and spatially—was rejected in a series of decrees nationalizing land and abolishing private ownership of property in Russia.[1] Collective forms of housing were not only adopted as a matter of exigency, but also trumpeted as the democratization of space. Large pre-revolutionary apartments in Moscow, Petrograd and elsewhere, once occupied by the wealthy and their servants, were divided to provide homes for a number of working-class and peasant families. Similarly, thirty years later one of the key slogans of the new Soviet-backed authorities in Central Europe was that cities would be wrested out of the hands of landlords and capitalists, and given back to the workers. The benefits of city life were to be extended to those to whom they had been denied. To materialize this promise of welfare and culture, Warsaw, for instance, acquired a new hotel and cultural centre at its heart, Dom Chłopa (House of the Peasant). First conceived in 1946 but built more than ten years later, Dom Chłopa was created as a place not only of rest but of improvement. The building was designed to contain not only bedrooms and a restaurant for 500 guests, but also a library, a *świetlica* (political education room) and a cinema / theatre as well as a medical centre, a photographer's studio, and a hairdresser.[2]

The redistribution of space was not simply to be a measure of social justice: space itself was to be organized like a machine for the production of better citizen-comrades. Old habits had to be broken and new ones forged. Just as today we talk about 'digital natives'—people too young to remember a time before the Internet—Soviet architects and social reformers in the 1920s imagined that all children born into socialism would be brought up in communal housing where the desire for privacy and private ownership would never be felt, such was the indisputable virtue of an architecture which served collective needs. Writing in 1929, architects Moisei Ginzburg and Ignatii Milinis described the new collectivity:

1
See L. Attwood, *Gender and Housing in Soviet Russia* (Oxford: Oxford University Press, 2017), 34.

2
See D. Crowley, 'The Peasant in the City', in *PRL – A Country of Folklore*, exhibition catalogue (Zachęta National Gallery: Warsaw, 2016), 31.

3
M. Ginzburg and I. Milinis (1929) cited in 'Moisei Ginzburg's constructivist masterpiece: Narkomfin during the 1930s', online, available HTTP: https://thecharnelhouse.org (accessed February 2019). See also V. Buchli, 'Moisei Ginzburg's Narkomfin Communal House in Moscow: Contesting the Social and Material World', *Journal of the Society of Architectural Historians* (June 1998) vol. 57.2, 160–181.

4
K. Marx, 'Critique of the Gotha Program', *Selected Writings II* (Moscow: Progress Publishers, 1951), 23.

5
I. Dworakowska, 'O Parku Kultury Na Powiślu', *Architektura*, II, (1953), 278.

st-Socialist Cities

> The individual bourgeois apartment is no longer appropriate for new dwelling relations, which are based on principles other than the unified patriarchal family with its petty individualistic conduct. The economic routines of the worker's family (nutrition, cleaning, washing) as well as the education of children, their care and control and the fulfilment of the cultural and sport needs of workers and children, can and must be collectivized, that is, produced on a collective basis. Therefore all those rooms that for their functional destination and their character must serve entire collectives and not only single individuals, must be reshaped into corresponding highly collectivized premises: the canteen, common resting rooms, reading rooms and libraries, gyms, child care rooms and nurseries, etc.[3]

Their design—the celebrated Narkomfin House in Moscow (1929) —was presented as a prototype of a new type of building, the communal home, that would eventually flourish throughout the Soviet Union.

Other instruments for the production of socialist beings included the parks of culture and leisure which were created throughout the Eastern Bloc. Following a Soviet model laid down in Gorky Park in Moscow in 1928, such parks were created in various Central European cities after the Second World War including Katowice (Wojewódzki Park Kultury i Wypoczynku/Provincial Park of Culture and Rest, est. 1951) and Bratislava (Park kultúry a oddychu/ Park of Culture and Rest, est. 1954). Decorated with open-air theatres, leafy avenues and classical statuary, facilities for studying astronomy, zoos and botanical gardens, they were like microcosms of the communist future announced—but never detailed—by Marx in his writing. When labour was in a harmonic relation with culture and education, alienation would, according to the German political philosopher, be a matter of the past, and 'factory work ... [will be] an activity to which all people devote some time. It [will be] something which everybody, without exception, wants to do'.[4] In Moscow, Katowice or Bratislava, the worker was to be reinvigorated by the experience of visiting the park, ready for everyday challenges in the workplace and, ultimately, the great work of proletarian progress:

> Socialist parks of culture should not only compensate for social injustice, but they should also be landscapes created by the invention of artists; humanist landscapes in which man plays the main role; landscapes created with the conviction of the existence of knowable and objective facts about the world, as well as the marvellous possibility that the world can be shaped by humanity for the good of mankind.[5]

Whether or not such parks ever came close to the kind of enlightening effects that were claimed for them is perhaps not important. What is clear is that they provided means of escape from the often claustrophobic and inhibited conditions of life; places for being together and, importantly, apart too.

Late Socialist Spaces

The vision of shared space proclaimed by ideologues withered over years: the project of building communal homes was replaced by the mass production of conventional single family apartments throughout the Bloc (meagre traces survived in the residents' committees which had oversight of blocks). Similarly, the voluntary urban improvement efforts once loudly promoted by the authorities faded too. With a lineage that can be traced back to the Civil War and to Vladimir Lenin himself,[6] the Soviet tradition of the 'subbotnik'—days of unpaid, voluntary labour given over to public works such as rubbish-clearance or tree-planting—was widely trumpeted as a living demonstration of the investment of ordinary citizens in their environment. The enthusiasm of the *subbotniki* was supposed to be infectious, and the practice was exported to the Eastern Bloc in the 1940s. The tradition had, however, become little more than a late-socialist reflex by the 1980s or perhaps even a cliché. Voluntary labour schemes came to occupy one or perhaps two days a year, typically on May Day or around the anniversary of Lenin's birthday in late April. And each spring, Hungarian, East German and Soviet newspaper editors reserved a few column inches for a portrait of young, fashionably-dressed women wielding forks and spades. These images of socialist voluntarism appeared in marked contrast to the unloved state of many late socialist spaces. Unlit hallways in housing blocks, flickering neon advertising signs, broken playground equipment and the dismal waiting rooms in bus and railway stations testified to the anomie and disconnection often felt by citizens. Far from being shared spaces, these were non-places of a dismal kind. When sharing did emerge in this impoverished environment, it was often, as Polish sociologist Kacper Pobłocki has described, *despite* rather than because of the activities of the state.[7]

Coerced voluntarism was usually described by critics of Soviet order as one plank in a raft of measures that robbed citizens of their human rights to privacy. Václav Havel, the Czech dissent, wrote:

> The bureaucratic regulation of the everyday details of people's lives is another indirect instrument of nihilization. It is here that public matters infiltrate private life in a way that is very 'ordinary', but extremely persistent. The sheer number

6
V. Lenin, 'Pervomaisky Subbotnik', *Collected Works* (Moscow: Progress Publishers, 1965), 123–125.

7
'The Eastern Roots of Sharing. Interview with Kacper Pobłocki', *Cities Magazine* (2018) vol. 2, 12–15.

8
V. Havel, 'Stories and Totalitarianism' (1987), in: Paul Wilson (ed.), *Václav Havel: Open Letters. Selected Prose* 1965–1990 (London: Faber and Faber, 1991), 331–2.

9
A. Bátarová, 'Interview with Katalin Cseh and Adam Czirak about the second public sphere in the former Eastern Bloc' (August 2014), online, available HTTP: http://www.artmargins.com (accessed February 2019).

10
G. Konrád cited by K. Cseh-Varga and Adam Czirak (eds.), *Performance Art in the Second Public Sphere: Event-based Art in Late Socialist Europe* (London: Routledge, 2018).

11
Rajk in conversation with fellow architects Dezső Ekler, Katalin Gyarmathy, Katalin Pikler, Bálint Nagy, curator Szilágyi Gábor and writer György Konrád, 'Beszélgetés a Keszthely-pályázatról' (26 September 2001), online, available HTTP: http://beszelo.c3.hu/ (accessed February 2019).

> of small pressures that we are subjected to every day is more important than it may seem at first, because it encloses the space in which we are condemned to breathe. There is very little air in that space. But not so little that we might suffocate, and thus create a story.[8]

Havel's view was not only that privacy had been eroded but that that publicness—in the sense of openness and civic-mindedness—had been damaged too. Despite a loudly-voiced commitment to equality, the communist authorities had created zones of privilege for their 'elites': special stores where only party members could shop; entire housing districts where only the powerful lived; and luxury hotels and restaurants that were not only beyond the means of the majority but were widely viewed as evidence of corruption. Moreover, in the suspicious atmosphere of the most paranoid regimes (above all the USSR and the Socialist Republic of Czechoslovakia), it was almost impossible to exchange views freely, to gather or to act independently without some kind of license from the state. Much dissenting activity in Central Europe under communist rule—whether samizdat publishing, underground theatre, or illicit lectures—took place outside the official zone (or 'illicitly' within it). This web of activity has been described as the 'second public sphere'; 'a social and cultural field of strategies for alternative action that existed parallel to the official and controlled publicity of late socialism.'[9] As Katalin Cseh-Varga and Adam Czirak note—citing Hungarian dissident György Konrád writing in the 1970s—advocates of the second public sphere imagined that it 'extends the possibilities of a given public system.'[10] In other words, it created an 'authentic' publicness in a world circumscribed by the actions of dogmatic and often irrational power. Konrád was himself involved in an unofficial urban design project in the early 1980s in which 72 architects contributed designs for Keszthely, a town at the westernmost point of Lake Balaton. An explicit rebuttal of the impersonal and industrial forms of architecture that were constructed across the country in the 1970s, the project also issued an objection to Soviet-style masterplanning. Allocated 'virtual' sites in the centre of the town and with no expectation of being commissioned to build, architects made their own, individual propositions, often to rehabilitate existing structures for homes, cafés, bookstores and theatres. Directed to work within the building codes that had operated in Budapest around 1900 by the project's organizers, the scheme was a critique of the National Building Codes of the People's Republic at the time. It was also a living demonstration of the pluralism and potential of the second public sphere. Notwithstanding its critical view of official spaces, this scheme was hardly a form of proto-capitalism. In fact, László Rajk, one of the organizers, admitted twenty years later that 'we did not think about capital, not even for one minute.'[11]

New Forces

The turn of events which led to the collapse of communist rule in the 'satellite' states of Central and Eastern Europe in 1989 and then, in 1991, to the end of the Soviet Union, ushered in a new set of forces. Of course, the most spectacular images of the period were of jubilant crowds filling city squares to proclaim their opposition to communist rule and, most dramatically, passing through the checkpoints in the Berlin Wall on the night of 9 November 1989. This wholesale reorganization of space was seen as a kind of triumph of the popular will, and a harbinger of a new kind of publicness (if only for a short, euphoric period). Other instances of spatial revolution included the occupation of communist party buildings: in January 1990 in Warsaw, for instance, protestors from the Solidarity Union called for the nationalization of the Polish United Workers Party headquarters and other assets, a demand rejected by the communist leadership even though power had already slipped from its hands. With hollow irony, they accused the union of 'seeking to carry out a "Bolshevist" confiscation'.[12] The sense that this monumental building at the heart of the city was understood to be public property was accentuated by the fact that deductions had been made from the wages of ordinary Poles in the 1950s to pay for its construction. In return, they had received 'share' certificates inferring part-ownership. When the matter of the future of this building was debated in the early 1990s, Poles sent their shares to Warsaw University, demanding that the former party headquarters be given the civic function of education. In the event, the building became home to the revived stock exchange—a sign of things to come.

Across the former bloc, public hopes and expectation that democratic politics would bring about an equitable and transparent distribution of resources were often at odds with new forces shaping space, namely those of privatization and consumerism. Spaces and buildings which had once—at least in name—been public property were sold to developers to stimulate investment and dock the economies of these former Eastern Bloc states with the West. The case of the Praha Hotel in the Czechoslovak capital provides a somewhat typical example even if the building itself was exceptional. Commissioned in 1971, and opened a decade later, the hotel was a powerful sign of the privilege that the communist elite reserved for itself—a near-private space in the public setting of late socialism. With bespoke interiors and fittings, some created by celebrated Czech decorative artists, like glass artist Stanislav Libenský, supporters of the hotel claimed that the artistic merit of this late communist *Gesamtkunstwerk* outbalanced its dubious past. The story of the hotel's privatization in the 1990s is indicative of the operations of capital in the Czech Republic after communist rule. Becoming property of Prague City

12
S. Greenhill, 'Upheaval in the East: Poland; Protesters Occupy the Communist Party Headquarters in Warsaw', *New York Times* (25 January 1990), online, available HTTP: www.nytimes.com (accessed February 2019).

13
W. Shepard, 'A Look At Abu Dhabi's "Bad Joke": The Belgrade Waterfront Project', *Forbes* (8 December 2016), online, available HTTP: https://www.forbes.com (accessed February 2019).

Council in 1992, the hotel's swimming pool and grounds were welcome additions to the public spaces of the city. However, in 2002, the hotel was sold to Falkon Capital, an investment company established by Georgian and Armenian businessmen in 1996, with close ties to Russian energy interests. Then, in spring 2013, a Cyprus-based investment company Maraflex bought the hotel, before quickly selling it on to Petr Kellner, the richest individual in the Czech Republic. He then announced plans to demolish the hotel to build a private housing and a school. At the same time, petitions to list this late Socialist building were turned down, on the basis that the hotel—completed in 1981—was too recent to warrant protection. In the end, the structure was destroyed, providing photographers with the opportunity to add to the fashion for post-socialist 'ruin porn'. Private housing and a private school were erected on its former site.

For many critics of the activities of local and international property developers in post-socialist Europe, the power of money has corrupted representational politics. Public planning mechanisms which, at least in principle, ought to facilitate discussion of urban development and set checks in place to stop the damaging effects of development on lives, on existing businesses, on historical buildings and on the environment, have often proven to be chronically weak when confronted by powerful developers and ambitious politicians. Describing the grandiose plans for a new waterfront district in Belgrade of towering offices, luxury apartments, and an opera house proposed by an Abu Dhabi development firm with the backing of the Serbian state, *Forbes* in 2016 reported:

> The people of Belgrade were caught off guard. The entire project was reputedly planned in secret, with no public participation. Having been classified as a project of national significance—like an airport or military base—Belgrade Waterfront was fast tracked, which meant that certain bureaucratic hurdles could be sidestepped—such as the otherwise mandatory competition for the project's architectural design. (The government claimed that there actually was a competition, but it was held in Abu Dhabi and no Serbian architects were apparently invited, and who actually designed the project is still unknown). There was also no open bidding process for the tender, as is standard operating procedure. When it was highlighted that Serbia's government was violating its own laws, such as the building codes which are outlined in Belgrade's General Urban Plan, they reputedly just changed the laws.[13]

At the time of writing (Valentine's Day 2019), the project is underway, with the building permits signed and cranes erected.

In the hands of developers, urban parks that were once integral parts of the socialist city have become commercial opportunities. The addition of shopping centres, offices, hotels and spaces on what were green sites introduced new forms of gated privacy to settings that once offered open access. The small pavilions and theatres of Bratislava's Park of Culture and Rest were, for instance, demolished in late 2015 and early 2016 to make way for the River Park (the anglophone 'brand' underlining its exceptionalism). In this 'luxury' development, overstuffed buildings squat by a tree-lined strip along the Danube which the developer, Cresco, disingenuously calls 'komunitné záhrady' (community gardens).[14] Kitsch bronze monuments nearby are offered as unconvincing evidence of a commitment to the city's 'vibrating' cultural life.

Inflatable Ducks and Golden Calves

It is important to note that these developments have *not* been met with indifference. In fact, one of the striking features of public discussions of urban space in post-socialist Europe in recent years is the boldness and commitment of those who have protested against the operations of private capital in public space. Curiously, it was often the threat to communist era architecture—often of the elite kind—that was a rallying focus for protests by groups which often combine architectural historians, community groups and Occupy Movement activists. In June 2013 protests were mounted outside the Praha Hotel with a banner with the words 'Vekslák Bourá Prahu' (Racketeer Destroys Prague) draped over the entrance by anti-capitalists. Similar banners appeared outside the headquarters of Kellner's office in July too. Derived from the German word Wechsel, 'vekslák' (racketeer) is often used to label those who have benefited from the precipitous privatization programmes after 1989, often—though not exclusively—members of the former elite. The term points not to the productivity of capitalism but its interest in accumulation and asset-stripping. This—ultimately unsuccessful—campaign had the paradoxical effect of turning anti-capitalist protesters into the defenders of a luxury hotel. One activist, Dominik Forman, wrote:

> Events that promote the preservation of Hotel Praha are important—not only because they are attempts to save a unique building, but mainly because the anger of the people is finally pointed in the right direction. The target of this anger is the richest oligarch, a financial speculator, who wants to demolish the hotel. He represents exactly the class of people responsible for the financial crisis ... which falls on the shoulders of the poorest and weakest.[15]

14
Cited in M. Dugovič, 'Na mieste PKO vyrastie Riverpark 2, developer na seba privolal hnev kritikov' (27 July 2017), online, available HTTP: https://dennikn.sk (accessed February 2019).

15
D. Forman, 'Mají argumenty pro bourání hotelu Praha smysl?' (2013), online, available HTTP: http://solidarita.socsol.cz (accessed November 2016).

16
See P. Althamer and G. Macuga, *Park Rzeźby na Bródnie Rozdział X. Weneckie Biennale na Bródnie* (Warsaw: Muzeum Sztuki Nowoczesnej, 2018).

Similar reflexes have been felt in Belgrade and elsewhere. The Abu Dhabi-financed scheme for the city's waterfront was met in 2016 by protesters carrying giant inflatable ducks (duck sounds like the Serbian word for fraud). Angered by what they saw as the complicity of the media in its failure to report the way in which the deal had been struck behind closed doors and the abuse of compulsory purchase orders, they protested in front of city hall and various media outlets. In March 2014, artists Cecylia Malik, Mateusz Okoński and Marta Sala organized a rolling demonstration through the streets of Kraków to the door of the Cracovia, a communist era modernist hotel that was slated for destruction. A shopping centre was planned for the site, much to the distress of historians, activists, and community groups. Around 300 people dressed in gold masks and clothes—some carrying banners or playing instruments, others transporting a golden calf in a shopping trolley—took part in a rally that the artists called 'Chciwość Miasta' (Greedy City). Approaching protest in an emphatically ludic and spectacular manner, Malik and her friends were highly effective at attracting the media and, as a consequence, public attention too.

Much is shared in such protests, not least a darkly sardonic sense of humour. But what does all this effort to attract public attention achieve? Much of this activism is predicated on the idea that images—whether of inflatable ducks or golden calves—can change attitudes and that developers, local authorities, and architects can be held to account in the 'court of public opinion'. On that basis the results are mixed (though the Cracovia appears to have been 'saved' by being acquired with state funds and is now the property of the National Museum nearby). Other attempts to share space have taken the form of material interventions into the cityscape, many of which are outlined in this book. At Bródno, a working class district in eastern Warsaw, for instance, local officials and artist Paweł Althamer established a sculpture park with the residents of the communist-era housing blocks nearby. Working with local people (particularly children), ten artists from around the world have made additions to the park since 2009 in the manner of what the scheme's champions call 'social sculpture'.[16] Youssouf Dara, an artist from the Dogon tribe in Mali, for instance, created a wooden structure with a thick roof on carved columns. Known as a 'toguna', this structure serves as a traditional place of gathering in Dogon culture. In Bródno Park, it serves a triple function as an artwork, as a social space, and as a bus stop. Tapping the considerable attention that the scheme has drawn, the Park was declared a 'Biennale' in June 2018 with more than eighty locations selected by Bródno residents as sites of significance that they wished to share with visitors. The event was a project of re-enchantment for visitors and residents alike.

Disenchantment with social housing and other shared spaces, and the march of developers are not exclusively post-socialist phenomena. In fact, one of the striking features of this age is precisely the global reach of multinationals channelling Russian, Chinese, Malaysian, and Saudi money into international property portfolios. Oliver Wainwright calls them an 'international development force, supercharged by the untold riches of sovereign wealth funds, national pension funds, and the gushing pump of petrodollars'.[17] Writing in *The Guardian*, he has pointed to the ways in which property development has squeezed Londoners out of their city despite planning controls and social housing targets. At the same time, many cities around the world face a housing crisis as result of the success of Airbnb's so called 'community' model. So what, if anything, distinguishes the post-socialist city? And what are the legacies of the historical experience of state socialism in Central Europe, whether positive or negative? What can be retrieved from the visions of collective life proposed by the avant-garde of the 1920s or the social networks of dissent? What are the conditions needed to ensure that people feel that they have the right to shape their environment (or equally to contest the actions of others)? What kind of spaces allow us to be together but also apart? What might a 'second public sphere' be in an age when the social world is increasingly organized according to the interests of data capitalism? And what tools are required to encourage spaces to be shared in viable and fulfilling ways? This book—itself a tool—provides many thoughtful reflections on these questions.

17
O. Wainwright, 'The truth about property developers: how they are exploiting planning authorities and ruining our cities', *The Guardian* (17 September 2014), online, available HTTP: www.theguardian.com (accessed February 2019).

Bratislava

1.01

Population
(millions of inhab.)

2016 (metropolitan regions)
2016 (Belgrade)
2017 (other cities)

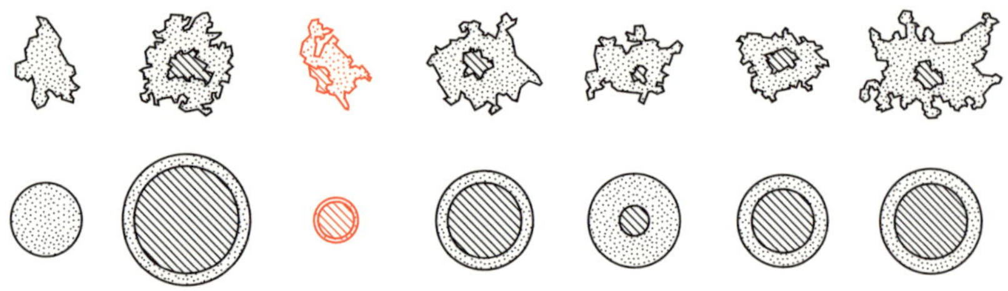

	Belgrade	Berlin	Bratislava	Budapest	Katowice	Prague	Warsaw
City	1.68	3.54	0.43	1.76	0.30	1.27	1.75
Metropolitan region		5.21	0.64	3.00	2.71	2.62	3.37

1.02

Built-up area footprint

City
2016
Total area: 368 km²
Population density:
1,159 inhab./km²

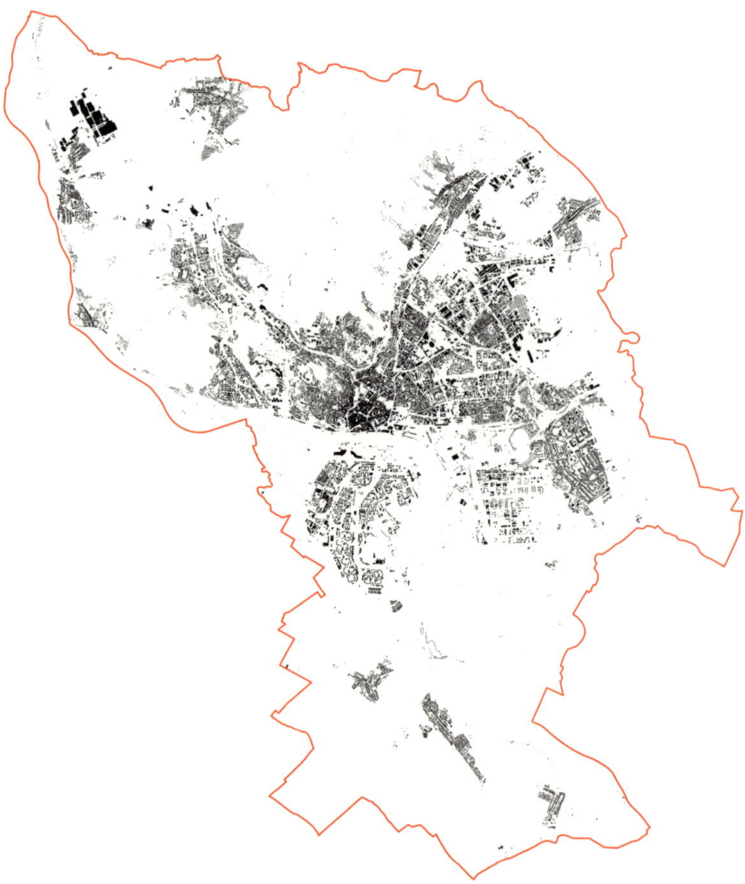

0 5 km

1.03

GDP per capita
(USD)

Metropolitan regions
2000–2012

→ Economy
Chart D.01, p. 24

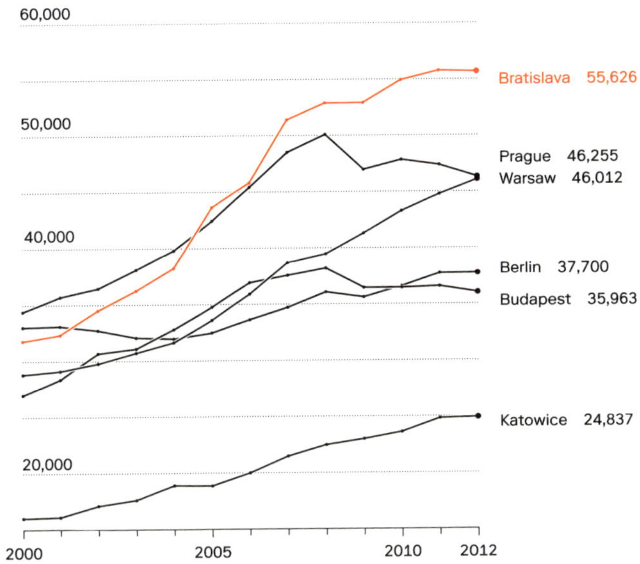

1.04

Local elections turnout
(per cent)

Cities
2016 (Belgrade, Berlin)
2014 (other cities)

→ Society
Chart B.09, p. 18

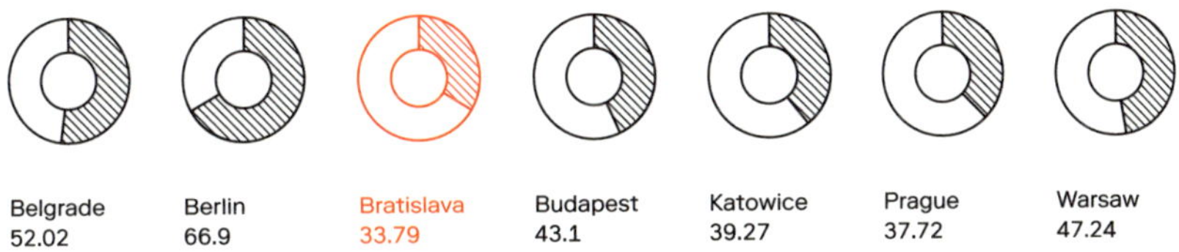

1.05

Average area of living accommodation (m²/inhab.)

City
2011

26.10

◆ = 5 m²

1.06

Average monthly net salary
(EUR)

City
2018

944.78

▧ = 100 €

1.07

Registered passenger cars
(cars/1000 inhab.)

City
2016

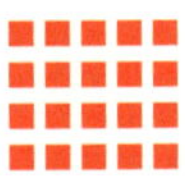

400

■ = 20 cars

1.08

Tourists
(number/year)

City
2016

1,226,385

= 1 million tourists

STARÁ

SLOVENSKÝ ROZHLAS

my
my
bratislava
F&F
obchodné domy
TESCO
Nech máte chuť na čokoľvek...
Dove
60 rokov

Iconic Ruins

Organization	Academy of Fine Arts and Design in Bratislava, Department of Architecture
Address	Hviezdoslavovo nám. 18, 83104 Bratislava
Authors	Benjamín Brádňanský, Petr Hájek, Vít Halada, Zoltán Holocsy, Danica Pišteková, Kristína Rypáková, Ján Studený, Students of the Department of Architecture, Academy of Fine Arts and Design
Partners	Belgrade International Architecture Week – BINA, Czech Centres, City of Trnava, Medialab Katowice
Dates	1 June 2016 – 31 May 2019

Activities				
	Workshops	2	Discussion	1
	Exhibitions	2	Lectures	14
	Publications	2	Film screening	1
	Conference	1	Study trips	5

1
See D. McLaren and J. Agyeman, *Sharing Cities. A Case for Truly Smart and Sustainable Cities* (Cambridge and London: MIT Press, 2015).

2
For further information see L. Králik, *Stručný etymologický slovník slovenčiny* [Concise Etymological Dictionary of Slovak Language] (Bratislava: Veda, 2015) 226, 227–228, 514.

Iconic Ruins in the Sharing Paradigm and the Creative Ways of their Revitalization

Marian Zervan, Monika Mitášová

Introduction

In their book *Sharing Cities. A Case for Truly Smart and Sustainable Cities* Duncan McLaren and Julian Agymen draw on ideas of a global networked society,[1] which is becoming increasingly dominated by a paradigm of sharing. They forget that the world was still divided into two political systems in the twentieth century. They build on the assumption that sharing or a shared paradigm is functional within the network, since the network emerged with equal positions for everyone, although it soon became clear that restrictive, subversive, and often politically motivated platforms are also starting to emerge. *Cyber polis, smart polis* or *metapolis* are not yet similar to a social polis in the case of global cities or metropoles. Cities in post-socialist countries increasingly resemble those in developed countries; however, the former socialist city is in many ways still part of the multi-layered city structure.

The Shared Cities: Creative Momentum[2] initiative highlights such distinctions, searches for creative ways of sharing layers of post-socialist cities, and participates in their revitalization and reconstruction. Iconic ruins are part of the former socialist city, and at the same time, they are an example of its reconciliation with this layer, a suitable 'pathological' diagnostic sample. Our hypothesis is that when a problem called 'the iconic ruin' is successfully diagnosed, and creative possibilities of its revitalization have been designed, one might gain a better understanding and deeper knowledge of how to share a socialist city in the multi-layered structure of contemporary cities in post-socialist countries.

Identification

The first step of our project is the identification of iconic ruins. This unusual phrase is best understood through the meanings of the words it contains. It is seemingly an oxymoron which combines the adjective 'iconic' and the noun 'ruin'. The adjective is derived from the Greek word *eikon*, an image, so the correct adjective form would be 'imaginal'. *Eikon* has a similar root to *eidos*, which means shape, model, appearance, idea or thought. If we allow for the hybridization of these words, which undoubtedly occurred, then the adjective form could also have been *eidolon*—'imaginal', 'appearance-imaginal', etc. Thanks to this hybrid meaning, in Byzantine times, an image containing a proto-design could be called an icon. The word 'ruin' is of Latin origin, from the verb *ruere* 'to roll', 'tumble', 'tear down', and the cognate noun thus means 'a ruin'—not merely that of a building, but also human, physical, or symbolic. Taking into an account these two short etymological digressions, the meaning of the word-compound 'iconic ruin' would be an '*eidolon*—imaginal ruin'. However, we are not referring to *eidola* or imaginal ruins, but to buildings from the second half of the twentieth century, which share certain characteristics.

These buildings have been deserted due to various reasons: they no longer fulfill current technical norms; their former use is no longer desirable; they were shut down. They might also be considered symbols of the socialist regime by politicians or the public; they became unacceptable or associated with a certain nostalgia. This is their first common periodical characteristic. The second characteristic is that they were designed during the political liberalization of the 1960s, but they were built during the 'normalization' of the 1970s.[3] Their plans and projects followed current architectural trends, but the execution was informed by a very different and conservative political, social, and economic situation. Their noteworthy, innovative, and unorthodox form and spatial organization was opposed by the conservative taste of normalization-era politics as well as parts of the general public; at the same time, these designs were never built in their full extent, or in full accordance with the original architectonic project. This meant that these buildings were (and still are) left unfinished rather than ruinous, but they might have 'ruinized' contemporary taste. Most had a unique yet recognizable shape, which dominated the surroundings.

Iconic buildings, a term coined by Charles Jencks,[4] epitomize the Bilbao effect—they are able to attract contemporary nomads and generate money. They are more ostensively iconic[5] and formally representative than semiotically representative through iconic signs, and they are in no way physical or symbolic ruins. What visibly distinguishes iconic ruins from iconic buildings is the decrease in their capacity to generate money. Therefore, they are an example of the negative Bilbao effect, even though their new owners might attempt to advertise them as retro or pseudo-nostalgic. Another distinct feature is that iconic ruins—unlike iconic buildings—have dialogical, intra-architectonic meanings, which are not enigmatic and can be experienced and explored.

The third characteristic of iconic ruins is that at the time of their construction they already differed from contemporary typification and prefabrication. Typologically, they were cultural, sports, or administrative facilities, travel, leisure or recreation building

3
The term 'normalization' (Slovak: *normalizácia*) refers to the era following the Warsaw Pact invasion of Czechoslovakia in August 1968.

4
Charles Jencks started to write about iconic buildings in 2005 (Ch. Jencks, *Iconic Buildings: Power of Enigma*, London: Francis Lincoln, 2005). According to his theory, iconic buildings are not necessarily a contemporary phenomenon, and they can be identified thanks to their exceptional form or architectonic solutions. Moreover, these buildings are not iconic in the sense of cathedrals which operate with generally acknowledged codes and iconic symbols that were easily deciphered and affirmed their formal and functional importance. Cathedrals represented Gothic spirituality and their structure mimicked the organization of theological sums. The form of contemporary iconic buildings is exceptional, ceremonious and significantly different from the twentieth-century internationalist style, however their iconicity and figurativeness are not easily understood due to the absence of shared codes. Iconic buildings are symbolically and semantically enigmatic, and recipients or users tend to project multiform and often contradictory meanings onto them.

5
See *ostension* in I. Osolsobě, *Ostenze, hra, jazyk* [Ostension, Performance, Language] (Brno: Host, 2002[1981]).

6
See M. Zervan, 'Za interpretáciu a proti interpretácii. Stav a perspektívy' ['For Interpretation and Against Interpretation. State and Perspectives'], *KUDĚJ* (2019) In print.

7
For more information about social field see P. Bourdieu, *Les Règles de l'art. Genèse et structure du champ littéraire* [The Rules of Art: Genesis and Structure of the Literary Field] (Paris: Seuil, 1992).

complexes, or ones of special political importance such as embassies, municipal councils or school buildings, and in rare cases also housing complexes and transport structures—mostly bridges. Their use transgressed the typified solutions and prefabrications. Iconic ruins were therefore of exceptional form and authorship, and their construction operated in different economic and builder-contractor relations than regular buildings. For architects they presented an opportunity to escape socialist state-controlled unified urban planning and design, and a promise of return to the architectural profession, so they paid special attention to them. This ensured that apart from conventional meanings, architects also concentrated on intra-architectonic meanings.[6] The communist regime often used these innovative works as propaganda and a form of political pride in socialist building construction. This meant that the buildings, which were iconic in their outward appearance and internal organization, became the target of political attacks after 1989. The public no longer recognized their architectonic qualities and started to perceive the pseudo-iconic symbolism of the former political regime, which was historically misused against them, as real. As a result, iconic ruins were and continue to be subjected to current iconoclasms and diverse modes of ruinizations.

The Social Field of Iconic Ruins[7]

Our relation to both ancient and recent historical architecture is currently shaped by heritage preservation, activists, as well as a conservative or nostalgic general public: three counterforces to the often ruthlessly expansive active force of developers and investors, who are well-connected to politicians both on the municipal and state levels. While the reactive force of heritage preservation seemingly represents the position of universal principles that do not distinguish between historical and modern architecture or architecture of the second half of the twentieth century, activism does not distinguish between architecture and non-architecture in general. Universal principles of conservation are to a certain extent able to cope with the dilemma of architecture as a sample book of historically valuable layers, or to unify an artwork according to the most valuable layer. However, in the case of twentieth-century architecture they are unable to decide which layers are to be protected and which are the most valuable. For example, heritage protection conserves modernist staircases instead of protecting *spatialist modernism*: spatial constellations and elements of spatial composition. Meanwhile, they oppose the protection of architecture from the second half of the twentieth century due to perceived architectonic or urban 'faults', instead of focusing on its unique features such as the hybrid connection of atypical forms and materials and spatial clusters of various provenances. Activism succeeds at winning the public opinion, or with bricolage, but not with architecture. In a world dominated by financial profit, rigid conservation, and naïveté of activism, architects are pushed away from the centre of interest and are only invited to consult or advise on the projects. We understand the attempts of architects to gain attention; however, they will not succeed unless they present elaborate concepts and strategies, and better and more efficient results.

The 'Iconic Ruins' project is an emerging platform fostering a change of roles: activists become consultants or advisors, and heritage protection is replaced with continuous consultations between affiliated disciplines (architecture, history and theory of urbanism, art history); attempts to 'save' architecture are replaced with tailored solutions, strategies, and tactics for the integration of architecture of the second half of the twentieth century into the socio-cultural environment.

Strategies and Tactics

Drawing on research of parallel modernism of the second half of the twentieth century, the Department of Architecture at the Academy of Fine Arts and Design (AFAD) in Bratislava conducts systematic research of iconic ruins in the structure of contemporary post-socialist cities. Among the first results, which were presented to both Slovak and international audiences, was the exhibition *Care for Architecture: Asking the Arché of Architecture to Dance* in Pavilion Cecoslovacchia at the 2016 International Biennale of Architecture in Venice. The exhibition was dedicated to the iconic ruin of the Slovak National Gallery (SNG) in Bratislava, represented by a metal model of the building complex, and to the analysis of responses it has provoked from architects and the general public. The results of architectonic competitions for the reconstruction and completion of the Slovak National Gallery were exhibited there as well; they all searched for the genetic code of this important work by Vladimír Dedeček.[8] The intention of *care* (*sorge*) confronted the attitude of heritage protection, which required architectonic enclosure of the building complex with a front wing according to the plans of a historical four-wing object of water barracks; and the iconoclastic intentions of parts of the public and investors to destroy the buildings they considered unsatisfactory. As a follow up, academic studio assignments were launched by architects Petr Hájek and Vít Halada (Studio of Ján Studený and Benjamín Brádňanský, AFAD, Bratislava) and parallel assignments / studio tasks of Petr Hájek and Jaroslav Hulín (Czech

8 See M. Zervan (ed.), *Care (Sorge) For Architecture* (Prague: CTN ČVUT, 2016).

9 See M. Zervan and M. Mitášová, 'Ikonické ruiny ako architektonická úloha' [Iconic Ruins as an Architectonic Task]. In print.

10 See 'Transformácie (Ikonické ruiny)' [Transformations (Iconic Ruins)], *Projekt* (2017) vol. 1 and 2, 3–4.

Technical University, CTU, Prague) for the Slovak National Gallery. The Studio of Ján Studený and Benjamín Brádňanský enriched the selection of iconic ruins with the Slovak Radio Building, Slovak Television and Istropolis in Bratislava; and later on with the Embassy of Czech Republic in Berlin. In Studio Hájek/Hulín at CTU the assignments also covered the shopping malls Máj and Kotva and the Congress Centre in Prague.[9] In 2017, the Department of Architecture at AFAD in Bratislava and the Department of History and Theory of Art at Philosophical Faculty at University of Trnava organized a workshop together with activists and the public. Its main objective was a search for possibilities of revitalization of the Hviezda cinema building in Trnava. During the year 2017, the Studený/Brádňanský and Hájek/Halada studios developed projects for Dezember Palast in Katowice. The former House of the Unions Istropolis building in Bratislava and its public space was tested for future development in the reconfigured AFAD studios of Ján Studený/Danica Pišteková and Vít Halada/Benjamín Brádňanský. The studio tasks and both Slovak and international researches resulted in a double-issue 3–4 of *Projekt* magazine entitled *Transformácie (Ikonické ruiny)*, edited by Ján Studený.[10]

In 2018, the Department of Architecture at AFAD organized a workshop in Belgrade that dealt with a neglected public infrastructure—Bezistan. The Studio Halada/Brádňanský provoked the revitalization of The Supreme Court of the Slovak Republic building, National Archive, New Market, of the surroundings of Hotel Kyjev and shopping mall Prior in Bratislava by implementing a new residential programme. The Studio Studený/Pišteková envisioned strategies for the redevelopment of the Incheba expo complex in Bratislava. The results were presented at an exhibition *Iconic Ruins/Strategies* at the Medium gallery in Bratislava and later in final research publication. In contrast with the demolitions and new projects by real estate developers, temporary revitalizations by activists and rigid proposals of heritage protection, the following three strategies are crucial: a) an extension of intra-architectonic methodologies and meanings and their further development; b) a transformation of buildings in terms of their programmes and use, shapes, appearances, but also their context in an analogical gesture to the creation of an iconic building, or its suppression; and c) hybridization by reconstruction, annexes and completion of construction, which can be spread into several differentiated tactical steps and revitalization techniques. All three strategies are founded on the metaphor of *dance*: *interplay, cooperation and surrender* of oneself to music and its rhythm. They significantly differ from the metaphors of *fight* as represented by all types of radical real estate development, protective or activist solutions. The strategies of dance initiate creative moments in design processes.

Slovak Radio—Transformation

Miroslav Búran, Martin Mikovčák
Studio Ján Studený, 2016

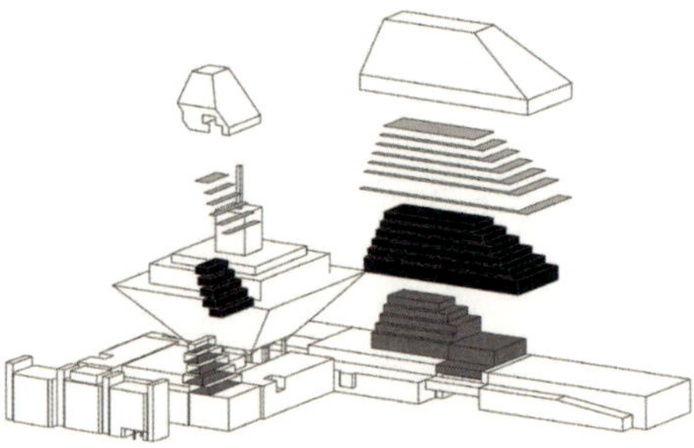

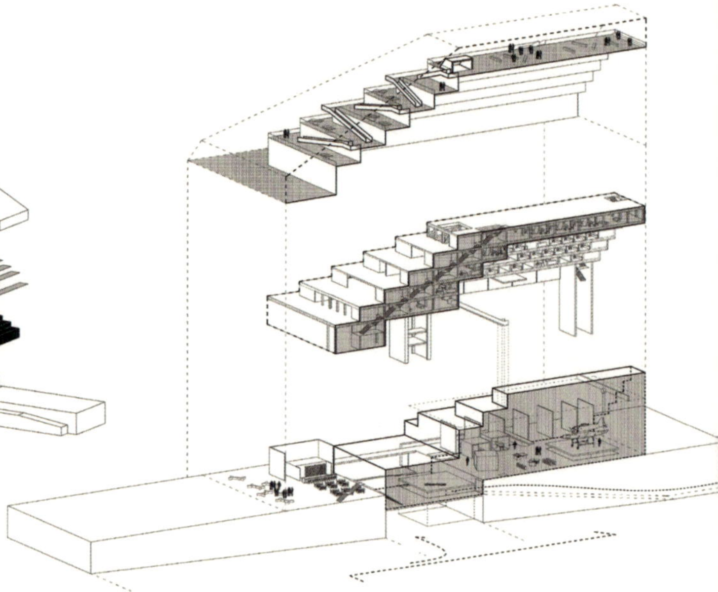

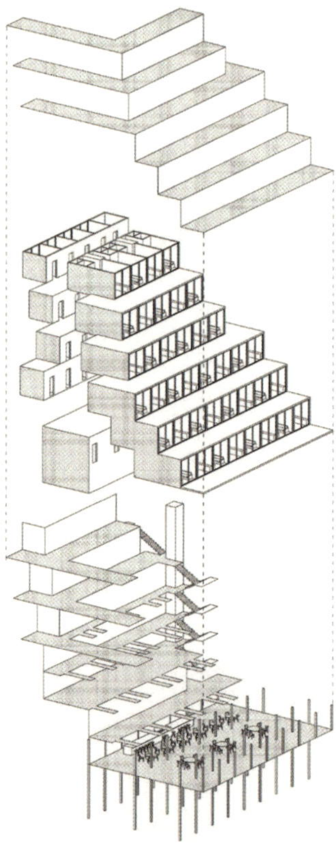

Slovak National Gallery—Spider
Jakub Kubát, Ivana Nechajová
Studio Hájek/Hulín, 2016

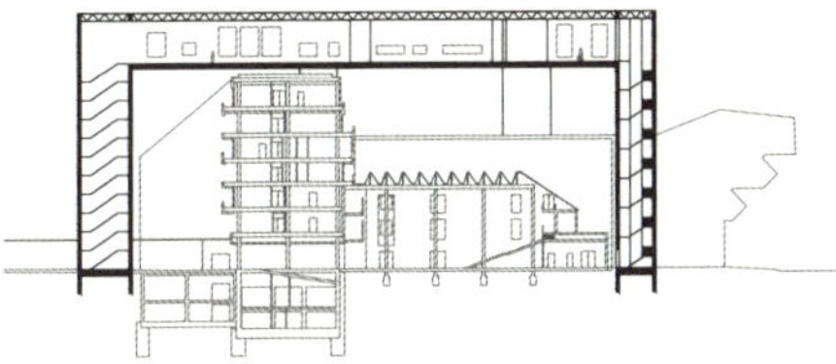

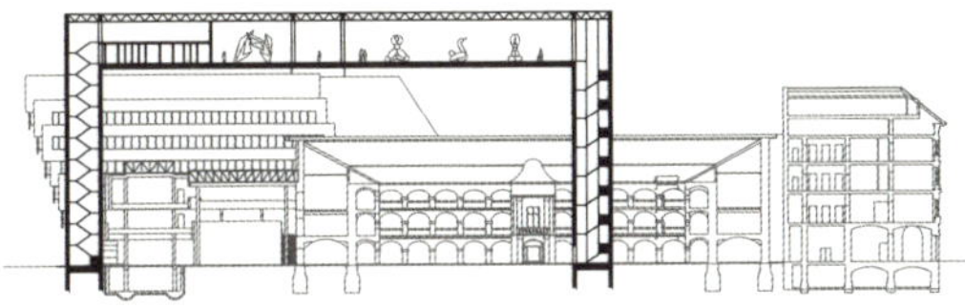

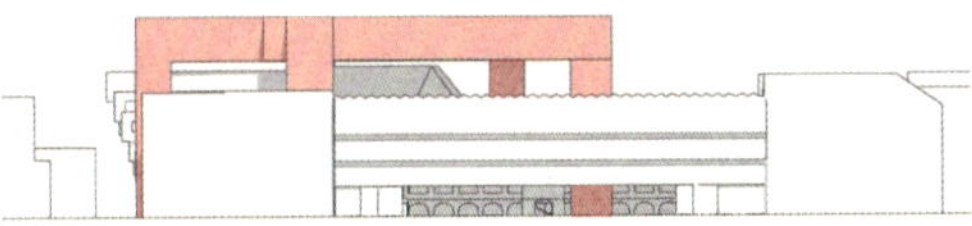

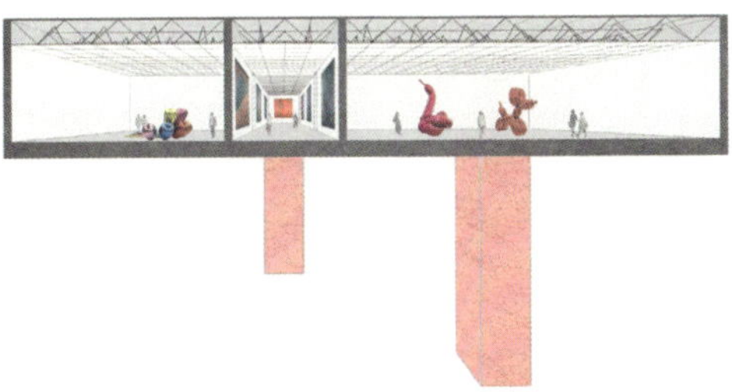

Slovak National Archive—Inhabit Iconic Ruin
Dávid Nosko
Studio Halada/Brádňanský, 2018

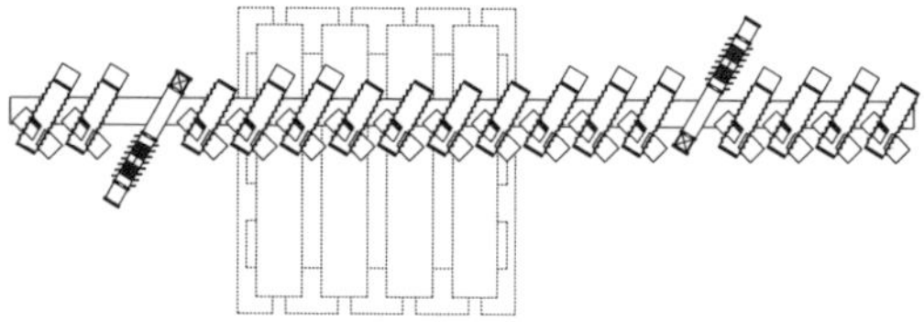

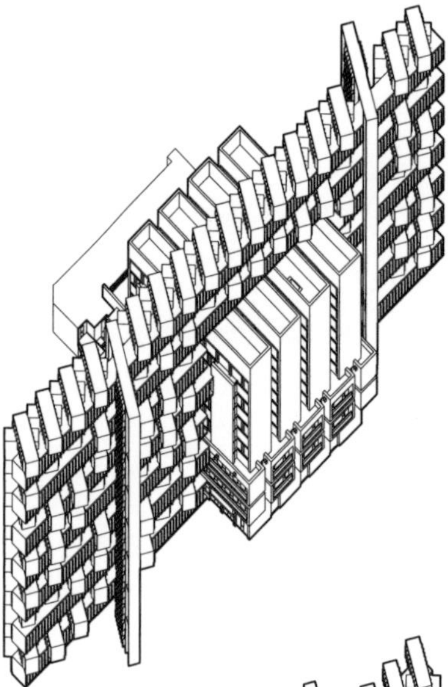

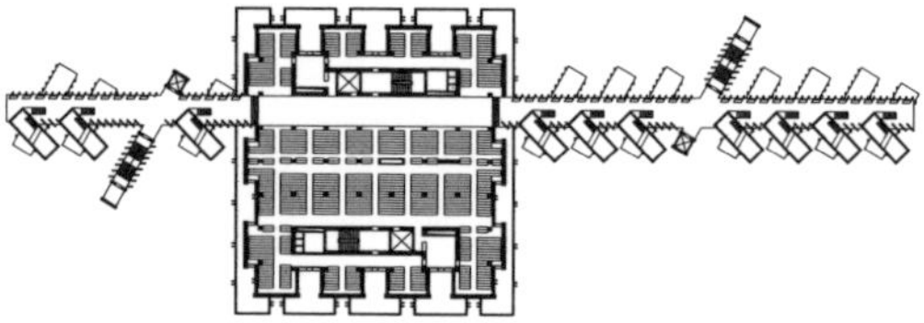

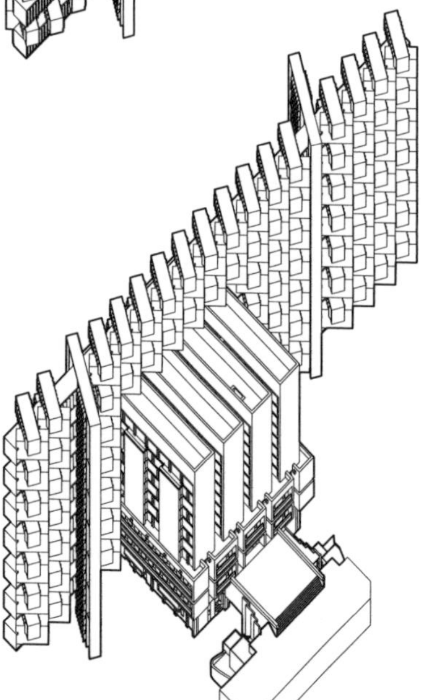

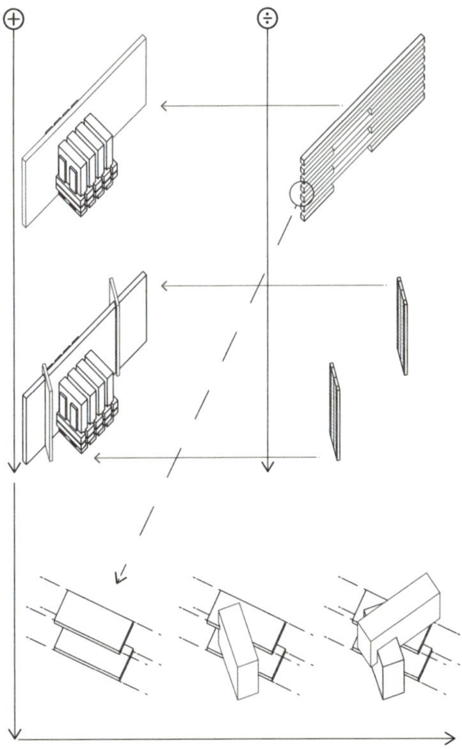

STV Tower—Start Up Centre
Gabriela Lenďáková
Studio Ján Studený, 2016

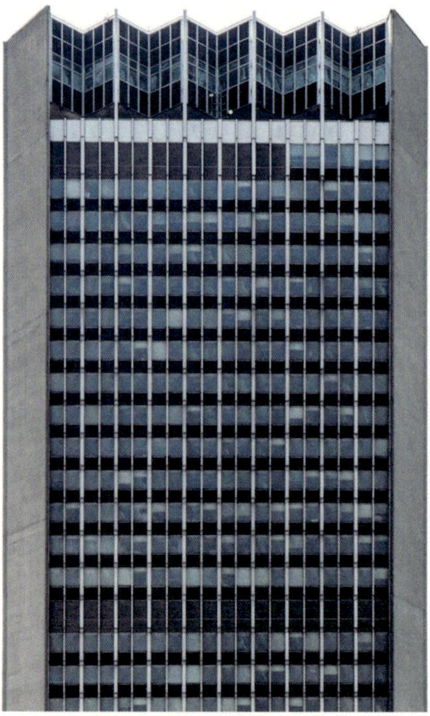

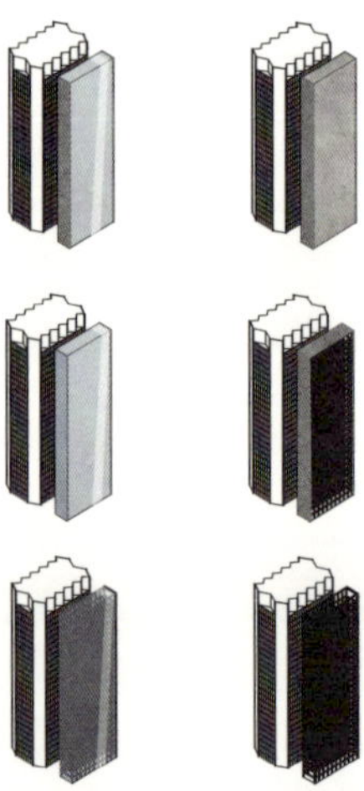

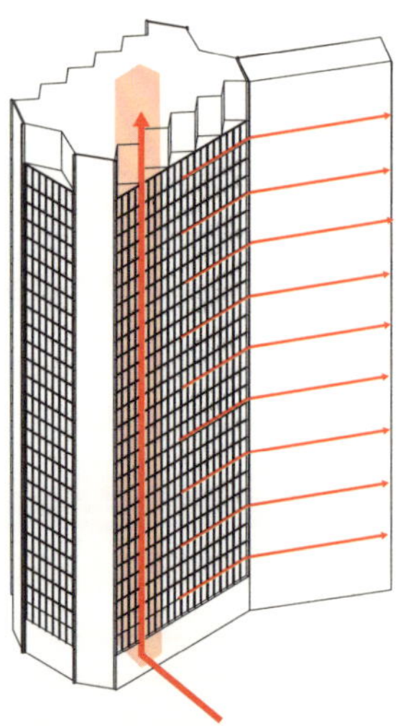

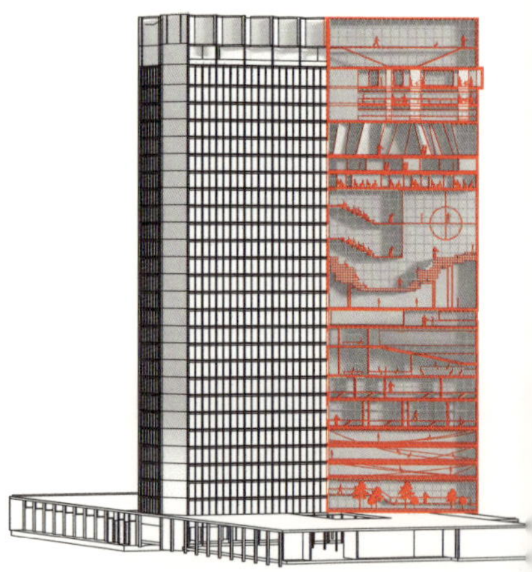

Kamenné Square—Crossing
Filip Kusák
Studio Ján Studený, 2017

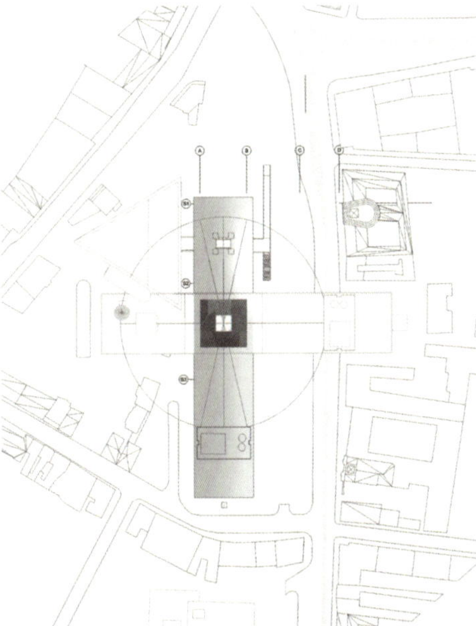

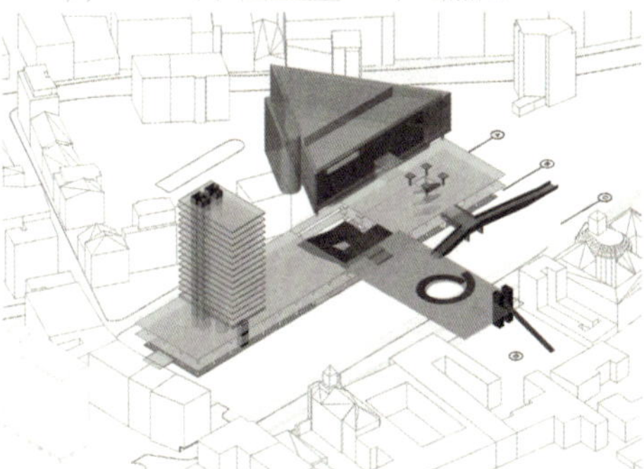

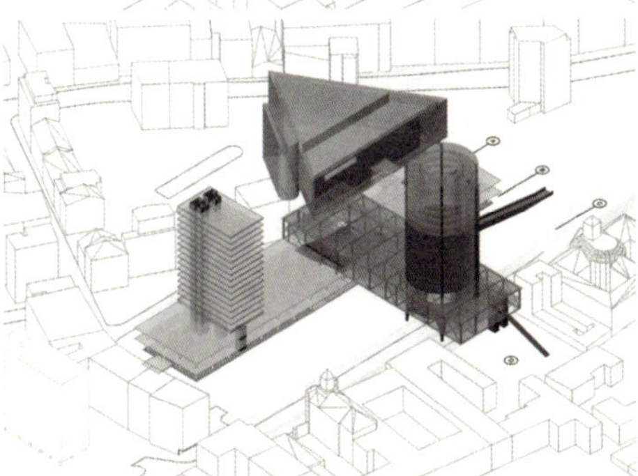

Vivid Square

Organization	Old Market Hall Alliance
Address	Námestie SNP 25, 811 03 Bratislava
Authors	Gábor Bindics, Veronika Hliničanová, Juraj Hurný, Ctibor Košťál, Peter Lényi, Ján Mazúr, Veronika Prachárová, Michal Marcinov & collective, Ondrej Marko & collective
Partners	Slovak Governance Institute
Dates	1 June 2016 – 31 December 2018

Activities				
	Workshops	5	Working group meetings	150
	Publications	17	Presentation sessions	5
	Discussions	4	Conference	1

Vivid Square. Public Space Through Participation

Ján Mazúr, Veronika Hliničanová

In 2016, the Old Market Hall Alliance started to work on a major political space in Slovakia, the Square of the Slovak National Uprising (SNP Square). It was a natural extension of efforts to rejuvenate Old Market Hall, turning it into an important cultural venue in the centre of Bratislava. The Alliance envisions the square as an elegant central space in Bratislava, re-claimed and pedestrian-friendly. The square serves as one of the primary commemoration spaces; important events of Slovak history have their memorials here, such as the Slovak National Uprising, the victim of the 1968 occupation, the 1989 Velvet Revolution protests, or the recently assassinated journalist Ján Kuciak and his fiancée Martina Kušnírová. Last but not least, it would be a space for gathering and contemplation, and not just for transferring or parking.

For hundreds of years, the square served as a marketplace, as evidenced by its historical names: Prot Marckht (1461), Bozapiacz (1658), Vásártér (1880). Gaining a political meaning later during the Austro-Hungarian Empire, the square ceased to be a market. The end of the twentieth century was a missed opportunity to restore its communal function. It remains a broken public space characterized by visual smog, an incoherent use of street furniture, and illegal construction, and it is used predominantly for parking and for public transport transfer. These are the results of layers of random interventions which lack a clear vision.

The case study has two main objectives. First, to prepare the grounds, material and political will to invite competition proposals for lasting solutions to what is probably the most important public space in Bratislava. The competition must fulfill rigorous international standards in order to attract relevant evaluators, architects, and studios. Second, to prepare and implement small-scale interventions—quick wins. Clustered into seven coherent packages, the interventions will make the space more livable and useful to pedestrians and locals. They include taking away 10–15 per cent of parking spaces, removing illegal constructions, harmonizing street furniture, and installing new street lights in the darker parts of the square. In any case, the quick wins must be practical and politically feasible, easy to implement, inexpensive and short-term. They also have to provide short to medium-term value and must not hinder future complex solutions offered in the competition.

For the case study, we reviewed documents and publicly available data and those that were available to the city authorities.

Unfortunately, most of the data were either outdated, incomplete or missing. As a result, we had to run numerous surveys, analyses and studies. For instance, we reviewed hundreds of reports from the public space maintenance app called *Message for the Mayor*; most of them concerned illegal parking and destroyed street furniture. We charted the whole area, creating a 3D map of the buildings, maps of objects, maps of functions etc. We also procured a dendrological survey and collaborated on an ethnographic research of the area.

We also ran a series of participatory surveys. The first one included over 40 in-depth interviews with area stakeholders and institutions, as well as experts on urban planning, architecture and related social sciences. We followed with a massive public survey on the preferences of area locals and visitors, reaping over 1500 responses—potentially the largest participatory endeavour in Bratislava. Finally, upon discovering that certain social groups remained underrepresented in the surveys, we created four focus groups of senior citizens, visually and physically impaired persons, and parents of small children. We orchestrated dozens of additional workshops, public discussions and presentations, and a conference.

Together with our project partners and stakeholders, we decided to create an official local stakeholders' association. It should partner with the municipality in the future implementation of quick wins and represent a unified stakeholders' position. It will also provide members with assistance such as cleaning and security services and advocate for the area in dialogue with the municipality.

It is hoped that the case study will become a prototype for creating public spaces through extensive participation in Slovakia. Should the association succeed in championing locals' and stakeholders' interests, the model could be used in other public spaces, creating an additional layer of (self-)governance between the municipality, stakeholders, and users.

Quick Wins – Small-scale Urban Interventions

Unify Urban Furniture

The analysis shows that there are different types of objects and furniture including: 16 kinds of flower pots, 7 kinds of waste bins, 5 types of cycle stands, 7 types of seating. The aim is to reduce the array of furniture from 61 to 12 standard types.

Restrict Car Parking

Canceling even 9.5 per cent of parking places in the area in the first phase would bring significant change.

Prioritize Pedestrians
More than 40,000 people pass through the square each day—arriving mainly by foot or public transport. Only about 5 per cent of people reach the area by car. In the narrower part of SNP Square, the pedestrian pavement should be widened at the expense of parking space while raising adjacent pedestrian crossings.

Year-round and Seasonal Seating
Creating year-round seating in places where barriers are already present or where such barriers are desirable (e.g. at the proposed playground). From April to October, mobile seasonal seating will be provided.

Social Control
A new playground should be built in the unused space of Kamenné Square. To achieve better visibility, it is necessary to trim the trees, cut the shrubs underneath, and install lighting as well as new information boards on the squares. Establish new kiosks—the goal of diverse local businesses is to attract customers all day and year round.

Square of the Slovak National Uprising

Old Market Hall Alliance
2021 Architects

Colour Codes in Architecture Visualizations

Street lighting	Yellow
Playground	Blue
Bicycle lanes	Dark green
Greenery	Light green
Pedestrian walks	Red
Pedestrian crossing	Purple

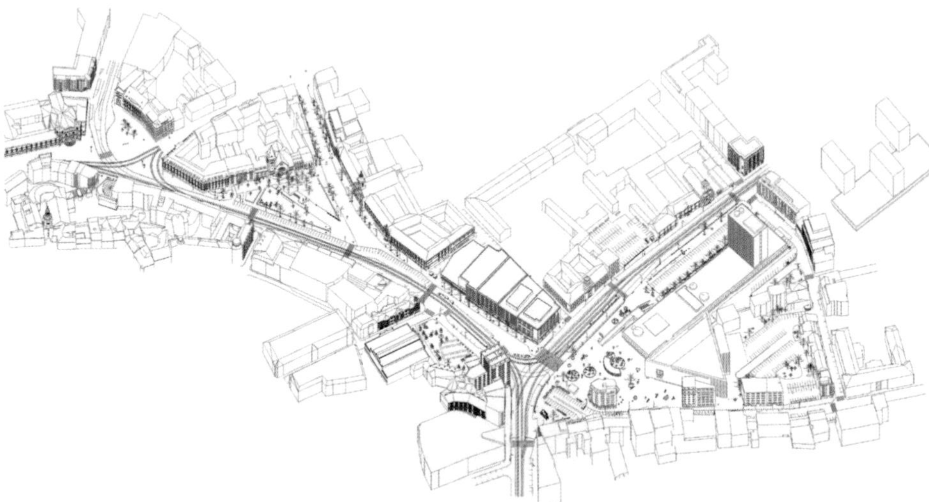

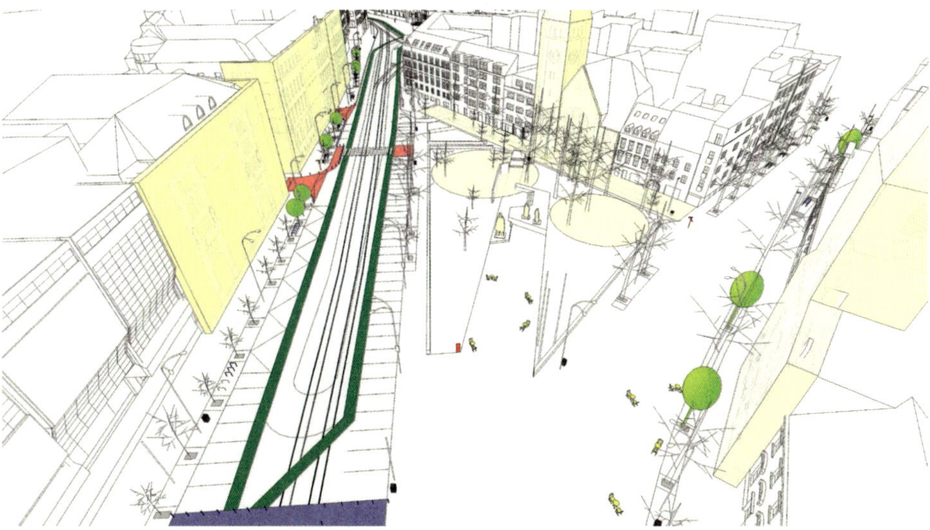

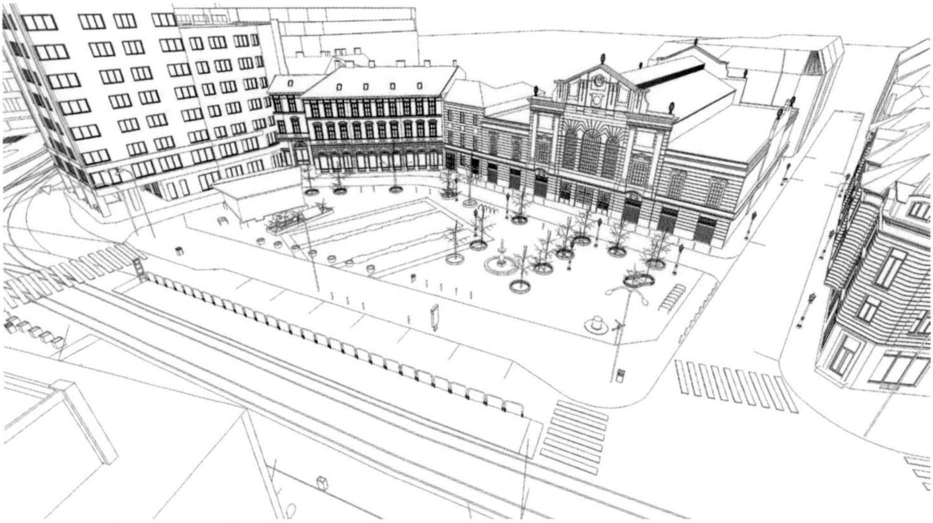

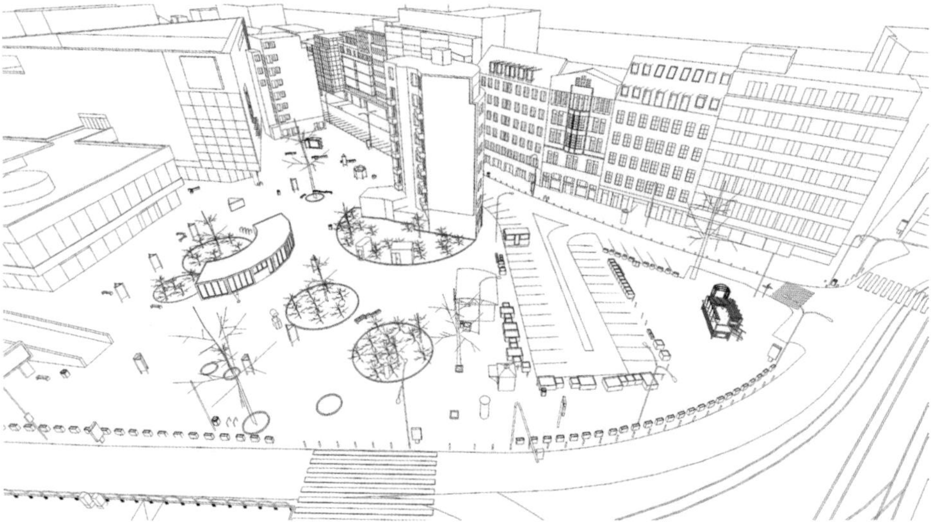

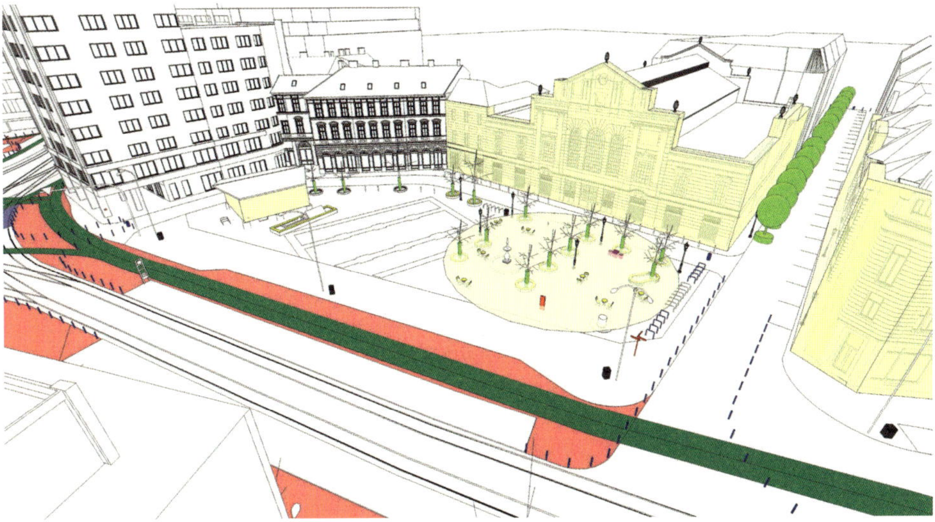

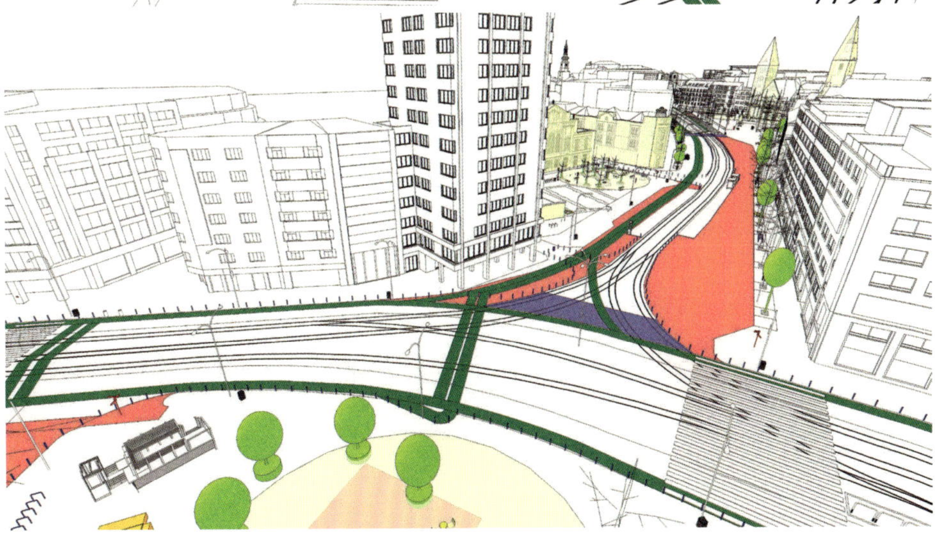

A Message for the May Crowdsensing Platform Public Space Managem

The poor state of public spaces has become a typical feature of Bratislava and, with a few exceptions, most Slovak cities. At the same time, citizens are now able to spot, report, and even fix problems in their areas before municipal maintenance systems even respond to them. Jan Mazúr states that crowdsensing tools are the result of bringing together participatory sensing tools and a large number of participants.[1] They can be delivered via mobile networks to district residents and, enhanced with semantic legal categories, they can cut the transaction costs of municipalities reporting public service issues to citizens, and have issues automatically assigned to authorities.

A Message for the Mayor

Odkaz pre starostu (A Message for the Mayor, MfM) is an online communication platform for reporting public space issues. It was designed by two IT specialists, who were inspired by the UK-based platform *FixMyStreet*. Launched in 2010 by the NGO Slovak Governance Institute, it streamlines the communication between citizens and municipalities. Issues are communicated to the local government, and their solutions are communicated to the users. Largely operated by volunteers, the tool has processed 47,000 reports since its release.[2] Feedback (reports, complaints) is provided by hundreds of individual users in a semi-structured form, which allows for a broad categorization of the reported issue or situation.

1
J. Mazúr, 'Crowd-Sourced Participatory Sensing of Legally Relevant Situations under Smart City: The Case of Bratislava' (June 2017), unpublished.

2
As of September 2018.

Chart 1
Complaint analysis in time

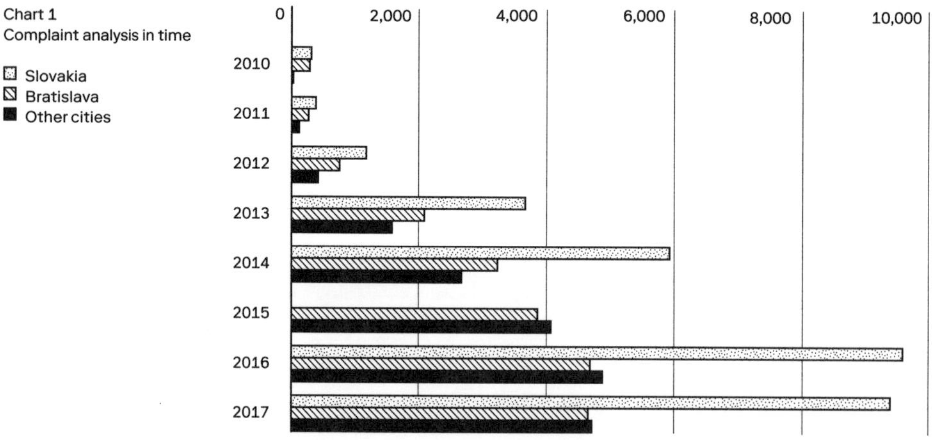

r:
s for a More Efficient
ent

Chart 2
Content analysis of the complaints

■ =100

Content analysis of the complaints	Bratislava		Slovakia (other cities)	
Roads and pavements (potholes, stairs, barriers, obstacles, curbs)	5,883	27%	27%	5,679
Illegal buildings, structures and their changes (buildings, walls)	677	3%	2%	426
Traffic signs, crosswalks, traffic lights	1,734	8%	8%	1,653
City's movable property (trash bins, playgrounds, benches, statues)	1,468	7%	8%	1,691
Abandoned cars and wrecks (old cars)	1,888	9%	3%	671
Parking (places, problematic parking)	1,525	7%	7%	1,414
Public services (drainage system, lighting, schools, public transport)	1,716	8%	10%	2,162
Public order (silent hours, advertising, graffiti)	1,501	7%	5%	1,002
Green and environment (illegal landfills, animals)	4,637	21%	20%	4,179
Other	1,163	5%	9%	1,886

Users

The app is used by more women than men in the 25–55 age group. It is least used by the youngest (15–25) and eldest (60+) citizens.[3] Young people are unaware of public space issues and the existence of the platform, while the elderly are unfamiliar with the technology. This limits the use of the tool in participatory planning processes. The distribution of user reports follows the typical fat tail distribution: most users report once or twice, while a smaller number of loyal users and followers report dozens or even hundreds of issues.

3
Slovak Governance Institute, 'Age and Gender profile of the users. Google Analytics for Message for a Mayor', 2017.
Note: Age and gender has been calculated from approximately 60% – 190,000 users.

Chart 3
Age and gender structure of the users

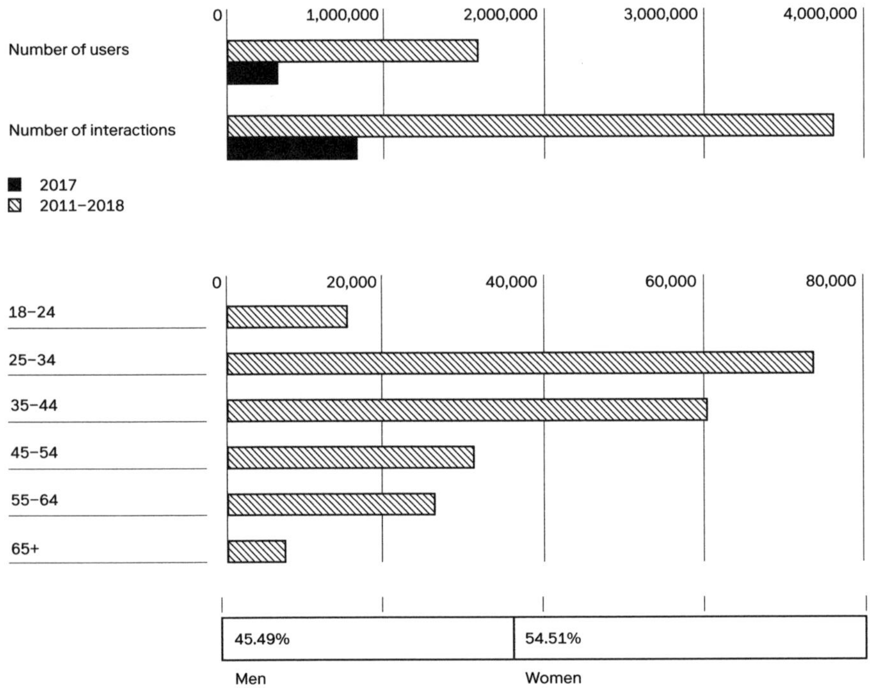

How it Works

There is a discrepancy between the simple process of receiving the message (via the free app) and the low success rate of issues solved by Bratislava City Hall. This is due to several reasons: too many areas of responsibility (compared to municipal districts), complicated and unsystematic responsibility structure, and little or no communication between departments. As there is no official stance on managing reports from the outside, reported issues often reach the director of the Mayor's office, politicians, or department heads. As a result, it takes a long time to solve issues in areas that City Hall is directly responsible for. On average, municipal districts have higher success rates, which could be attributed to fewer reports and/or people involved in the solution.

Chart 4
MfM process diagram

Step 1 →	Step 2 →	Step 3 →	Step 4
Report uploaded by user (location, description, image).	Report is analyzed by MfM volunteers and/or by municipality employees, passed onto the responsible clerk either at the municipality, other public authority (e.g. the police) or a private service provider.	Problem is marked 'pending'. Municipality has a 14-day period to respond to the reported problem.	• Municipality responds > problem is marked as 'solved' or 'being solved'. • Municipality does not respond > 'not solved' (or 'pending' for a given period of time).

Chart 5
MfM types of responses

In process	Closed	Solved	Unsolved
The issue pends for a period of time in which the municipality is expected to respond.	The issue is not relevant anymore, an unknown party (not the municipality) has solved the issue or the problem reporter is not satisfied with the solution provided by the municipality.	The municipality has addressed and solved the problem. If the solution is not considered to be satisfactory by the MfM team, the volunteer addresses the municipality again.	The issue automatically becomes unsolved, if there is no response to the problem in 14 days, if a municipality does not fulfil a given promise or if a problem reporter or other reporter provides feedback that the issue was not solved.

Uneven Balance

What is Most Problematic in Bratislava?

Chart 6
Submitted cases in different municipal districts of Bratislava

Resolved cases in different municipal districts of Bratislava.

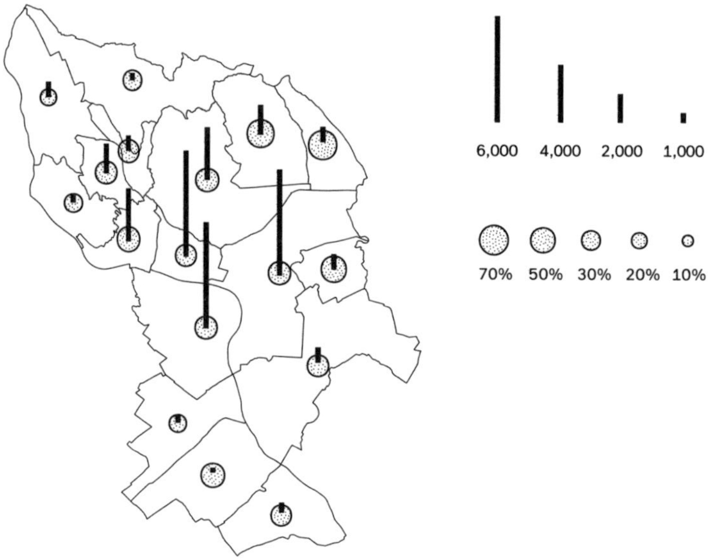

> 'I myself was an active user of the platform, until today. The weakness of the whole initiative is that it can't change the behaviour of the municipality and make them solve smaller, but equally important issues. This however is a value problem, since installing a bike stand is not an issue of money or competences, but simply of willingness on the part of the municipality.'
>
> Matúš Čupka, former volunteer, candidate for Mayor of Bratislava-New City

Impacts

The app has become the most important tool for reporting issues with 114 municipalities adopting it in Slovakia.

Chart 7
MfM participating cities in Slovakia

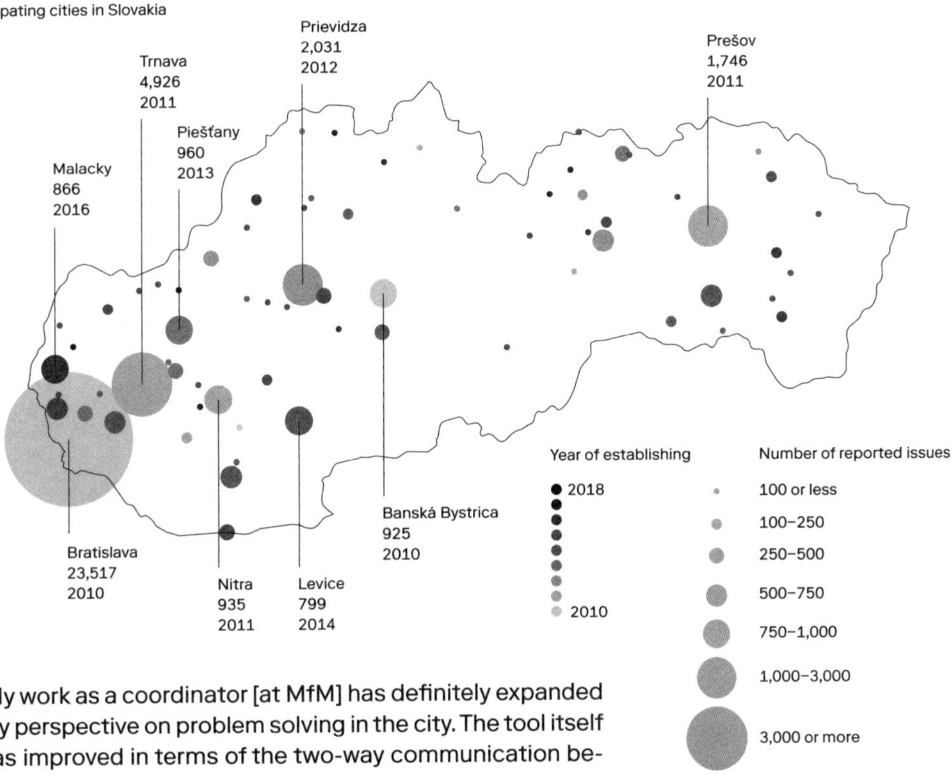

'My work as a coordinator [at MfM] has definitely expanded my perspective on problem solving in the city. The tool itself has improved in terms of the two-way communication between citizens and municipalities.'
Peter Brocka, MfM volunteer, Mayor of Trnava (2014–2022)

Chart 8
MfM status of reports in participating cities (per cent)

Status	Bratislava	Košice	Trnava	Prievidza
Unsolved	26	41	2	8
Closed	3	2	1	3
In solution	27	23	24	25
Solved	43	33	73	63
Posted by self-government	1	1	0	1

Volunteering. For How Long?

The application is currently provided free of charge, though a cooperation contract that comes with the free service binds municipalities to a long-term commitment. But how long can a team of 30 volunteer administrators provide this service in over a hundred municipalities? A few additional paid positions are currently being funded by an EU grant. In the past, the resources came from different projects and donations. The question of financial sustainability is essential; the application should offer a paid upgrade in the future. Real change is only possible if municipalities include public-reported issues in their regular agenda, and not see them as extra workload. It is a matter of commitment and of efficient restructuring of resources.

Prague

2.01

Population
(millions of inhab.)

2016 (metropolitan regions)
2016 (Belgrade)
2017 (other cities)

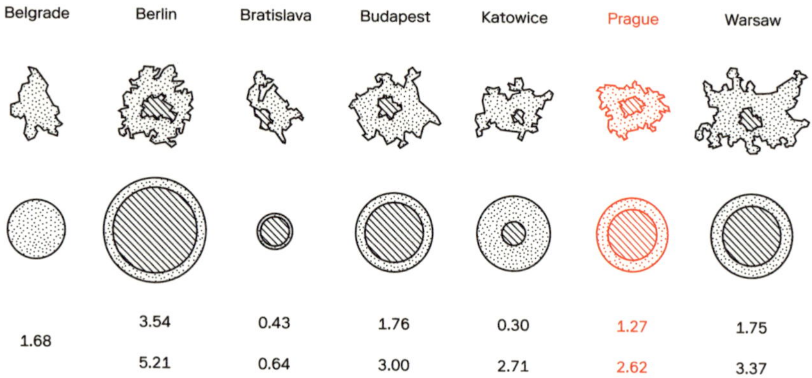

City
Metropolitan region

2.02

Built-up area footprint

City
2016
Total area: 496 km²
Population density:
2,581 inhab./km²

0 5 km

2.03

Population projection
(per cent change)

Metropolitan regions
2016–2040 (Belgrade)
2016–2050 (other cities)

→ Population
Chart B.03, p. 16

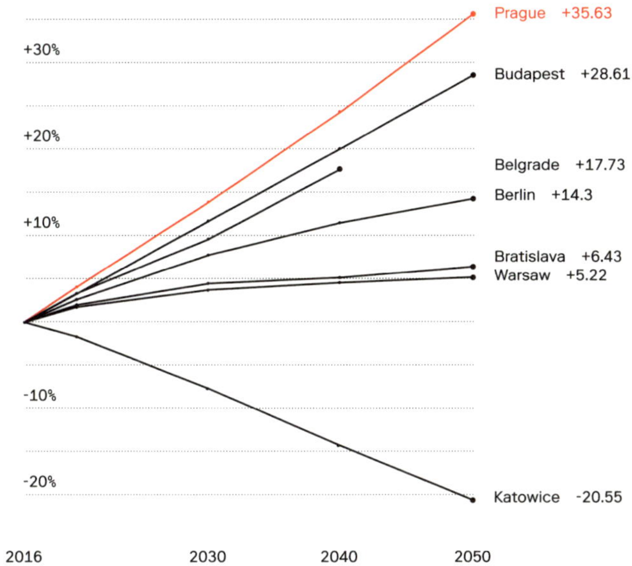

2.04

Population density
(inhab./km²)

Metropolitan regions
2015

→ Spatial Development
Chart E.09, p. 29

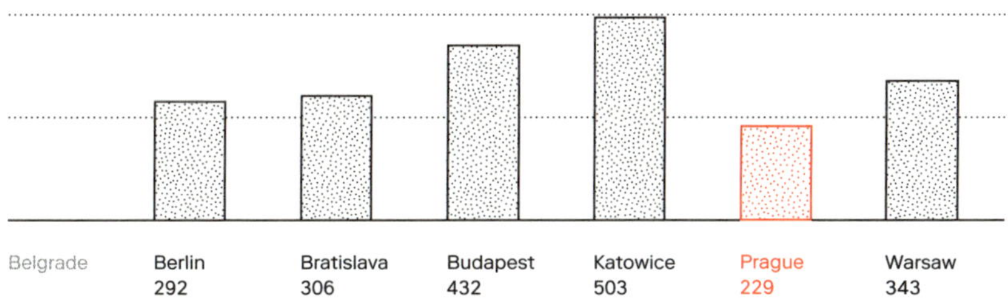

2.05

Average area of living accommodation (m²/inhab.)

City
2011

22.08

◆ = 5 m²

2.06

Average monthly net salary (EUR)

City
2018

1,033.23

▧ = 100 €

2.07

Registered passenger cars (cars/1,000 inhab.)

City
2016

621

■ = 20 cars

2.08

Tourists
(number/year)

City
2016

7,127,558

= 1 million tourists

PLASTY

LÉKAŘ.cz

LODĚTERIA
PIVO & DRINKY
GRILOVANÉ
DOBROTY
PIZZA
BURGER
TYRŠ

Foyer²

Organization	Goethe-Institut
Address	Masarykovo nábřeží 32, 11000 Prague
Authors	ifau, Jakob Ráček, Stefanie Heublein, Milota Sidorová, Zuzana Čermáková
Dates	1 June 2016 – 28 February 2020

Activities				
	Workshops	7	Discussions	10
	Publication	1	Film screenings	3

Foyer². A Space for Negotiation

Jakob Ráček, Kamil Pavelka

Architecture is never neutral. It emerges through a negotiation process that shapes the way we carry out discourse. As Winston Churchill said: 'We shape our buildings; thereafter they shape us.' For the Goethe-Institut in Prague, *Shared Cities: Creative Momentum* also initiated a long journey of self-reflection, culminating in efforts to change the institute's institutional agency.

One of the main tasks of the Goethe-Institut is to provide a space for discourse. Mostly, these kinds of premises are academic and one-sided, pitting an active speaker against a passive audience. For a few years now, the Goethe-Institut has been trying to deconstruct these traditional debate formats and replace them with a more democratic space for negotiation.

The architecture of the Goethe-Institut in Prague is a perfect example of early twentieth-century Art Nouveau. The entrance and the publicly accessible space on the first and second floors are impressive to the point of intimidation. The ceremonious air of the building collides with the general policy of the Goethe-Institut to be an open institution with low thresholds.

The second-floor foyer used to be the sore spot of the whole institution. This attractive space with a beautiful panoramic view of Prague's Hradčany was being used for multiple but contradicting purposes such as a gallery, an event space, a formal venue for receptions, and even a storage room. To understand and develop the full potential of the foyer, the Goethe-Institut invited and commissioned the Berlin-based architects from the ifau (Institut für angewandte urbanistik), as ifau works on two levels: spatial transformations and user-oriented negotiations of cultural institutions, such as the Grazer Kunstverein, Artists Space in NYC or Casco in Utrecht, or large-scale co-housing and social housing projects in Berlin and Hamburg in various co-operations and with different stakeholders. Both elements of their work were highly relevant to us: the sharing of public space combined with the re-shaping of institutional agency are present in ifau's work and in *Foyer²* on the second floor. Or, as they put it themselves:

> The Goethe-Institut in Prague is a heritage protected building, so you can't change it structurally—you work with minor or exchangeable interventions such as furniture. We tried to create a common space for co-working and co-operation in all its senses—for guests, artists-in-residence, the public, and the members of the Goethe-Institut. The idea of

> a 'meeting and productive working situation' in a non-commercial space has been crucial.
> We understand the city as an open system where every process is negotiable. In light of this we are examining our work as planners, and how to intervene and react to the problems and contradictions of a city.
> City spaces should be open to the public. But in reality, there are very few truly public and truly open spaces. With *Foyer²* we need to work step by step to create programmes that invite people to shape what's happening within the space.

Having analyzed the different activities taking place in the second-floor foyer, ifau has suggested an architectonic intervention composed of a hung infrastructural ceiling grid and a flexible, cross-shaped bar-height table. The idea was to create a space for multi-scale and multi-purpose events—small and concentrated dialogues with a high degree of intimacy, as well as large panels with various speakers and engaged audiences, making *Foyer²* one of Prague's common coordinates, an indoor public space. The result is an open structure that can be shaped to meet the needs of its users or programme. The circular design activates the audience and invites participation. The *objet barré* forms and informs future events.

Another new addition to *Foyer²* was the 'communal fridge'. It was a kind of a McGuffin to the whole process of creating a shared space for employees, partners, and the public. The idea was to have an empty and accessible fridge to trigger everyday appropriation of the space. One could have (or share) a drink and use this space with the best view of the city as an ad-hoc bar for meetings with friends, colleagues or guests of the Goethe-Institut. But the idea did not catch on. It is currently abandoned and certainly does not bode well for the institute's ecological footprint. But even without the fridge, *Foyer²* has so far hosted and shaped numerous discussions about architecture, as well as other events.

The process of transformation did not stop with the opening of the transformed space and its rebranding. It has generated an important discussion about appropriation. Also, the idea of blending physical and digital space was rather relevant to the design of *Foyer²*. Events at the Goethe-Institut are going to be either recorded or streamed online as much as possible. Thanks to the new architecture, it will be much easier to make debates accessible to an online audience participating through streaming services.

The situative design for the Goethe-Institut in Prague is to some extent scalable and transferable to other places. As an architectural intervention, it refers to a site-specific constellation within the premises of a cultural institution, but what can be adopted for the design and use of similar spaces is the approach of negotiation, problematization, and appropriation.

Spatial elements of *Foyer*[2]
Designed by ifau Berlin

1 A cross-shaped bar table
Manufactured by Master & Master s.r.o., Prague
The cross-shaped bar table (450×450 cm, height: 115 cm) is made of four single bar tables. These four functionally diverse tables are joined by screw connections and levelled by screw threads at the bottom of the table legs.

2 A grid ceiling
Manufactured by Master & Master s.r.o., Prague
To provide the bar table with electricity, light and display options, a hung grid ceiling is installed 50 to 60 cm below the existing ceiling of the second-floor foyer.

3 A curtain screen
Manufactured by couturereal, Berlin
To provide shade, acoustical improvement and intimacy, a screen-like curtain folded in deep pleats is hung in an offset of 70 cm to the panoramic bay window of the foyer.

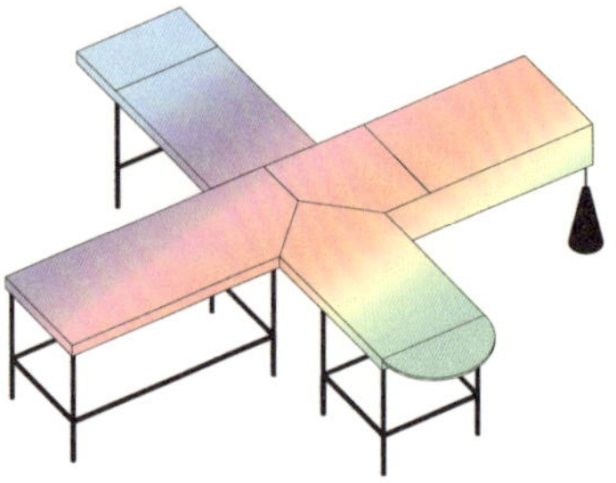

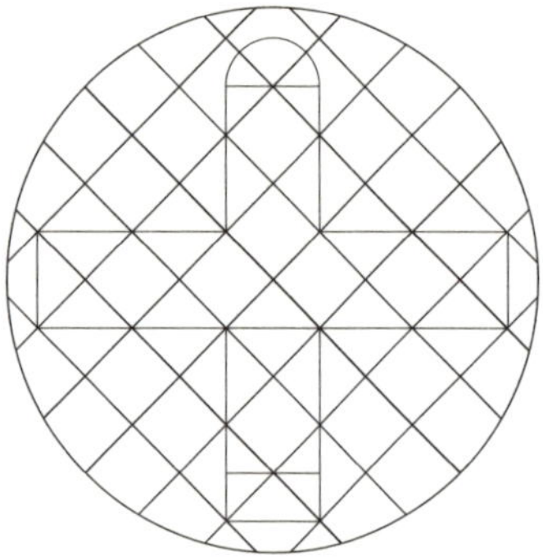

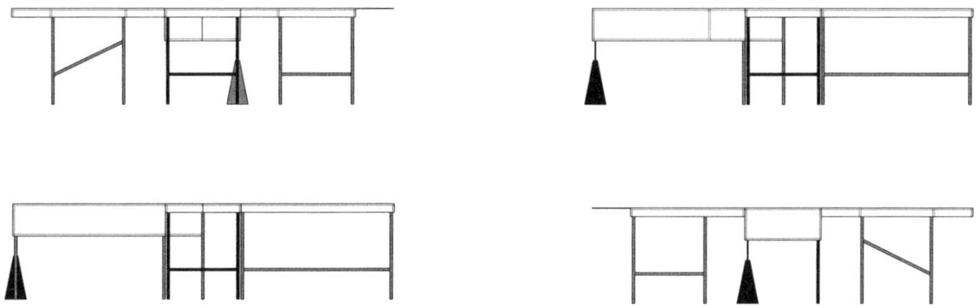

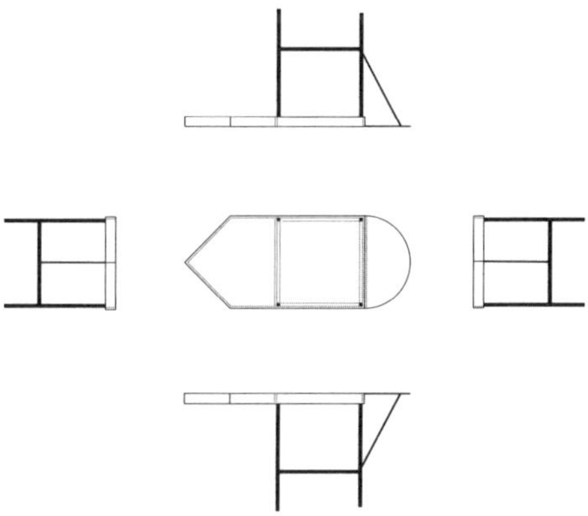

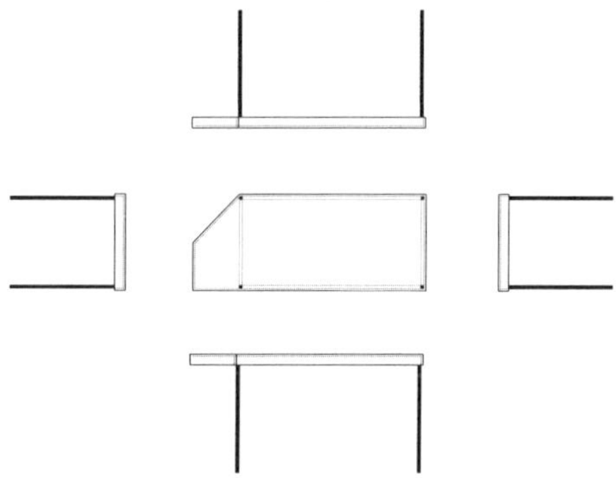

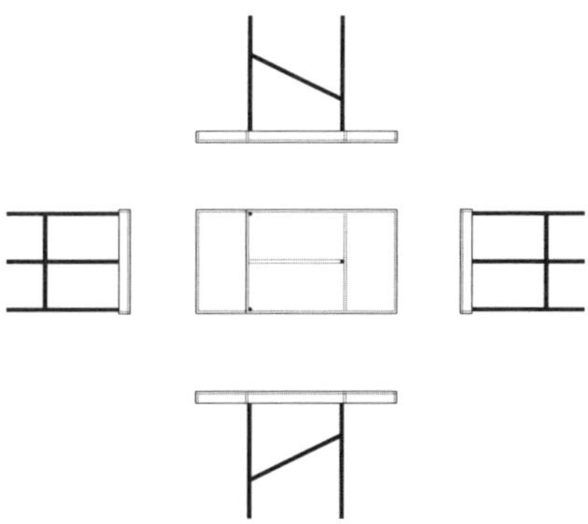

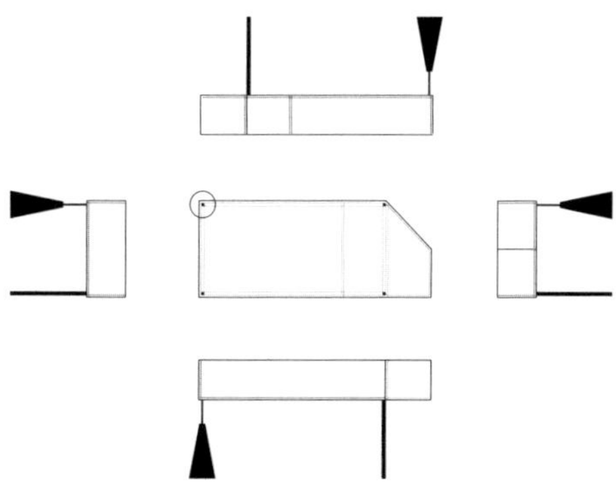

Curating Architecture

Organization	reSITE
Address	Voršilská 130/10, 110 00 Prague
Authors	Martin Joseph Barry, Helena Doudová, Lída Hasmanová, Osamu Okamura, Radka Ondráčková; Lila Athanasiadou, Anastasia Eggers and Ottonie von Roeder, Lydia Karagiannaki, Olga Labovkina
Partners	KUNSTrePUBLIK
Dates	1 June 2016 – 28 February 2020
Activities	Conferences 3 Residencies 4 Workshops 3 Publications 4

~~Architecture~~ Experience First. The Art of Sharing

Martin Joseph Barry, Osamu Okamura

Today's Central European cities face a growing polarization between an imminent demographic decline and the inability to benefit from increasing local and global migration. Slowly deteriorating older neighbourhoods are abandoned in favour of developing new land. The urban tissue is thus becoming frayed and more difficult to maintain effectively.

Is it possible to return to the principles that define a city, the ability to benefit from mutual cooperation and mutual proximity? Enriching one another not at the expense of others but through diversity, promoting various approaches, knowledge and skills? How can creativity be supported while responding to the challenges facing humanity in the near future?

Let's debunk a myth. Sharing is not always great. It is messy. It can be uncomfortable and can be a pain in the neck if people ask us to share too much or too often. The space or architecture of sharing loses significance if the experience is uncomfortable or poorly curated. The experience is where the magic lies. Sharing protects us from ignorance, and the space we design helps provide an environment stimulating the exchange of knowledge. But architecture in and of itself does not extend knowledge or understanding.

reSITE has a mission to connect people, bridge the gaps and create dialogue. Through unique experiences, events, discussions, and an extensive network of minds, we try to share best practices and ideas for sustainability and resilience, and ultimately push for the development of real places: the modern drivers and raison d'être of sharing, in opposition to the conventional top-down collective practice from the communist era.

We create spaces, both temporal and semi-permanent, that increase chance encounters among disparate groups. But above all, we create experiences. The location of our stage—in the centre of the audience, like a boxing ring, is a direct form of provocation. We put the speakers in the metaphorical ring and expect them to be comfortable presenting their views to all sides.

The space we create is not just a physical one. It is digital and virtual. We have hosted hundreds of thousands of people in physical spaces but hosted millions across multiple digital channels. Is the physical space more important than the virtual one? They only truly make sense when they complement each other and are merged into a seamlessly unified experience.

Before we consider the physical space for our events, we have in mind several archetypal architectural structures. These structures provide the canvas or ingredients for the experience.

We think of a bridge to encourage communication and collaboration among different interest groups. While crossing that bridge—usually over a mental, professional, or institutional divide—we want to make them discover the advantage of one interest we all share in the urban context: the public interest.

We think of a forum, a forum where we listen to and present inspiring ideas and positive solutions. Where we recognize someone's great work. Where we share different opinions. Where we push the limits of how we think about our cities and about living in our cities.

We think of a marketplace. A bustling, sometimes chaotic crossroads where everyone can test their chances of succeeding with a concept, a service, a tool. Where we can find partners and colleagues or the missing pieces to develop our ideas, to give the right direction to our investment, to choose the best of the possible ways and solutions. The market is where the idea magic really happens. It's where you explore the friction found in the forum and put the final pieces of the bridge together. This is where and how we convince our audiences, and it's highly choreographed—even if you can't sense it at first glance.

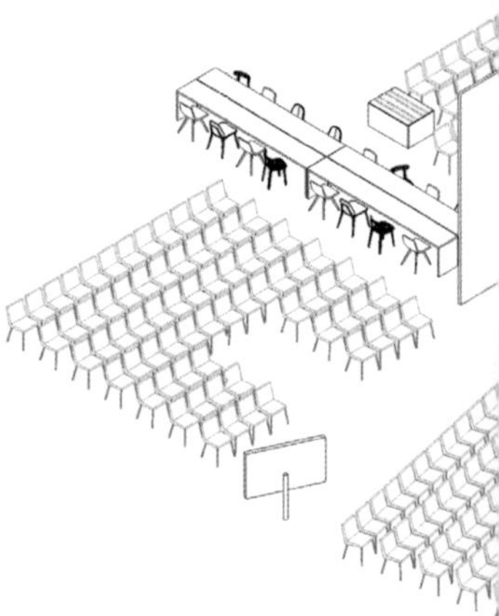

Our ideas and provocations are not meant to appease everyone. When we aim for collaboration, we often seek the middle ground by hearing both sides' arguments. The activists want us to be activists. The capitalists want us to be capitalists. We seek neither. We seek to find answers. We believe the best ones emerge through friction. This, for us, is increasingly important in a world dominated by loud polarities and folks being comfortable only in their bubbles, be they bubbles of the left or right, generational, or cultural. We despise bubbles.

The archetypes have one goal in common: open the eyes, open the minds, stimulate new relationships, and inspire design action that will have a positive impact on the future for us and the next generation of urban dwellers. Let's ensure that the experience of sharing is more important than the 'architecture of sharing'.

In addition, reSITE and KUNSTrePUBLIK explored the staging of architecture sharing and urbanism in contemporary artistic and curatorial practice at four two-month residencies at Zentrum für Kunst und Urbanistik (ZK/U) in Berlin in spring 2018. The aim was to produce contemporary artistic positions and analyses on the theme 'Share your heart. Share your city,' a task for the five residents (Lila Athanasiadou, artists' duo Anastasia Eggers and Ottonie von Roeder, Lydia Karagiannaki, Olga Labovkina). Their work at ZK/U was informed by theoretical and practice-based critiques in geography, anthropology, urban planning, architecture, urban policy, and the humanities.

360° Podium

reSITE

Conference scenario and space bring together leaders, mayors, architects, urban planners, developers / investors, artists and activists from around the world across the spectrum of urban development. Through panel discussions, keynotes, interactive workshops, urban games, guided tours, film screenings and dance performances, the event seeks to be a one-of-a-kind experience combining the best ideas in the world from the bottom to the top.

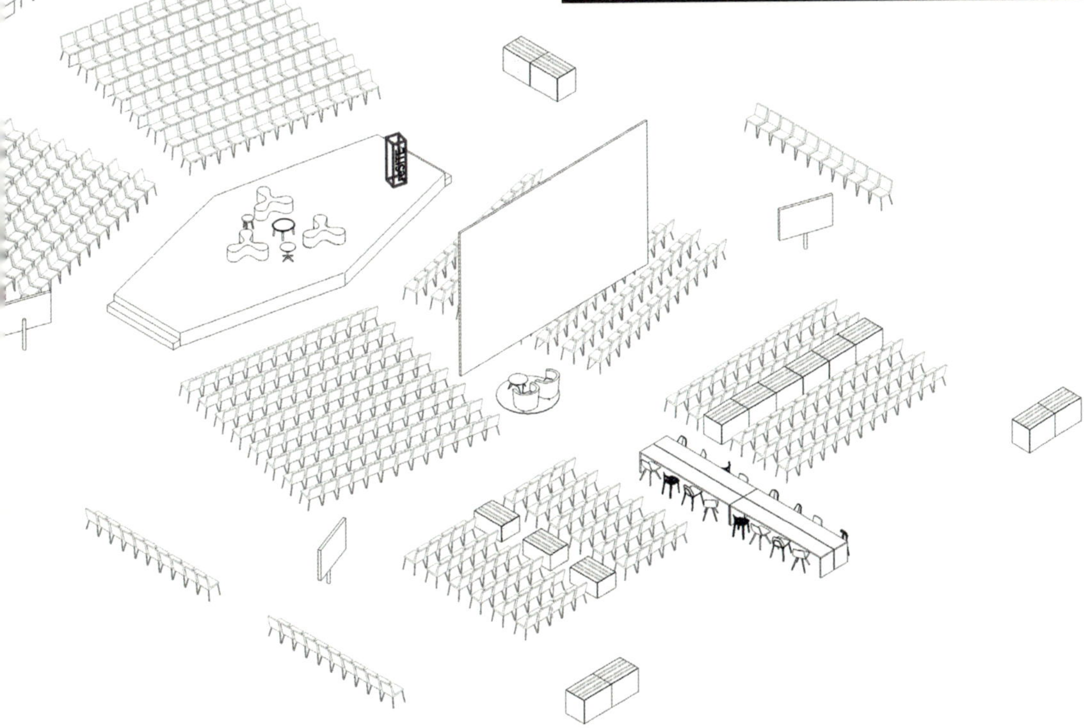

Live Mic Stage

reSITE

In 2018, reSITE hosted for the first time lively and popular discussions on its intimate Live Mic Stage simply made of 50 pallets and installed in a public courtyard to create a truly democratic space. Sou Fujimoto, Jeanne Gang, Ricky Burdett, Dara Huang, Michel Rojkind and other speakers shared what they learned in reaction to visitors' questions about what happens behind the scenes of their work.

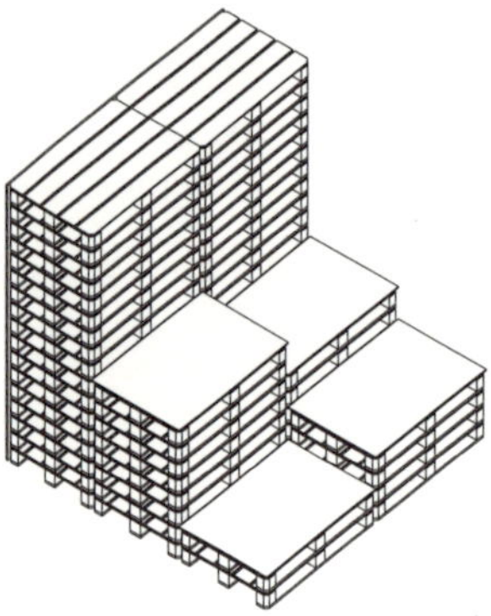

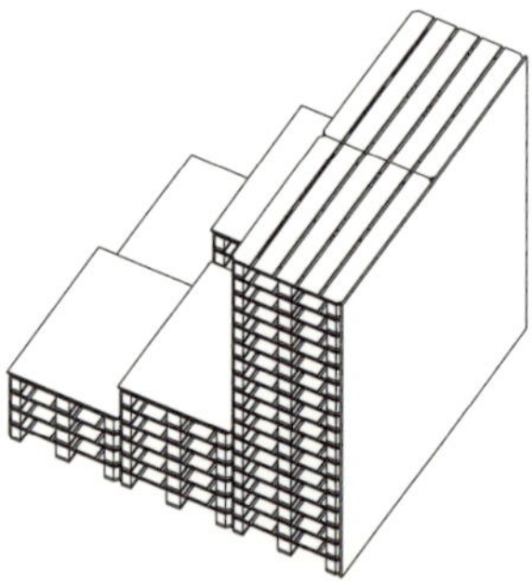

[right page]

Homage to the Residents

Lydia Karagiannaki

A site-specific installation, non-intrusive and almost invisible rests on the notion of sharing, or 'sharing over time' the same space and similar experiences in a residency studio. The room was kept in its original state, with no addition of external elements except for explanatory labels. The work was the visitor's experience, enabled by her/his imagination, sometimes leaving traces. The installation was an experiment: creating subtle environments and immersive experiences requiring personal interaction, re-enactment and empathy.

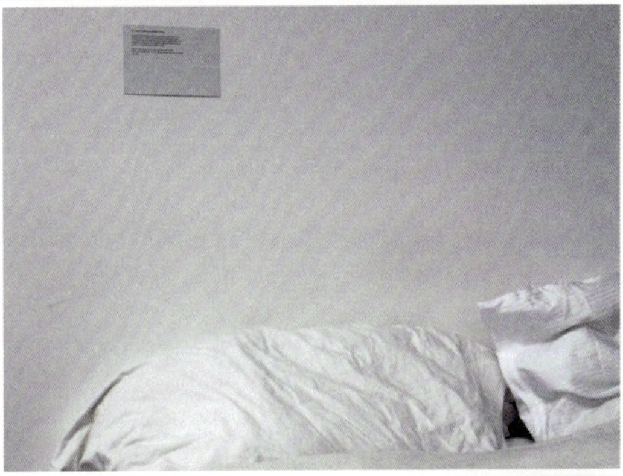
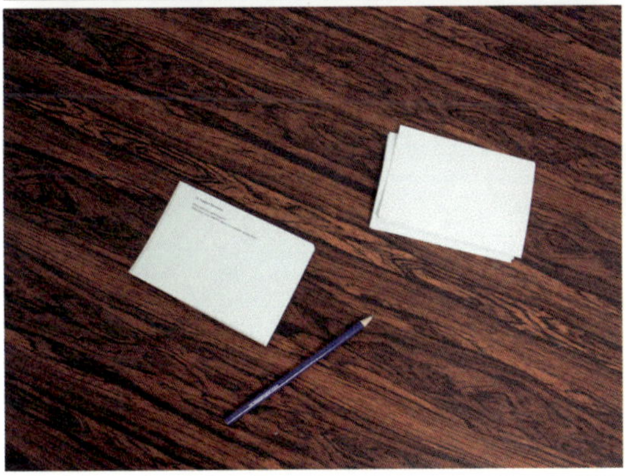

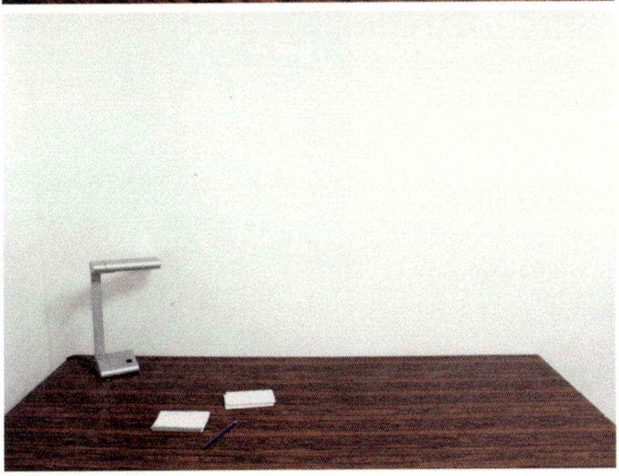

Waschsalon. Collective Washing in the Age of Warm Water Blockchain

Anastasia Eggers, Ottonie von Roeder

The intervention 'Waschsalon' is part of a speculative scenario wherein water is recycled and re-used. 'Waschsalon' hacks into public infrastructure and invites you to wash body and clothes together while exploring a possible future in which water and heat are no longer wasted but rather fed into a blockchain system. 'Waschsalon' makes the physical experience of collective public washing possible and creates an opportunity for informal community dialogue.

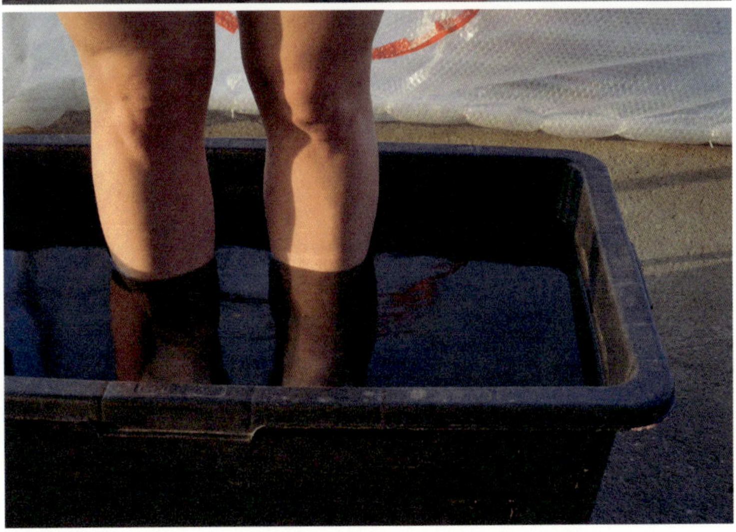

Milota Sidorová with Eva Ešnerová, Vladimír Lieberzeit (Prague Institute for Planning and Development), Tomáš Soukup

Affordable, Shared Nei How Long Can It Last?

A Typical Story?

Prague 7 has a seemingly typical history: a formerly industrial neighbourhood that gradually became a residential one.[1] In 2014, a local civic group *Praha 7 Sobě* won the municipal elections in this small yet popular Prague district. Privatization, restitution, and recurring floods (2002, 2006, 2013) have catalyzed its rapid transformation into a modern area fairly close to the city centre. It has attracted newcomers looking for affordable housing. While the district could easily have succumbed to free market pressures, the new municipal leadership was aware of the dangers if they did nothing to keep the district affordable.

Map
Prague 7 city district

Area: 7.14 km²
Population in 2017: 44,034
Population by 2030: 55,000

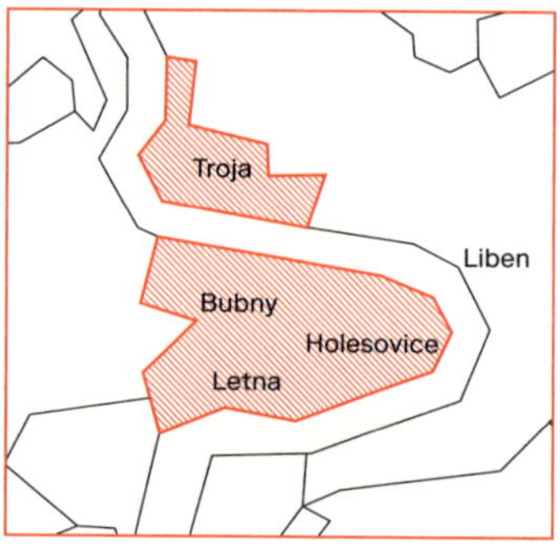

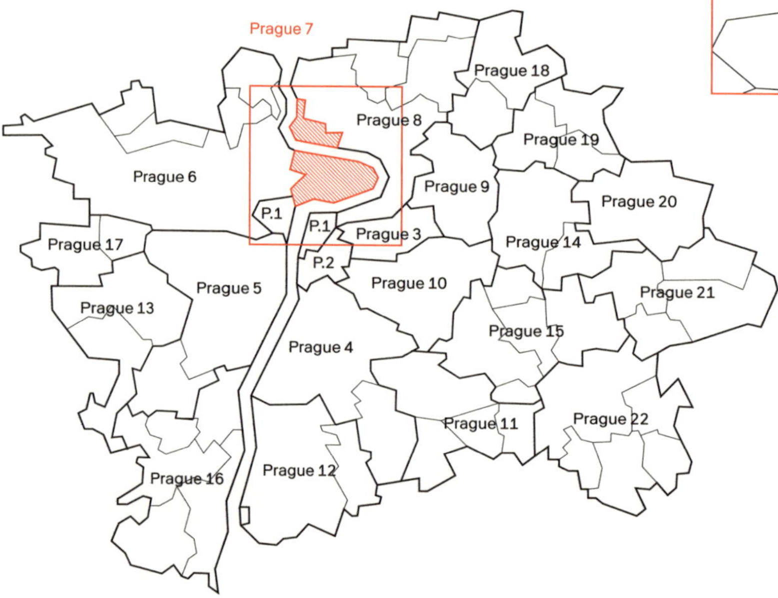

bourhood.

Chart 1
Prague 7 modern history

< 1989

- Industry declined in Prague 7
- Industry remained in Holešovice
- Letná became a mostly residential area

1989

The Velvet Revolution

1990s

- Privatization and restitutions of individual flats and properties
- First small and medium establishments opened in Holešovice

2002

- Major floods
- Holešovice under water
- Evacuation of citizens
- 200+ houses damaged
- Anti-flood protection in larger Vltava area

2006

Minor floods

2007

Continuous population growth in Prague 7

2008

Economic crisis, flat construction slowed down

2013

Minor floods

Yuppies' District

The number of residents has been on the rise since 2007. Among 57 city districts, Prague 7 has become one of the most popular for young residents to move into.[2] Compared to other Prague districts and the Czech Republic, there is a large proportion of residents aged 25–40.[3] By contrast, the number of people aged 50 years and older is below average.

1
'History of Prague 7', online, available HTTP: https://www.praha7.cz/volny-cas-prehled/o-praze-7/historie-prahy-7/ (accessed 31 July 2018).

2
T. Soukup, 'Number of residents in selected Prague districts', *Výzkumy Soukup* (June 2016), online, available HTTP: https://www.praha7.cz/wp-content/uploads/2018/04/Demografick%C3%A1-studie-M%C4%8C-Praha-7-%C4%8Derven-2016.pdf (accessed 18 July 2016).

3
T. Soukup, 'Age and gender structure of Prague 7 residents compared to Prague City and Czech Republic', *Výzkumy Soukup* (June 2016), online, available HTTP: https://www.praha7.cz/wp-content/uploads/2018/04/Demografick%C3%A1-studie-M%C4%8C-Praha-7-%C4%8Derven-2016.pdf (accessed 18 July 2016).

Chart 2
Internal migration of residents in selected Prague districts (2001–2015)
Source: T. Soukup, 'Demografická studie' (June 2016), online

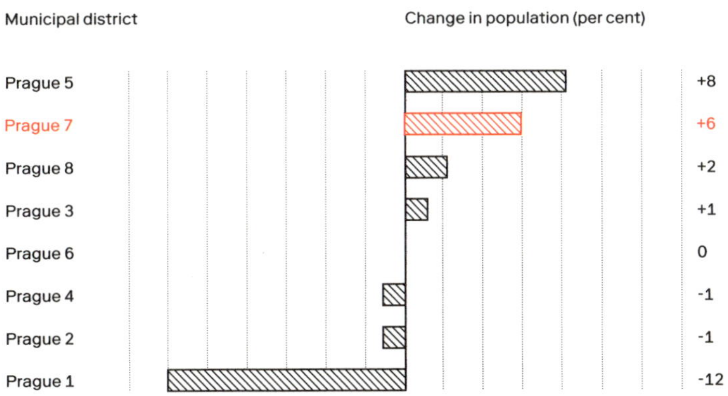

Chart 3
Age and gender structure of residents of Prague 7 compared to Prague city (per cent)
Source: T. Soukup, 'Demografická studie' (June 2016), online

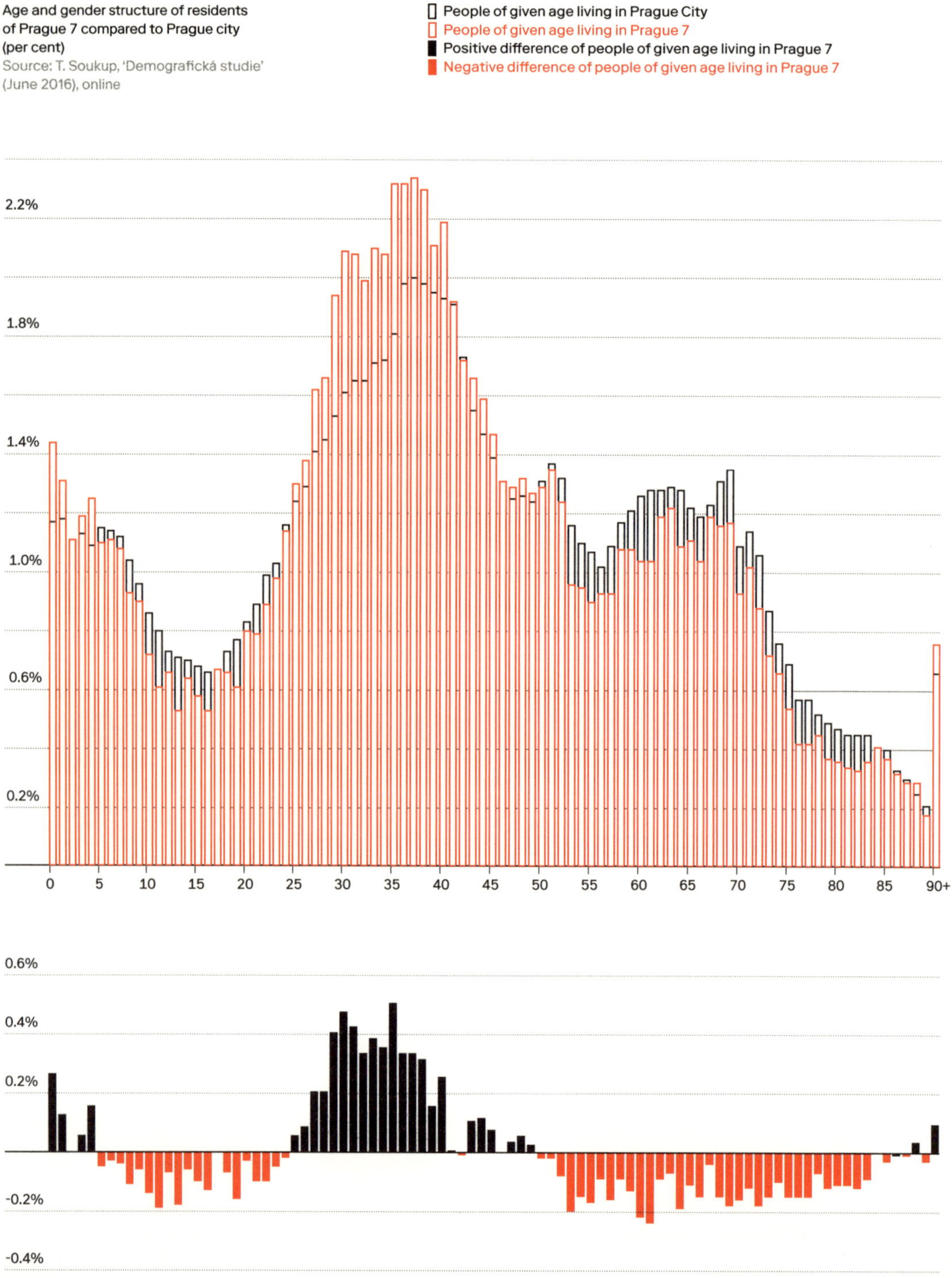

Chart 4
Mortality, natality and internal migration in Prague 7 (2011–2015) (thousands of people)
Source: T. Soukup, 'Demografická studie' (June 2016), online

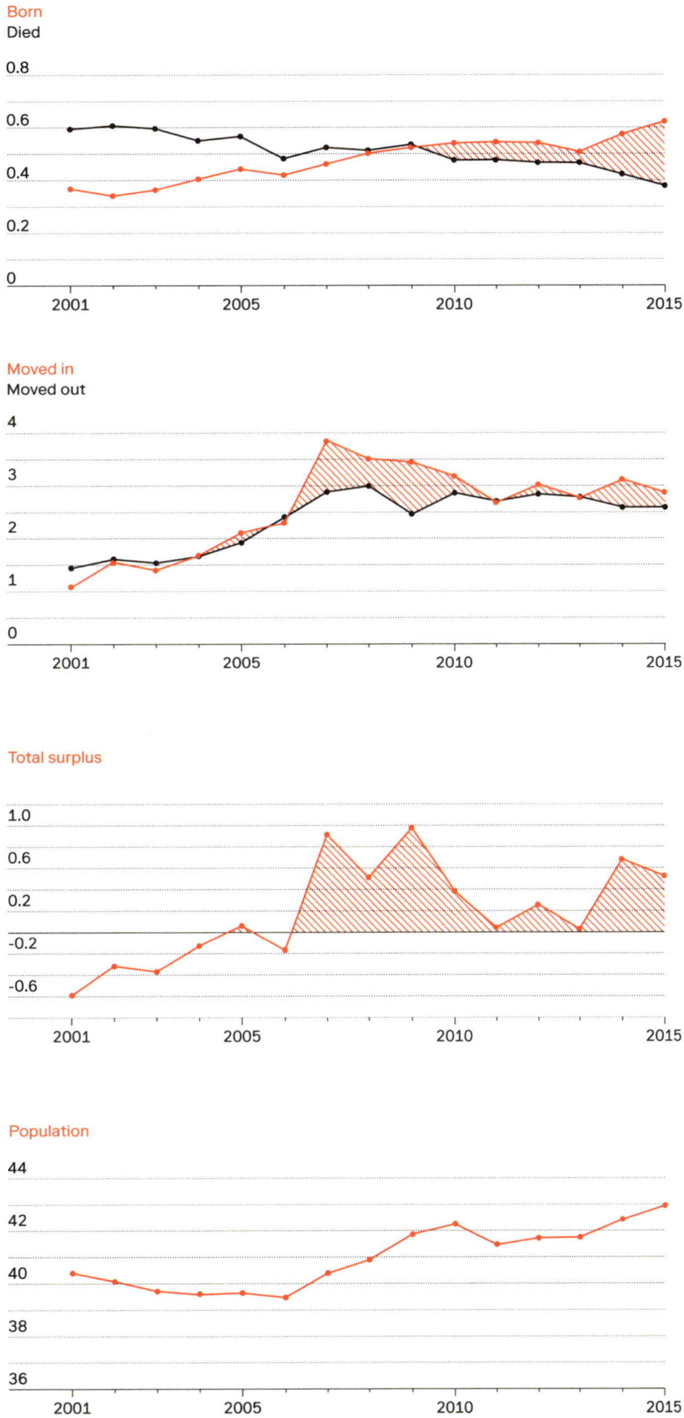

Art District 7

Local culture seems to be shaping the actions of the newly elected political representatives. One of the contributing factors to the victory of *Praha 7 Sobě* was Letenská parta,[4] a public Facebook group established in 2011 by independent film-maker and *Praha 7 Sobě* member Hana Třeštíková. It is one of the most popular online neighbourhood groups in Prague (and perhaps in the Czech Republic). Currently it has more than 22,000 members. People share diverse content: invitations to local cultural events, flats to rent, lost and found, complaints, and support. After the elections, the focus of the group expanded from Letná to the whole Prague 7 area. Třeštíková became Councillor for culture and neighbourhood relationships, and is now the driving force behind efforts to make the district the art centre of Prague while keeping it affordable for locals. The pilot project *Art District 7*[5] connects for-profit and non-profit cultural and art organizations and service providers, companies, schools and other subjects from a wide spectrum of art and creativity areas.[6] The project is set to redefine the cultural character of Prague by creating authentic spaces for authentic experiences.

4
Letenská parta, Facebook group, available HTTP: https://www.facebook.com/groups/137034543034563/ (accessed 31 July 2018).

5
'Art District 7', online, available HTTP: https://www.praha7.cz/temata/art-district-7/ (accessed 31 July 2018).

6
Milota Sidorová, 'Partnerships Database in Art District 7' (June 2018), unpublished.

Chart 5
Cultural amenities in Prague
Source: Database of cultural facilities, IPR Praha

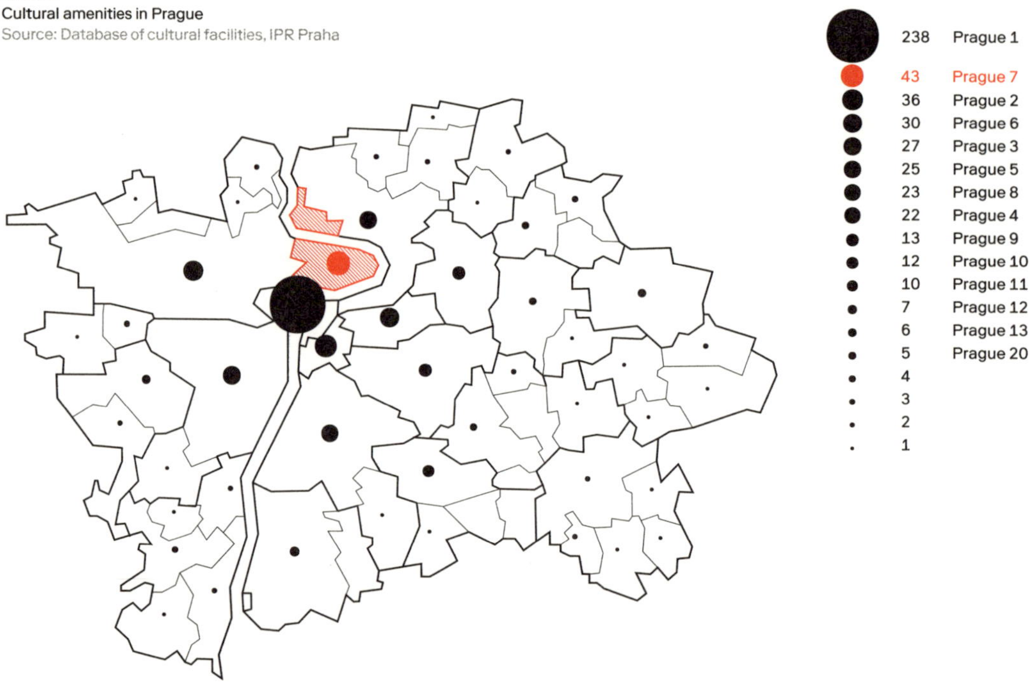

Chart 6
Art District 7 – Partnerships

Category	Number	Share
Galleries	27	38.57%
Theatres	12	17.14%
Leisure institutions	10	14.29%
Museums	5	7.14%
Music clubs	5	7.14%
Singing choirs	4	5.71%
Church, charities	3	4.29%
Art schools	2	2.86%
Cinema	1	1.43%
Library	1	1.43%

A blend of organizations participating in the project shows a wider understanding of neighbourhood creativity in Prague 7. Apart from traditional art- and culture-oriented organizations such as theatres and galleries, it includes traditional community-oriented institutions such as churches and charities.

Development

Major investments have been planned for the next 15 years in the residential district. More than 3,000 flats are planned to be built between 2016–2025 in Prague 7 – Bubny.[7] The hope is that young people will settle here and start families.

Chart 7
Migration in Prague 7
(persons)

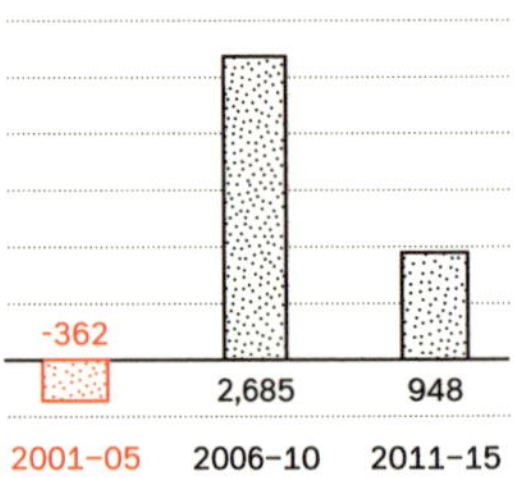

Chart 8
New and planned residential development in Prague 7
(number of apartments)

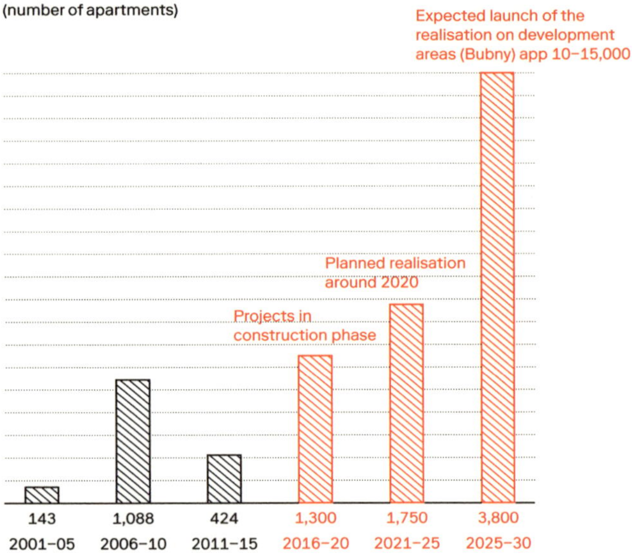

Tipping Point

With housing costs constantly rising in Prague and the ongoing popularity of the district, a question remains as to how projects like *Art District* 7 can be maintained.[8] Without the implementation of appropriate policies, the limits of sustainable cultural growth may easily be reached. Prague 7 is already exhibiting these symptoms. The listed building that once belonged to what is now the Prague Public Transit Co. Inc., and which is currently owned by billionaire Radovan Vítek's CPI Property Group,[9] is a good example of a temporary art and creative hub turned commercial corporate headquarters. More than 250 tenants (artists, studios, NGOs) were not given the option to stay and had to leave.[10] The erosion of social capital, the dispersion of cultural activities, and the consequent weakening of the cluster effect as well as of cultural identity may become real for Prague 7. Will this be the case in more spaces? How will the municipality respond to the issue?

Chart 9
Average rent prices of existing flats, Holešovice (CZK/m^2)
Source: IPR Praha based on data by JLL

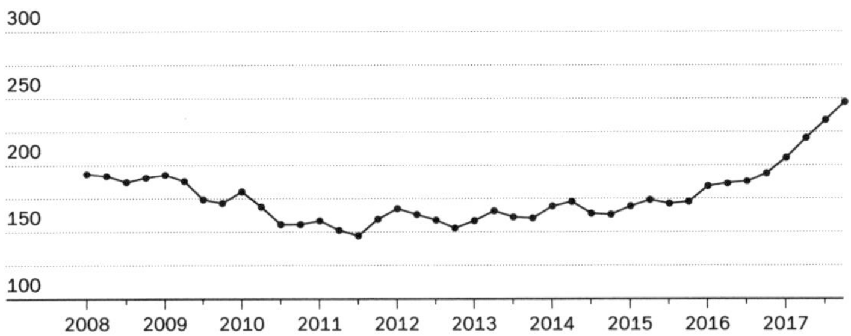

'Gentrification is sadly a phenomenon that follows urban development. Prague 7 has several tools to mitigate its negative consequences, namely owning sufficient housing stock with rent control so that students and the elderly can afford living here. The district should own enough non-residential spaces to maintain a diversity of services. Our last soft measure is the proactive inclusion of socially vulnerable residents into public activities, e.g. to offer activities for the elderly and to show them this is still their home, and they are welcome here.'
Hana Třeštíková, Prague 7's Councillor for Culture and Neighbourhood Relationships, 20 August 2018[11]

Future Prospects

Above all, a shared neighbourhood means an affordable one that accommodates a variety of functions and facilities for every group, and as such it necessitates appropriate tools and policies. These must be implemented and strengthened through cooperation with other parts of the city, or even the country. As for *Art District 7*, Třeštíková would like to see the project grow independent from the municipality. It should transform into a foundation uniting all the cultural stakeholders of Prague 7. By doing so it can gather independence from political will, and opportunities to apply for a wider range of public and international funds.

7
T. Soukup, 'Expected flat construction by 2030 in Prague 7', *Výzkumy Soukup* (June 2016), online, available HTTP: https://www.praha7.cz/wp-content/uploads/2018/04/Demografick%C3%A1-studie-M%C4%8C-Praha-7-%C4%8Derven-s2016.pdf (accessed 18 July 2016).

8
'Average rent prices of existing flats, comparison between various Prague districts', Institute of Planning and Development (August 2018).

9
O. Aust, 'WPP sestěhuje tucet svých agentur k Vltavské', *Mediář* (2018), online, available HTTP: https://www.mediar.cz/wpp-sestehuje-12-svych-agentur-k-vltavske-bubenska-1/ (accessed 3 August 2018).

10
L. Bíba, 'Místo umění kanceláře. Obrazy, tenisky i taneční lekce v Bubenské 1 končí', *Hospodářské noviny* (2017), online, available HTTP: https://archiv.ihned.cz/c1-65996090-misto-umeni-kancelare-obrazy-tenisky-i-tanecni-lekce-na-vltavske-konci (accessed 3 August 2018).

11
Milota Sidorová, Interview with Hana Třeštíková, 20 August 2018, Prague.

Urban Activ

sm

Berlin
Belgrade

Divided We Share: On t of Public Space

#unteilbar was the motto of a mass rally that took place on 13 October 2018 in Berlin. *#indivisible* was used to demonstrate unity against the surge of right-wing populism and against racism and xenophobia. In German, just like in English, *un-* is a negative prefix which means *not*. The suffix *bar* translates into the English *-able* or *-ible* meaning *capable of being* or *able to be done*. The centre syllable *teil* interests me the most here. The verb *teilen* has two meanings: *to share* and *to divide*. Public space is both shared and divided, and people are divided over how to share and divide it.

Sharing: Rituals of Citizenship in Public Space and the Making of the Nation State

Public space comes with complex layers of history. The *#unteilbar* march started at Alexanderplatz, then continued via the Brandenburg Gate to the Berlin Victory Column, adding to the history of eighteenth- and nineteenth-century imperialism, war, and commerce these places have witnessed.

It may not be possible *not* to share the history of a given site, but it is possible to change its function and meaning. Some histories have to be shared. The ways in which they are shared can lead to division and conflict. This presents as much an ethical as a political problem. The hashtag *#unteilbar* drew attention to *teilen*, which means *to share* and *to divide.* We are divided over what it is that we have to share. We have to share what we are divided over. This is the condition of public space. Again, this is as much a question of ethics as of politics.

When something is shared by a group of people, they all become part of it. The nation state was founded on public manifestations of sharing. A common culture, shared in the public space of museums, operas, theatres, parks, or squares, was essential to the concept of the nation state. In the historical context of European metropolises, shared cultures and their legacies were informed by imperialism, colonialism, and capitalism. The idea of the modern institution of citizenship was first formed during the French Revolution. Practising the 'ritual of citizenship' was firmly linked to the nation state's infrastructure of such new public spaces.[1]

The concept of citizenship as developed by the French Revolution was reserved for white, male persons. The idea of universal citizenship had exclusionary premises. Classed, gendered and racialized subjects were not citizens. The ritual of citizenship

1
See C. Duncan, 'Art Museums and the Ritual of Citizenship', in I. Karp and S. D. Lavine (eds.), *Exhibiting Cultures: The Poetics and Politics of Museum Display* (Washington: Smithsonian Institution Press, 1991), 88–103.

2
O. de Gouges, *Declaration of the Rights of Women and Female Citizens* (Lewes: Ilex Press, 2018).

3
S. Sassen, 'The Repositioning of Citizenship. Emergent Subjects and Spaces for Politics', *The New Centennial Review* (2003) 3(2), 42. See E. Krasny, 'Citizenship and the Museum: On Feminist Acts', in J. Ashton (ed.) *Feminism and Museums: Intervention, Disruption, and Change* (Edinburgh and Boston: MuseumsEtc, 2017) vol. 1, 74–99.

therefore reproduced these exclusions and spatialized them, making public space gendered, racialized, and classed. Looking back at the beginnings of public space as it gave rise to a shared nation state culture, we understand that being divided over what was supposed to be shared formed part of this public culture from the onset. One such example is Olympe de Gouges's 1791 *Declaration of the Rights of Women and the Female Citizen*, which contested and expanded the 1789 *Declaration of the Rights of Man and of the Citizen*, the blueprint of the Western idea of citizenship.[2] People are as much united as they are divided by and over public space and its rituals of citizenship. Finding new rituals of denationalized and informal citizenship and new cultural expressions in public space for such divided sharing without epistemic violence or militarized violence presents one of the biggest challenges today.[3] A history of the ethics and politics of public space would examine the formation of the culture of sharing to understand its long-term structures and its changes over time. Such a history of public space in European cities during the long twentieth century extends by far the scope of this essay. Political systems of the twentieth century—imperialism, colonialism, communism, fascist totalitarianism, socialism, or liberal democracy—have each in their own way made ideological use of public space; meanwhile the twenty-first century has witnessed much change of public space effected by globalization, capital-centric urbanization, and the shift to neoliberalism in urban governance. New gender relations along with diasporic or migrant ways of living play a major role in the transformation of public space, its everyday use and cultural expectations towards it.

Sharing: A Keyword for the Twenty-First Century

As seen above, the idea of sharing has been formative to the culture of public space at the beginning of the nation state. For example, the modern institution of citizenship has been shared and performed in public space. Sharing in the twenty-first century has taken on a different dimension altogether. Typing 'share' into the Google search engine on 26 December 2018 resulted in 13,480,000,000 hits. From Facebook to Airbnb, from Uber to open-source tools, from co-working spaces to a traffic concept where barriers between vehicles and pedestrians are removed, the paradigm of sharing has reshaped life, work, leisure, human relationships, friendships, affects and emotions. In short, sharing/shared are among the buzzwords of our time. In 1976, Marxist cultural theorist Raymond Williams published his seminal book *Keywords: A Vocabulary of Culture and Society*, in which he explored the social and cultural valence of words such as *bureaucracy*, *masses*, or *work*. In 2005, Tony Bennett, Lawrence Grossberg and Meaghan Morris presented *New Keywords. A Revised Vocabulary of Culture and Society.* Even though their update is helpful to understand widely used terms such as *mobility*, *participation* or *queer*, many of the keywords that have come to both define and describe our contemporary realities are absent.[4] Missing keywords include *Facebook*, *climate change*, *crisis*, *resilience*, *sustainability*, and, of course, with regard to the present topic, *sharing/shared*.[5]

When Facebook was first launched in 2004, it elevated the practice of sharing to a new digital lifestyle. *Share* next to *Like* and *Comment* came to constitute new digital subjectivities, including emergent forms of digitally mediated sociability with its concomitant attention and affect management. It soon became clear that digital sharing was about enhancing self-value, creating a digital personality, and investment in social capital networking. While such public sharing can definitely pass on valuable information or insights, it is also time-consuming and results in constant self-assessment based on likes, comments, or shares. This required new forms of affect management.

In 2008, Airbnb was founded. Even though the market was never far from home, this digital platform has completely transformed the home into a commodity. Airbnb's people-to-people platform turns homes into shares. This means that one inhabits a process of continuously reproducible commodification. Again, much like sharing on Facebook, Airbnb sharing has introduced a new form of lived subjectivity that requires new and skilful forms of personal representation and affect management.

Sharing has not only risen to prominence via digital social networks and sharing economies, but is also celebrated by austerity-based urban governance. When public funding is dwindling, when public infrastructure continuously fails, when private-public partnerships put the public realm last or transform it into branded and corporate landscapes, then the helping hands of the public are invited to share the responsibility for their public space. Social media, sharing economies, and austerity-based governance thus introduce new challenges concerning the relationship between ethics and politics. They are part of twenty-first century subject formations and profoundly influence feelings and expectations towards urban public space.

How to Practice Sharing in the Twenty-First Century City: Urban Hubs, Urban Hacking

While new cultures of sharing have emerged in the wake of digital social media and platform economies, the traditional notion of a shared culture as understood by the modern nation state

4
T. Bennett, L. Grossberg, and M. Morris, *New Keywords. A revised Vocabulary of Culture and Society* (Malden: Blackwell, 2005), 217, 252, 287.

5
Feminist scholar Sarah Bracke has drawn attention to the importance of resilience and has suggested that Raymond Williams would include it if he were writing his vocabulary today. See S. Bracke, 'Vulnerability and Resistance in Times of Resilience', in: J. Butler, Z. Gambetti, and L. Sabsay (eds.), *Vulnerability and Resistance* (Durham and London: Duke University Press, 2016), 54.

6
See D. Sekulic, 'Don't Stare So Romantically: On Extralegal Space in Belgrade' (11 March 2014) vol. 38, online, available http://volumeproject.org/author/dubravka-sekulic/ (accessed 26 December 2018).

7
Ibid.

8
Bina centar: Čuvari parka, Video (6 June 2017), online, available HTTP: https://www.youtube.com/watch?v=8VDF2pCJCf0 (accessed 26 December 2018).

9
See E. Krasny, 'The Domestic is Political: The Feminization of Domestic Labour and its Critique in Feminist Art Practice', in A. M. Guasch Ferrer and N. Jiménez del Val (eds.), *Critical Cartography of Art and Visuality in the Global Age* (Newcastle upon Tyne: Cambridge Scholars Publishing, 2014), 161–178.

has not disappeared. Quite the contrary, it has returned in full force. Right-wing populism and extreme nationalism make claims to a shared culture. This has resulted in new divisions, new forms of hate, segregation, separation, and exclusion. Therefore, new class divisions and rising inequality inform sharing in today's multi-ethnic, multi-religious, multi-generational urban societies. Sharing is an ethical and political battlefield. People are divided over what to share and how to share. Divided, they share. In the post-socialist city of Belgrade where public space gives testimony to the legacies of the Ottoman empire, the Habsburg empire, Tito-ist socialism, the Balkan wars, the dissolution of Yugoslavia and today's transition into accelerated capitalism, societal responsibility for public space as a commons does not come easily. Architect and researcher Dubravka Sekulic has written about the Yugoslav model of socialist workers' self-management that combined elements of communism and capitalism and made housing a 'social property'.[6] The same held true for public space. The Yugoslav wars and the post-war period meant the end of this model of socialism and the dawn of unbridled neoliberal capitalism. Privatization radically changed the built environment with the impact of developer-driven urbanization and widespread informal building practices. Privatization was an economic shift, but it also changed commonly held cultural values. 'The attitude towards space changed from societal ... to a more private form, so from "ours" to just "mine".'[7] The socialist legacy of the modernist housing stock, with apartments transformed into private property from the 1990s onwards, has retained its potential of in-between space. Despite being neglected, the buildings hold the promise of communal use, comfort, and pleasure. Such in-between public spaces test shared labour and the sharing of responsibility. In the spring of 2015, the collective Čuvari parka (Park Keepers) started to clean the Plato park, where they came to play with their children. Their activist clean-up led to their participation in *Shared Cities: Creative Momentum* as they responded to an open call put out by BINA – Belgrade International Architecture Week. A film made as part of their project starts with the following description of their public space in Plato: 'It is great inspiration, even though it is dirty.'[8] They wanted a clean space for their children. So they took their brooms and set to work. Like Mierle Laderman Ukeles, who in 1973 performed 'maintenance art' by cleaning the floors of a museum in Hartford, Connecticut, three Čuvari parka mothers turned maintenance into a public performance.[9] While 1970s feminist art exposed the gendered division of labour, the public activism in Plato in 2015 exposed the lack of public maintenance and the fact that social reproduction is not only needed in the home but also in public space. By overcoming the attitude of privatization of only taking care of what is 'mine', the three mothers initiated a process of shared labour so their public space suffered less from neglect. Located between the high-rise buildings, Plato at Mileševska Street became what architect Ivan Kucina calls an 'urban hub'.[10] These are responses to austerity urbanism and lack of public involvement. Kucina reasons that the achievement of such an urban hub is a change in '[the] relationship between the city and citizens in Belgrade', adding that '[it] has been taken for granted that public spaces have to be developed and maintained by the public authorities, and not by citizens. This general attitude has greatly affected passivity and lack of civic initiatives which would aim at improving them.'[11] The network of urban hubs seeks to promote and support citizens' initiatives and the idea of the city as a place of shared interests.

Together with anthropology students from the Faculty of Philosophy and with architectural support from the BINA team, the best place for communal gatherings at Plato park was identified and painted red. A large table was designed and built out of metal and wood. When asked about the park and the table, one of the interviewed partners in the 13-minute film on Čuvari parka calls it 'utopian and idealistic and great.'[12] But he also warns: 'Now what life will bring and how it will be maintained, how it will survive that is on us [sic] and the people who live there and use it.'[13] This example shows how local activism connects sharing with labour, urban space, and digital networks into an urban hub.

Since the fall of the Berlin Wall in 1989, Berlin has witnessed tremendous change. The buildings and public space of Berlin reflect the complex legacies of the Hohenzollern Kings of Prussia and their imperial and colonial empire, of the Weimar Republic, the Nazi regime, the divided city of West Berlin and East Berlin after 1945, and the decades following the reunification. In 1991, the Bundestag's Capital Resolution made Berlin the seat of the German government. The fallow land and empty buildings of the 1990s witnessed a period of activist temporary use and a new culture celebrating the temporary. From the late 1990s onwards, three major trends have changed Berlin: real estate developer-urbanism, gentrification, and mass tourism. In 1996 there were 3,272,888 visitors to Berlin; by 2016 the number had risen to 12,731,600.[14] Against this backdrop, the public space of the urban metropolis is of great interest to global capital. ZK/U, Center for Art and Urbanistics, the Berlin partner of the Shared Cities project, have identified that the revenue from street furniture (bus stops, benches) and outdoor advertisement (billboards), is shared by a few global players. Wall AG, part of JCDecaux since 2009, is Berlin's provider of street furniture and advertisement. This largely defines the appearance of public space as this forms part of corporate, homogenized, developer- and tourism-friendly branding strategies. ZK/U initiated *Hacking Urban Furniture* as an activist

10
I. Kucina: 'Urban Hubs – Infrastructure for Collaboration', *BINA Programme*, SCCM Belgrade, 2018.

11
Ibid.

12
Čuvari parka, 11'41".

13
Čuvari parka, 11'44"–11'57".

14
Senatsverwaltung für Wirtschaft, Energie und Betriebe, 'Tourismus in Zahlen', online, available HTTP: https://www.berlin.de/sen/wirtschaft/wirtschaft/branchen/tourismus/tourismus-in-zahlen/ (accessed 26 December 2018).

research project in collaboration with artists, urban researchers, administrators, and politicians to suggest new models of taking back urban furniture. The group included artists and artist groups Markus Ambach, Christian Hasucha, *umschichten*, *raumlaborberlin* and *KUNSTrePUBLIK*. Projects have been realized in cooperation with *AbBA* (Alliance of Threatened Berlin Studio Houses), *Refunc*, *OpenBerlin*, and *Wildau Technical College*. Ideas, knowledge, labour, and responsibility were shared through the collaboration of many individuals and groups in cooperation with institutions. Awareness raising, outreach, and visibility were shared across many different actors and spread widely much like in digital networks. *Urban Hacking* launched an open international single-phase idea contest, held an exhibition, a conference, and talks, and invited international research partners including Laura Sobral, Benjamin Cope, Mary Dellenbaugh-Losse, Surfatial, Jan Bovelet, Joanne Pouzenc, Mobasher Niqui, Alireza Labeshka, and Ali Reza Hemmat Boland.

Hacking is a tech term denoting an illegal form of sharing with someone, bypassing security, and gaining access to a computer system and network, often with the purpose of altering it. In this case, hacking taps into the globalized and closed system of street furniture and outdoor advertisement in order to reclaim it not illegally but in dialogue with urban administrators and policy makers. *Hacking Urban Furniture* sees the fields of design, community participation, urban administration, and economy as interconnected, and proposes a new model of locally self-managed urban furniture production including reinvestment of the revenue generated. Their concept makes urban furniture a field of production for local artists, designers and architects; includes open source models; lets the community have a say in the 'what' and 'how' of their public space, and allows for collective decisions about reinvestment of revenue into urban, social, or cultural infrastructure. Ultimately, today's model of Public-Private-Partnership, known as PPP, which aligns urban governance to the interest of global capital, could be transformed into Communal-Collective-Cooperations (CCC). *Hacking Urban Furniture* presents the model for a radical transformation of wrestling public space from the interests of global capital.

Sharing: Learning from the Broom, the Table, the Bench, and the Billboard

The *Urban Hub* in Belgrade and *Urban Hacking* in Berlin are both involved on a local level and start from tangible and concrete objects that define public space. All the key objects in these examples—the broom, the table, the bench, and the billboard—can be considered units of sharing in public space. They help people relate to each other, to share labour: the broom, to share sociability; the table, to share relaxation; the bench or the billboard, to share information. These objects occupy the world between the people who share them. This follows Hannah Arendt's metaphor of the table. She writes that in mass society, 'the world between them has lost its power to gather them together'.[15] She compares this to a vanishing table leaving people behind, 'entirely unrelated to each other by anything tangible.'[16] Once people have to position themselves around the table—an object that separates them —it becomes a shared object, a process of sharing. The table is just as much about ethics as it is about politics. *Urban Hubs* and *Urban Hacking* work on the local scale. They make public space a locally shared endeavour. Urban governance, developer-driven urbanism, and the interest of global capital put public space at a remove. The scale of the broom, the bench, the table, and even the billboard makes public space concrete, tangible, and manageable. The broom, the bench, the table, and the billboard imply sharing *and* dividing. The shared broom represents labour that is divided. The shared table is a table divided among a group of people. These examples are templates that can connect into networks and can be tested in different locations. They constitute a public practice beyond the scale of the local, while acknowledging the specific local conditions.

A public space, in the most general sense, refers to an area or a place which is open and accessible to all people, regardless of age, ability, class, ethnicity, gender, or religion. The model of the *Urban Hub* and *Hacking Urban Furniture* could be expanded and used in the future to address issues of sharing as they pertain to the notion of a truly intersectional public space, and the objects that bring people together could be used to debate how and why people who share public space and its objects are divided over their history, their present, and their future. Public space and its objects require working out shared notions of what is right, what is wrong, and what obligations they come with. They form part of governing the relations of people living together in a society. Therefore, public objects such as brooms, benches, tables, or billboards, which have to be kept in one piece and undivided to maintain their physical integrity, support practices of public sharing as they gather people together. Making the care for public space, its infrastructures, and its objects a continued process of sharing turns public space into an ethical and political process.

15
H. Arendt, *The Human Condition* (Chicago: University of Chicago Press, 1998), 53.

16
Ibid.

Berlin

3.01

Population
(millions of inhab.)

2016 (metropolitan regions)
2016 (Belgrade)
2017 (other cities)

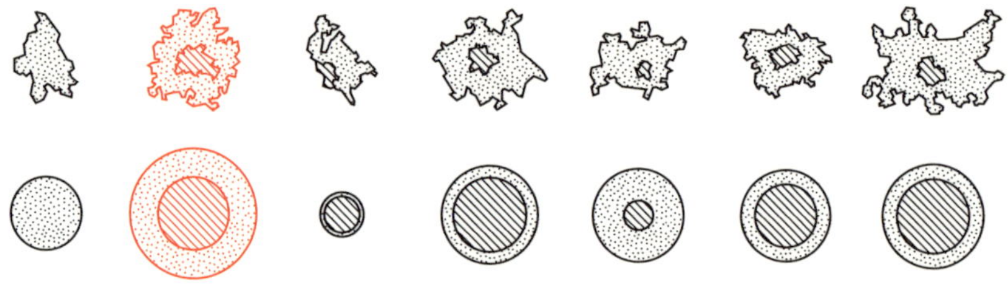

	Belgrade	Berlin	Bratislava	Budapest	Katowice	Prague	Warsaw
City	1.68	3.54	0.43	1.76	0.30	1.27	1.75
Metropolitan region		5.21	0.64	3.00	2.71	2.62	3.37

3.02

Built-up area footprint

City
2016
Total area: 891 km²
Population density:
3,948 inhab./km²

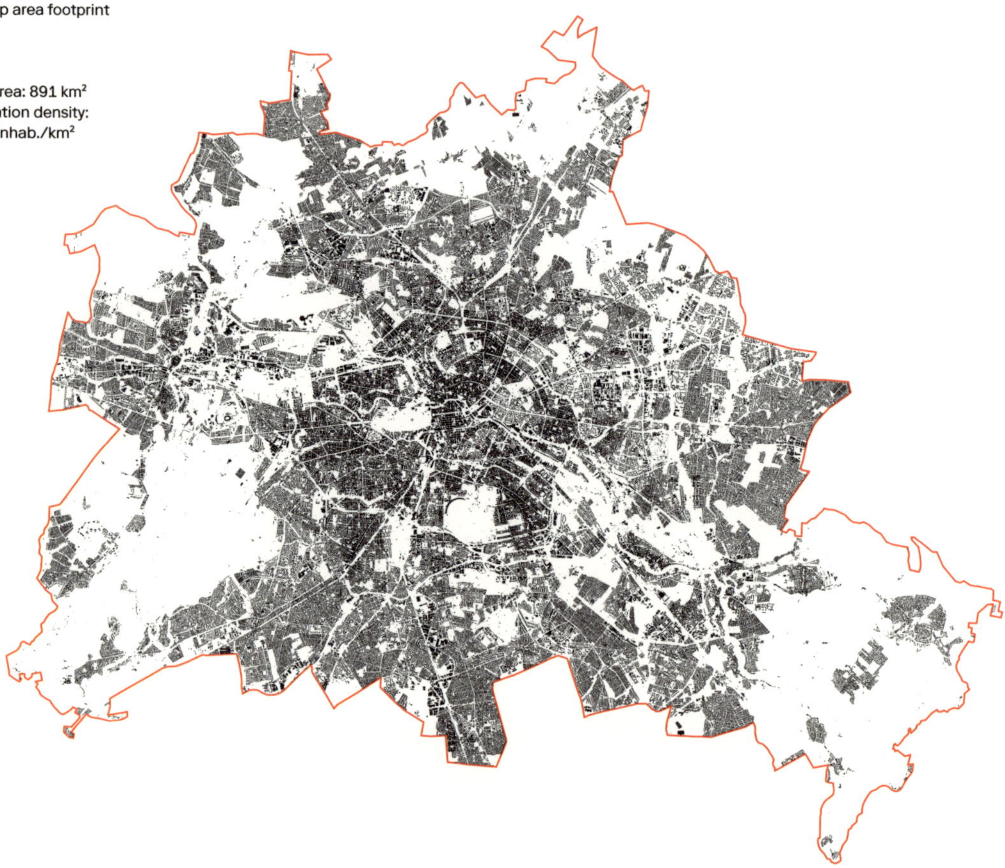

0 5 km

3.03

Patent applications in information and communications technology (applications/million inhab.)

Cities
2010–2012

→ Economy
Chart D.03, p. 24

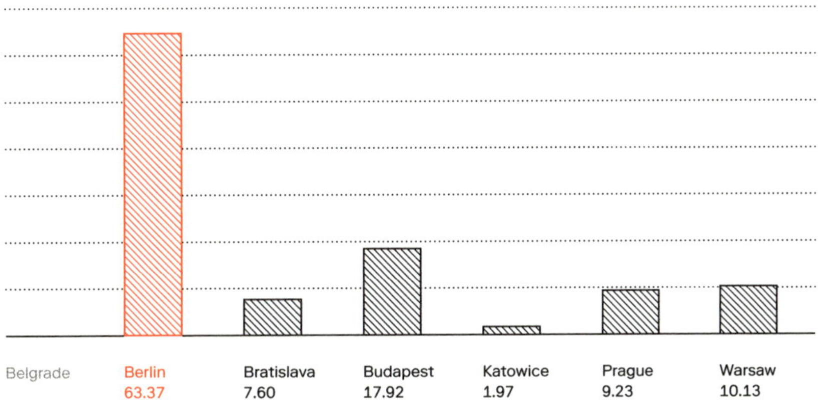

3.04

Public libraries and book loans

Cities
2016

→ Society
Chart B.14, p. 19

■ = 1 library; ■ = 1 book loan

	Belgrade	Berlin	Bratislava	Budapest	Katowice	Prague	Warsaw
(libraries/100,000 inhab.)	5.2	2.2	9.9	3.2	12.4	6.7	11.5
(book loans/1 inhab.)	1.2	5.9	4.0	2.1	4.5	5.6	3.5

3.05

Average area of living accommodation (m^2/inhab.)

City
2011

45.00

◆ = 5 m^2

3.06

Average monthly net salary (EUR)

City
2018

2,067.22

▨ = 100 €

3.07

Registered passenger cars (cars/1,000 inhab.)

City
2016

335

■ = 20 cars

3.08

Tourists (number/year)

City
2016

12,731,640

= 1 million tourists

ZENTRALFLUGHAFEN

RESTAURANT MOSKAU CAFE

Hacking Urban Furniture

Organization	KUNSTrePUBLIK
Address	Siemensstrasse 27, 10551 Berlin
Authors	Markus Ambach, Konrad Braun, KUNSTrePUBLIK, umschichten, raumlaborberlin
Partners	Hauptstadtkulturfonds, Straßen- und Grünflächenamt Berlin
Dates	16 December 2016 – 1 November 2019

Activities				
	Workshops	3	Publication	1
	Conference	1	Discussions	3
	Exhibitions	2	Web-platform	1

Hacking Urban Furniture. Inclusive Models of Creating Street Furniture

Matthias Einhoff

Street furniture and outdoor advertising have defined the grammar of our cities for over 30 years. Public-private partnerships (PPP) allow companies to advertise in public space, and to install and maintain street furniture such as bus stops, public toilets, benches, bins, and signposts. This business model is dominated by a handful of multinational companies, generating profits in the billions. In 2014, JCDecaux reached sales of 2.8 billion euro, 60 countries, and 11,900 employees. Berlin, Rome, Istanbul, St. Louis or Berlin: the feel is identical and a relation to the local identity is missing. A refined and perfectly marketable design language has become the international standard. Berlin, for example, has been serviced by Wall AG, which became part of the JCDecaux-Group in 2009.

There is a broad range of examples of citizens' growing demand to be more involved in public space and infrastructure design. In Berlin, there have been numerous petitions for the re-municipalization of public utilities, and citizens have reclaimed public goods in their neighbourhoods (city tree sponsorship, benches on public trees, etc.). The *Haus der Statistik* became a landmark for inclusive urban planning on the most central plaza—Alexanderplatz. Since 1989, the citizens of Porto Alegre have run participatory budgeting (*orçamento participativo*), a model adopted by the city of Córdoba, Spain in 2001; since 2006, the so-called 'citizens' budget' (*Bürgerhaushalt*) has been implemented in some places in Germany (such as Berlin-Lichtenberg). Also, 'Community Land Trust' models have been developed to produce and maintain communal infrastructure and housing. There has been a paradigm shift from increasing privatization of public services and goods, which came from austerity politics and economic theories typically clustered under the term 'neo-liberalism', to a more inclusive and community-oriented approach of space-production and public services.

Most recently, the city of Berlin renewed its contracts with JCDecaux. The process outlined ways towards achieving more communal responsibility, but also showed the limits of feasibility. JCDecaux was originally contracted to build and maintain public toilets, and in return got advertising rights for public spaces. It soon became apparent that the revenue from the rights outweighed the costs of maintenance. The city of Berlin had plans to take over the latter but soon realized that the years of austerity had resulted in a loss of administration skills. The new deal is a compromise: the city has reclaimed advertising rights, using the income to hire JCDecaux to continue and extend public toilet services. The decision-making power as to how much advertising is needed is now back in municipal hands, but the lack of competence has led to dependencies and compromises.

Over the course of three years, the 'Hacking Urban Furniture' project has brought exciting new perspectives to this area. The projects are based on the experience from a variety of artistic concepts already existing in the field, most notably 1990s and 2000s art which has been critical of the increasing privatization of city space. The renowned project 'Art in the Underground' (*Kunst im Untergrund*), for example, created site-specific works around the S&U-Bahn station of Alexanderplatz but was discontinued, since it did not correspond to the exploitation plan set out by the new license holder, WALL AG ('*Station Branding: U-Bahn stations become brand-name products*,' quote from the WALL AG website).

'Hacking Urban Furniture' explored a variety of new economic and inclusive models of creating street furniture through art projects, an open idea contest, and a variety of lectures and discussions. Artists, architects, and urban designers analyzed and reprogrammed the parameters of street furniture and outdoor advertising in close cooperation with an expert advisory board, with special focus on economic aspects. How can open participatory procedures for design, production, security and maintenance challenge for-profit business models and make public advertising obsolete? How can citizens identify and embrace these new structures? If there is no way around outdoor advertising, how should the revenue be distributed?

Artists Markus Ambach, KUNSTrePUBLIK, raumlaborberlin, Christian Hasucha, Martin Binder and others, in cooperation with researchers Laura Sobral, Benjamin Cope, Mary Dellenbaugh, Surfatial, Jan Bovelet, Joanne Pouzenc, Mobasher Niqui, Alireza Labeshka, and Ali Reza Hemmat Boland presented their results at an exhibition and at an international conference.

'Hacking Urban Furniture' was merely a starting point for a discussion that is long overdue: how can the demands of urban citizens for more democracy and direct involvement in the creation of their immediate environment be met despite the complexities of public space production—the economic, ecological, cultural and social aspects represented by local, federal and EU regulations that often limit the extent to which decisions can be made and citizens can be involved. The aim of 'Hacking Urban Furniture' was to explore these discrepancies, comment on the realities and outline new plans of action.

Happy Plurality

raumlaborberlin, Berlin, 2017

What if bollards, those commonplace bores, embodied an invitation to act? raumlaborberlin display excerpts of their speculative work as sketches on walls and in space. One of the bollard fantasies has been realized in bronze and made usable.

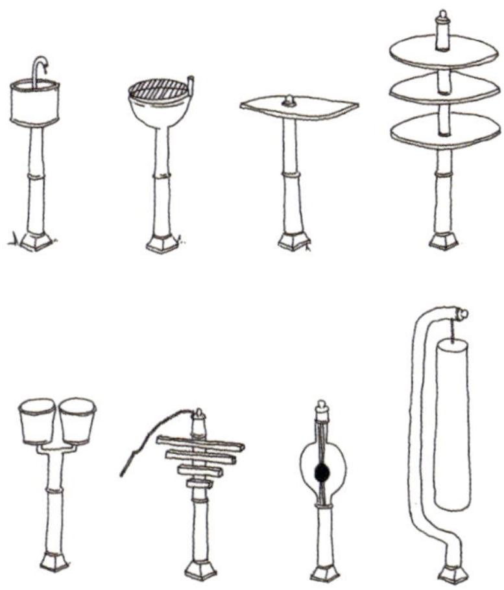

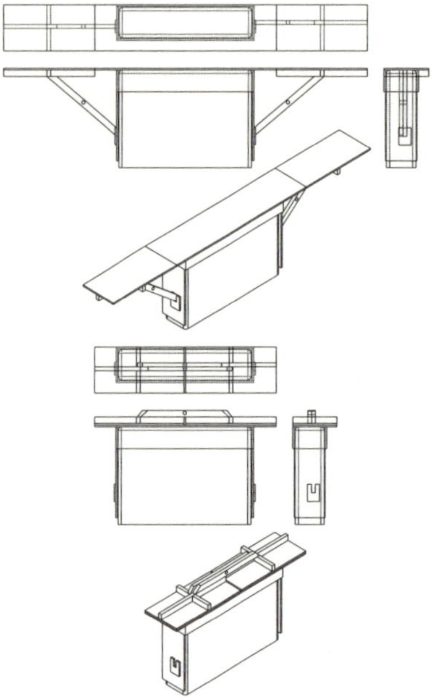

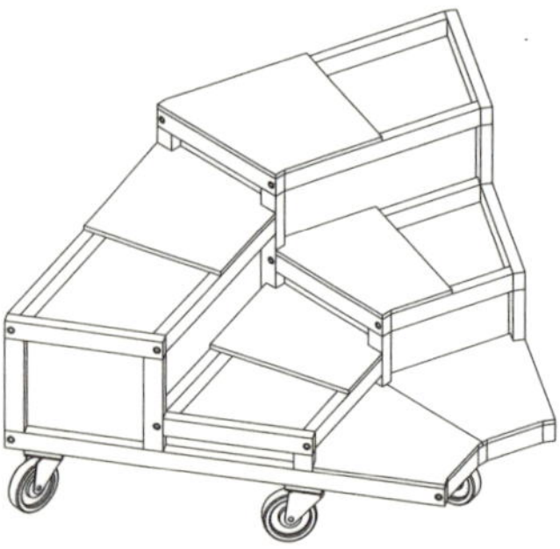

UUF – Upcycling Urban Furniture: Fix Your Park

Markus Ambach in Cooperation with Konrad Braun, Berlin, 2017

Ever so often, urban furniture and its space come under pressure. Vandalism, misuse, disinterest: good ideas are often left for dead. The small park at Bremerstraße in Berlin-Moabit once was a flourishing urban recreational area: its benches are now dismantled. The pergolas that surround the park are only partly conquered by nature, and the flower beds are deserted. The UUF project rethinks, reuses, and recycles urban furniture as a common good to repurpose the location. In a workshop open to neighbours, artists, citizens, and other stakeholders, UUF thinks about the possibilities this place has to offer today, which new functions are needed here, and that progressive and utopian imaginations of urban furniture can be tried out.

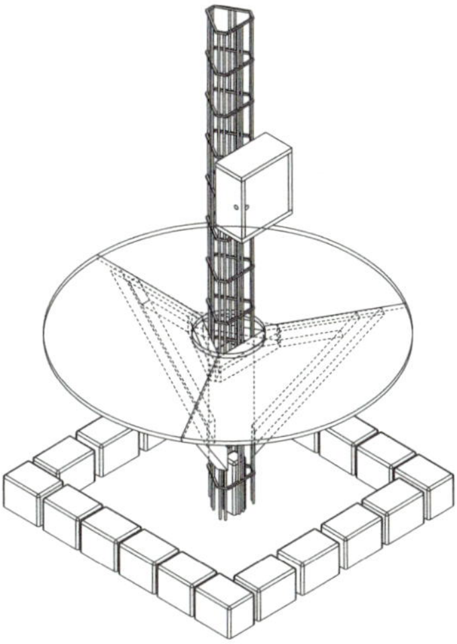

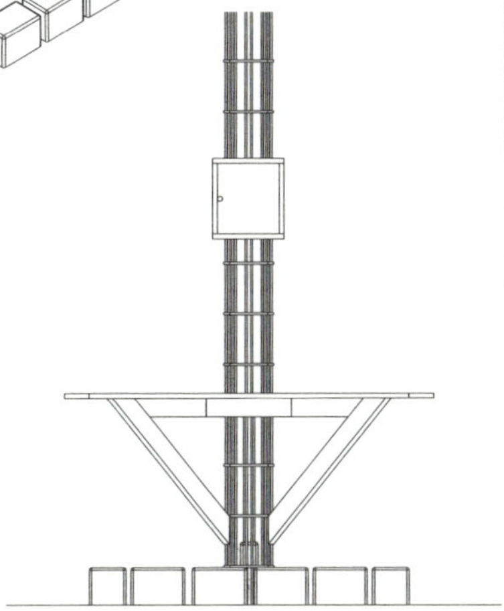

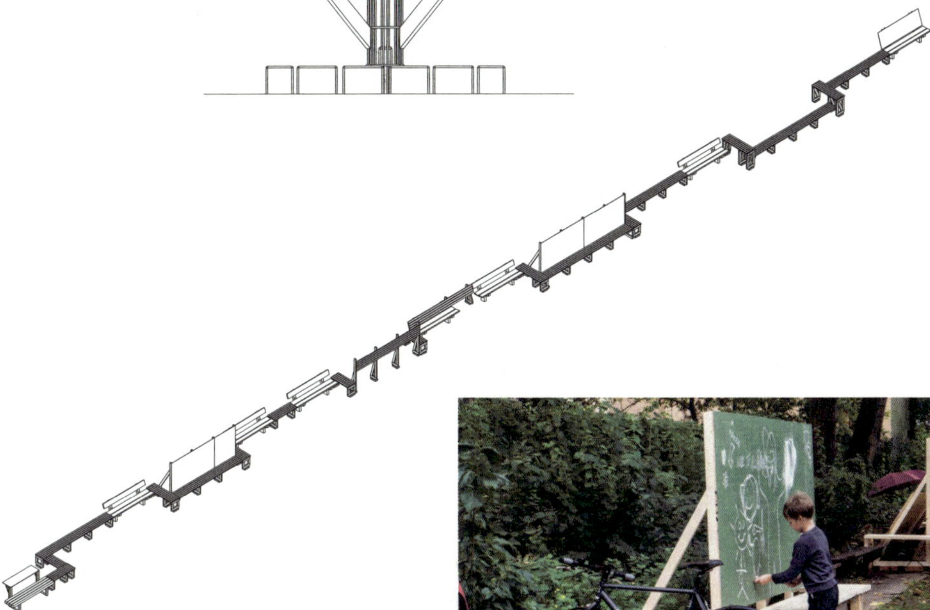

Stage to Go
KUNSTrePUBLIK, Berlin, 2017

There are over a million registered cars in Berlin. On average, each car is being driven for 15 minutes a day. Each car takes up the space of about 10 square meters. *Stage to Go* uses the parking space to set up a mobile stage. A lift system picks up a car body which, when lowered, produces energy for the stage light and audio installation, like an over-dimensional cuckoo clock with wind-up weights. 'Stage to Go' is a social generator. It is applicable to diverse locations in the city but the space of a parking spot suffices. Make plans with it; be spontaneous. The stage is freely accessible, an open space of exchange and performance. Being a public space, it is devoted to the interaction, negotiation and (re)production of different political and cultural voices. As a replicable prototype, 'Stage to Go' is a mobile stage for any form of everyday practice, an explicit amplifier of local voices, whose lyricism is often unheard in the urban narrative cacophony.

Next Stop Pony-Hof

umschichten, Berlin, 2017

Bus stops offer the public sector a full carefree package in return for advertisement revenues. Could a bus stop be used and shared by including a bike rent and repair station, an espresso bar, or anything else locals find useful? *umschichten* imagines an individualized, contextualized principle connected to sponsorship. Actors become sponsors of bus stops and their public functions. But they can also install a programme or feature with added community value. Sponsors become builders of 'their' bus stops, and together with architects, designers and mediators, they develop public space 'superspots'.

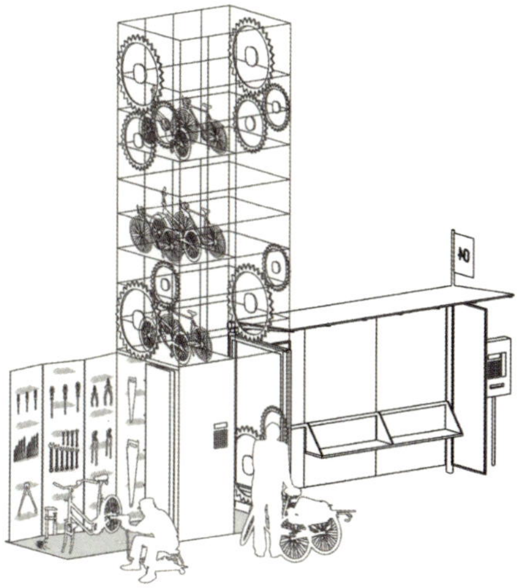

Bus Stops. Speculatior

A Leap Forward

In the recent shift towards the digitization of shared urban space, WALL AG, Berlin's major advertising company, is preparing a leap forward: from city advertising to an innovation company capitalizing on data extractivism. In the case of bus shelters, the previous business model generated value through advertising. With the new prototypes, the value becomes a speculation on data as a knowledge resource. Since the company is using public space and the public's data to capitalize on more urban services, it becomes urgent to rethink this model and argue for open data as a way to redistribute knowledge in the city.

Bus Shelters

Bus line 200 is known as the 'extended tourist line', stretching from the Berlin Zoo to the north-eastern suburb of Pankow. The 11-km bus ride lasts around 54 minutes and serves over 24,200 people per day.[1] The bus line is currently supported by 34 bus shelters in both directions, featuring a total of 49 spaces for advertising purposes. Even though the form of the bus shelter may appear as common-sense nowadays, its design intersects with the history of public-private partnerships and the gradual privatization of public spaces.

1 J. Helgard, K. Joachim, *Mobility in the City: Berlin Traffic in Figures* (Berlin: Senate Department for Urban Development and the Environment of the State of Berlin Communication, 2014), 54.

Chart 1
Bus line 200 – Number of passengers/hour and types of bus stops

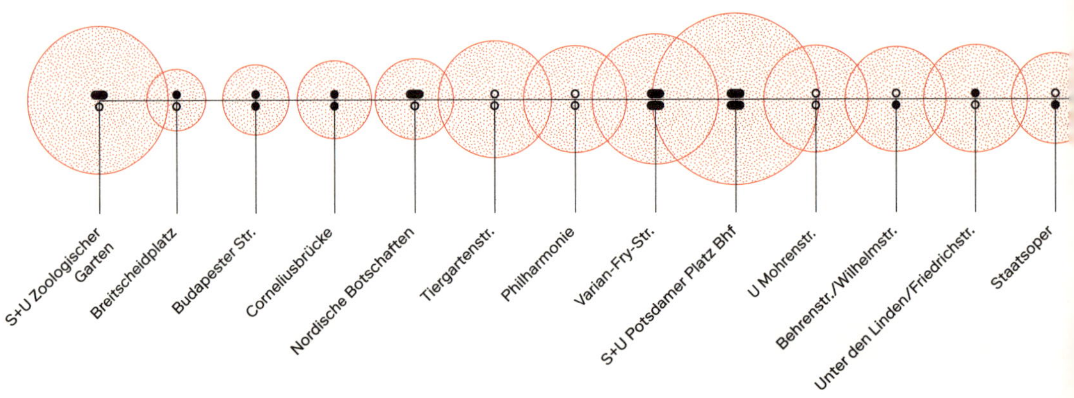

on Data Commons

Passengers/hour

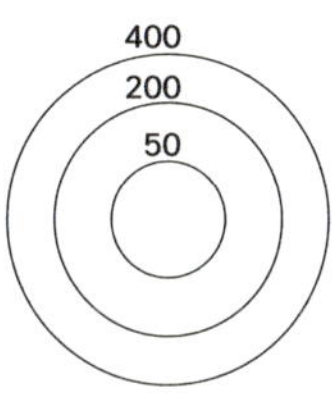

Types of bus stops

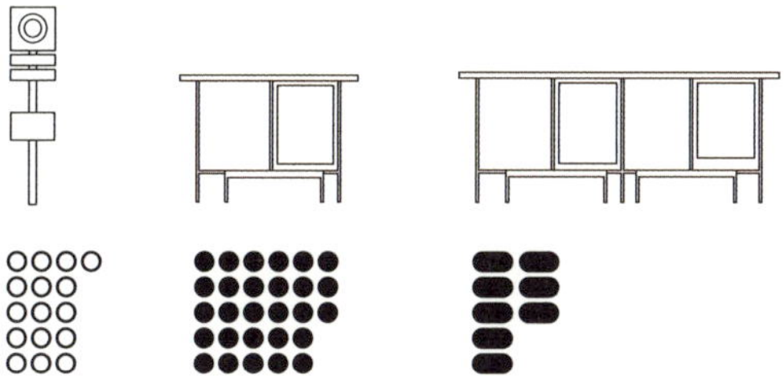

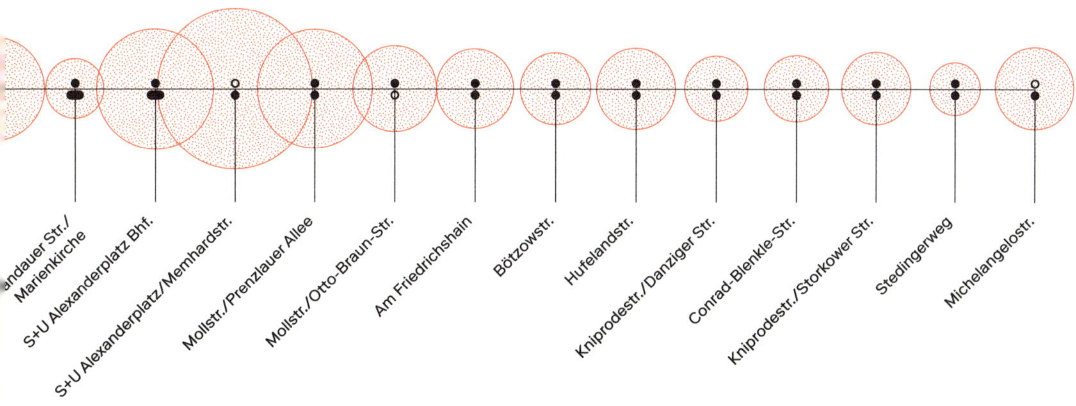

A Brief History

Until the 1960s, urban furniture was provided by cities, serving purely utilitarian purposes. In 1964, entrepreneur Jean-Claude Decaux partnered with the city of Lyon to install and maintain bus shelters that featured advertising that he would profit from, introducing the idea of public-private partnerships.[2] In Berlin, Wall AG adopted his business model in 1976 and became the sole provider of urban furniture in the city, winning the international competition for BVG (Berlin's main public transport company) in 1984.[3] An advertising facilitator as well as a technology innovator, the company made a digital turn in 2014, replacing paper format advertisements with screens in the subway station of Friedrichstrasse.[4] WallAG is launching a new generation of bus stops that incorporate a variety of new amenities as a prototype to be exported to Russia, Turkey, Egypt, and the USA.[5]

2
J. Pouzenc, 'JCDecaux, Public-Private Space', *Hacking Urban Furniture: Case Studies* (Berlin: Zentrum für Kunst und Urbanistik, 2016), online, available HTTP: http://www.hackingurbanfurniture.net/fileadmin/user_upload/HUF/Research/JCDecaux_HUF_article_JPouzenc.pdf (accessed 30 April 2018).

3
'Wall GmbH', Wikipedia (6 February 2018), online, available HTTP: https://de.wikipedia.org/wiki/Wall_GmbH (accessed 30 April 2018).

4
B. Hartmann, 'Berliner Wall AG will sich komplett digital aufstellen', *Berliner Morgenpost* (14 September 2014), online, available HTTP: https://www.morgenpost.de/berlin/article132236230/Berliner-Wall-AG-will-sich-komplett-digital-aufstellen.html (accessed 30 April 2018).

Chart 2
History of bus stops in Berlin

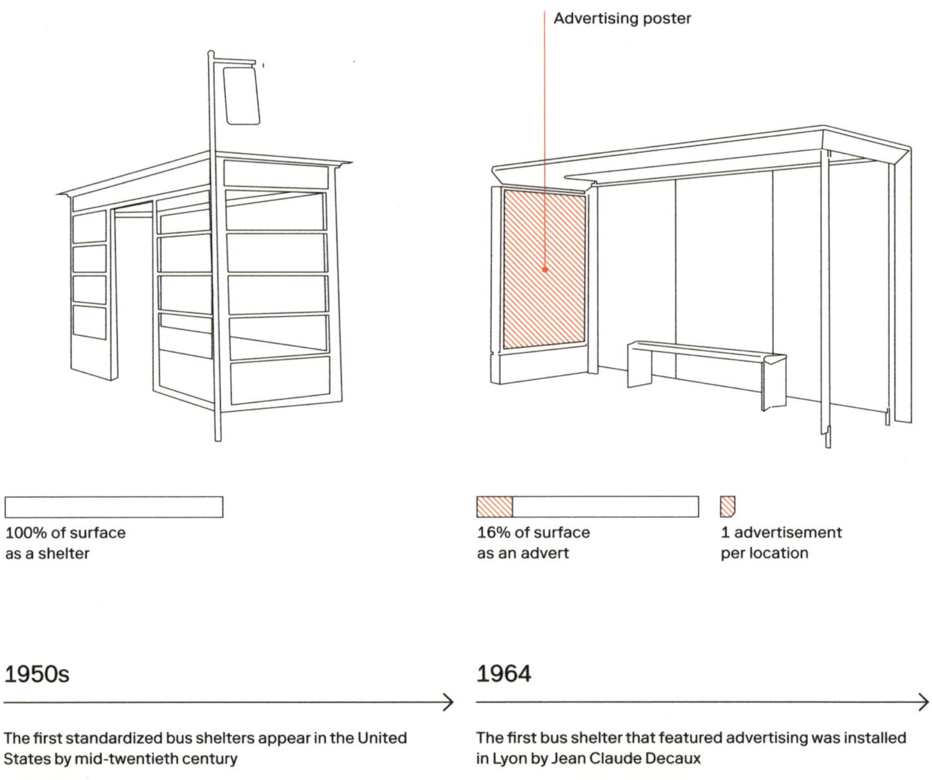

Value for Time

The changes in the amenities provided by the bus shelter become a diagram of the stakeholders' business model. Originally funded by the city, the bus stop served as a sheltered waiting room and its value lay in its function. However, once JCDecaux, a private company, becomes the main investor and introduces advertising to make a profit, the main value of the furniture lies in capturing the attention of its users and passers-by as its marketable advertising surfaces are expanded accordingly, generating substantial revenue. With the advent of screen advertising comes the running of six paperless ads per minute, allowing the company to serve more clients per location, thus increasing profit.[6] The new model not only exploits the overlapping of time/space that the screen provides, but also attempts to increase the number of amenities offered to users and passers-by in exchange for their data.[7]

5
Wall GmbH, 'Smart Berlin: Unsere Zukunftsstadt' (Berlin: Wall GmbH, 2017).

6
J. Stüber, 'Was die Wall AG unter neuer Führung in Berlin vorhat', *Berliner Morgenpost*, 28 February 2016, online, available HTTP: https://www.morgenpost.de/berlin/article207097491/Was-die-Wall-AG-unter-neuer-Fuehrung-in-Berlin-vorhat.html (accessed 30 April 2018).

7
When digital advertising joins forces with points that could extract personalized data, the advertising begins to target specific users with customized recommendations and message ads.

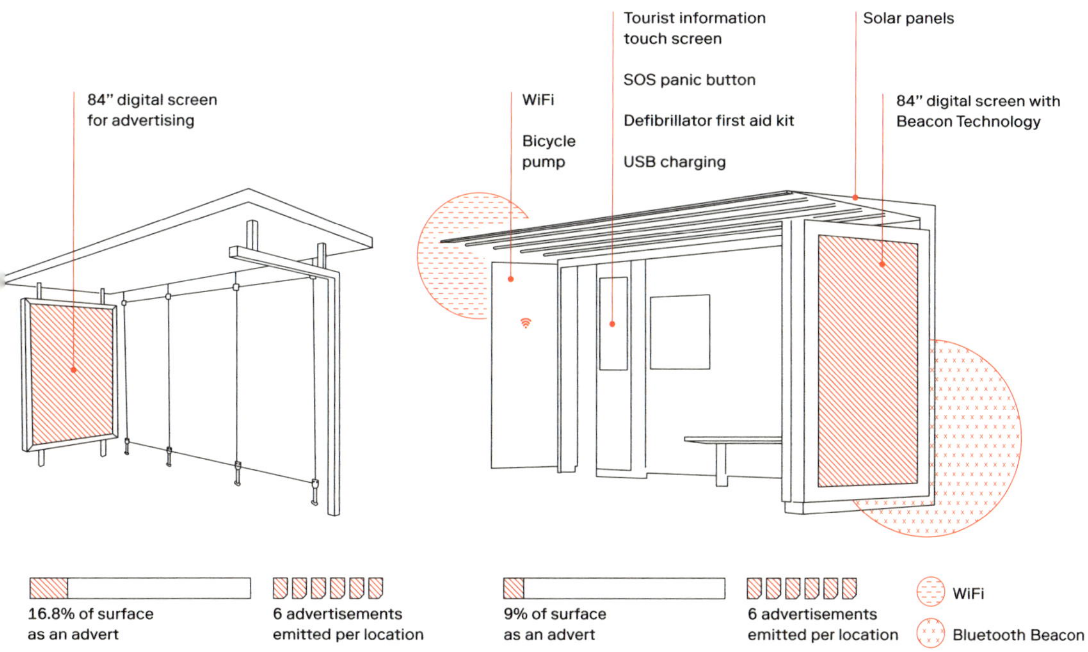

2014

In Berlin digital screens replaced poster adverts in selected bus shelters and S+U Bahn stations

2018

A super-hub autonomous bus shelter was designed for Berlin to be tested in Postdamer Platz

Chart 3
Change of bus shelter business models

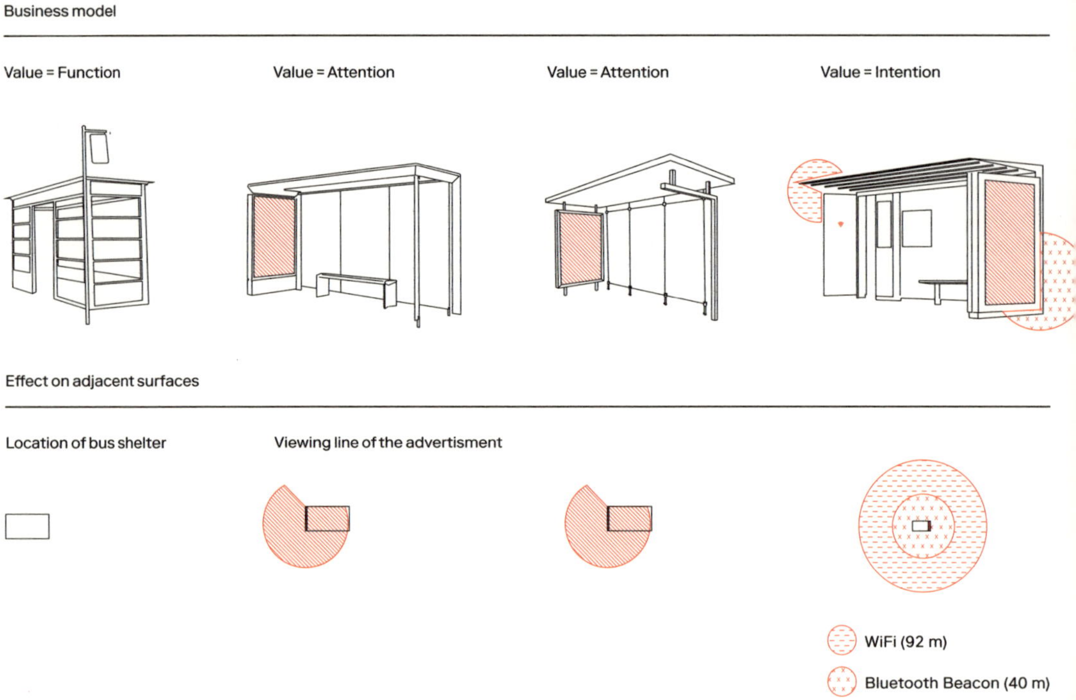

Intention and Attention

The main advantage of this model lies in the value shift from the attention of the individual to the intentions of larger groups, allowing Wall AG to provide new services to city dwellers. Within the framework of an attention economy, value is extracted from users and their ability to generate capital from the present (time-labour). Within an intention economy, capital is produced by speculation, and thus value becomes a future-oriented time-function. In the case of Wall AG, this tendency is illustrated by the company's expansion within urban services ranging from capitalizing on the sharing economy with a bike service and app, a more sophisticated commercial marketing service, and a live information service covering traffic, extreme weather conditions, and transportation disruptions. By having sole access to the public space for experimentation and exposure to a larger audience, the company also gains access to valuable data and is able to capitalize on other markets, scaling up and consequently maintaining a monopoly that cannot guarantee a better or more inclusive service.

Chart 4
Data and economic flow

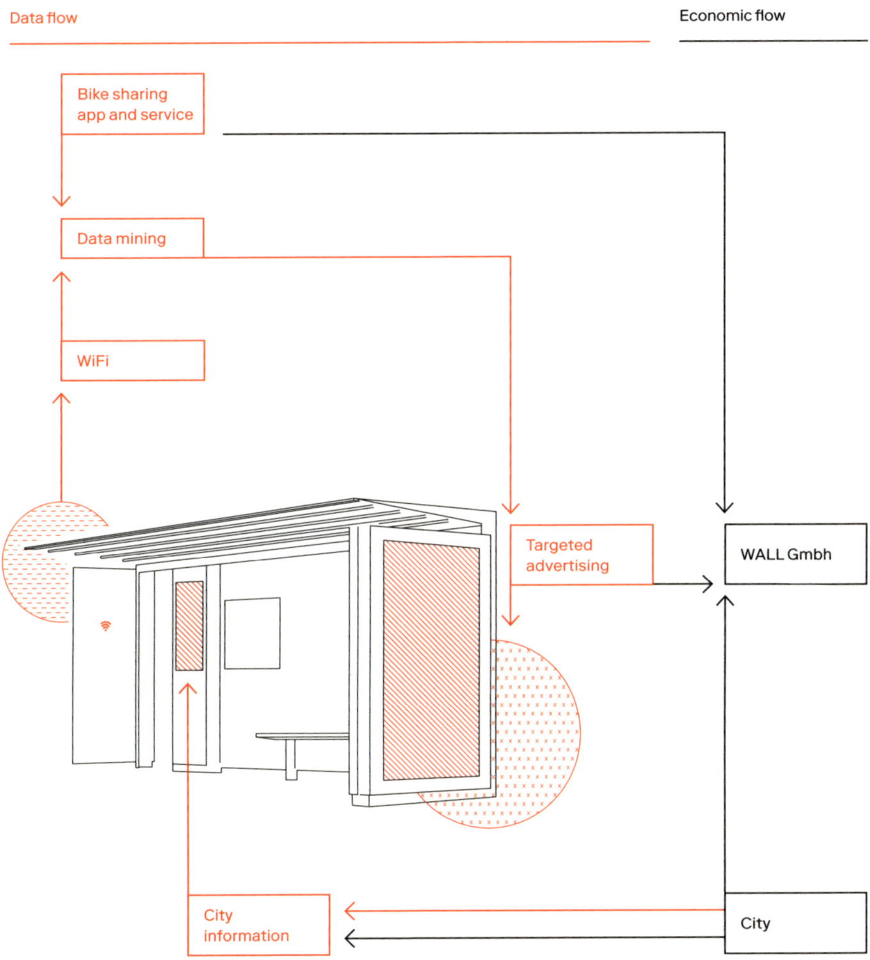

Open Data

Citizens may benefit from Wi-Fi, information services and extra battery life but neither they nor the city necessarily realize what they are giving up in exchange for these services. According to recent studies, the financial benefit that open data bring to the municipality can be up to 30 million euros per year.[8] The use of open data by local initiatives and community projects encourages the emergence of new services and applications, which have the potential to create a healthy competition, improving the quality of life and re-contextualizing the bus shelters.

8 B. Seibel, *Open Data in der Praxis: Bereitsteller und Anwender offener Daten in Berlin* (Berlin: Technologiestiftung, 2016), 5.

Chart 5
Open data local benefits

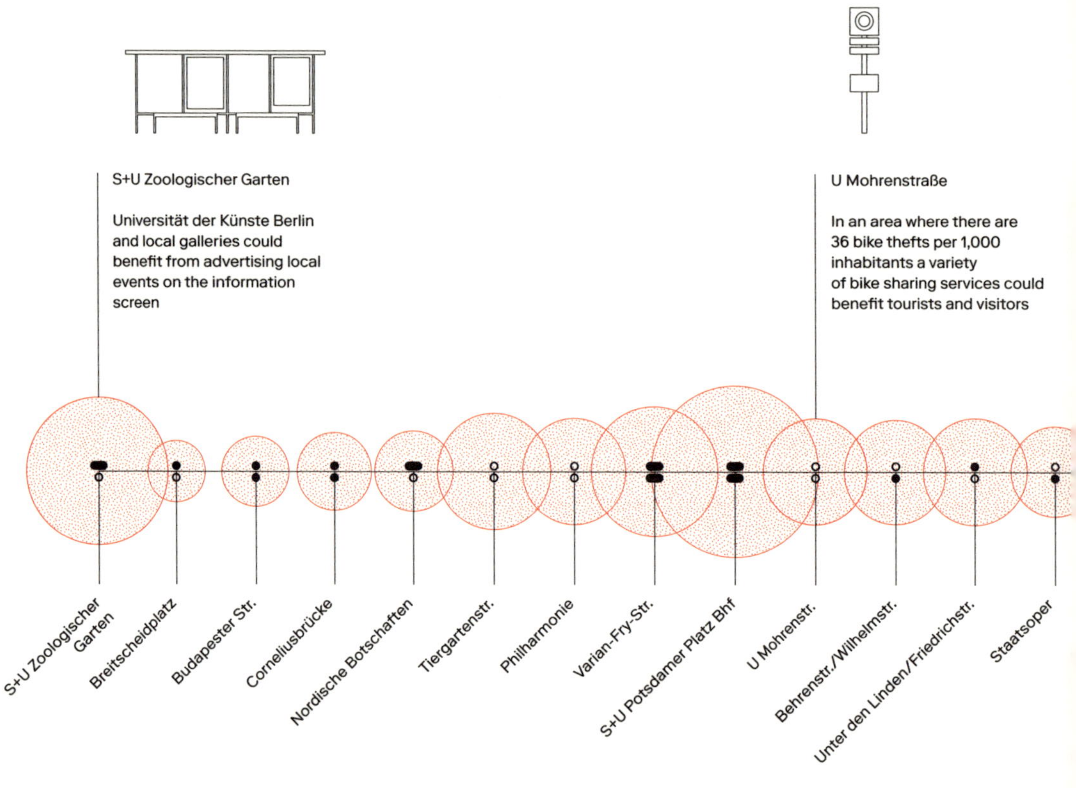

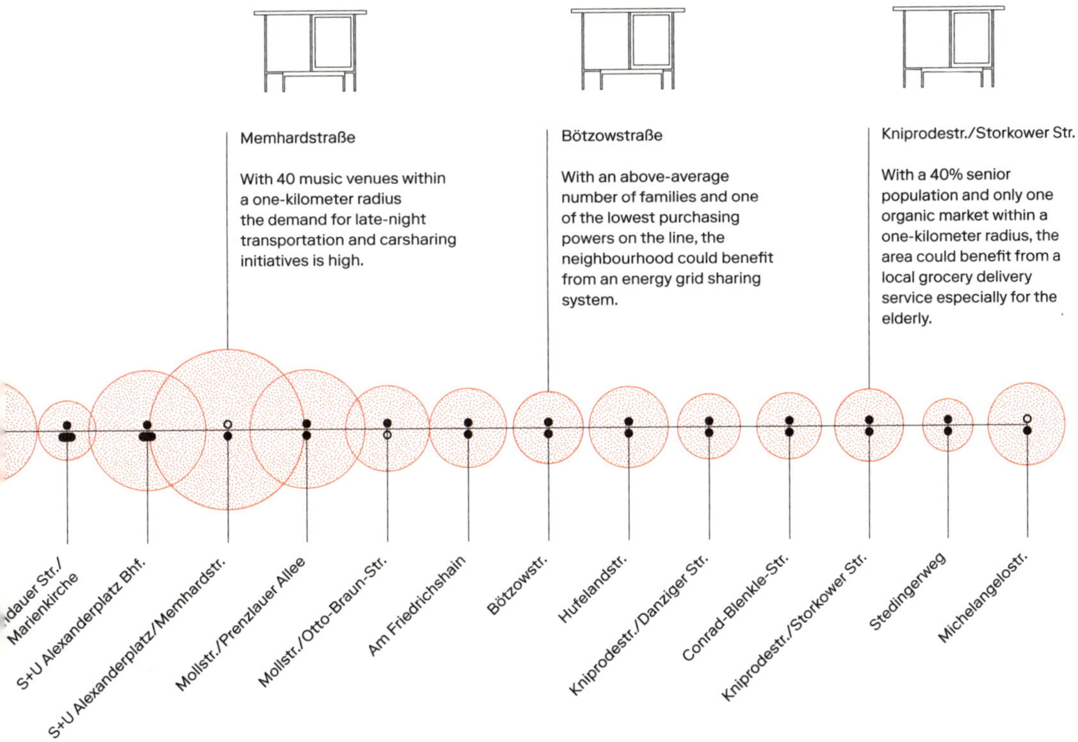
Memhardstraße
With 40 music venues within a one-kilometer radius the demand for late-night transportation and carsharing initiatives is high.
Bötzowstraße
With an above-average number of families and one of the lowest purchasing powers on the line, the neighbourhood could benefit from an energy grid sharing system.
Kniprodestr./Storkower Str.
With a 40% senior population and only one organic market within a one-kilometer radius, the area could benefit from a local grocery delivery service especially for the elderly.
dauer Str./ Marienkirche
S+U Alexanderplatz Bhf.
S+U Alexanderplatz/Memhardstr.
Mollstr./Prenzlauer Allee
Mollstr./Otto-Braun-Str.
Am Friedrichshain
Bötzowstr.
Hufelandstr.
Kniprodestr./Danziger Str.
Conrad-Blenkle-Str.
Kniprodestr./Storkower Str.
Stedingerweg
Michelangelostr.

Belgrade

4.01

Population
(millions of inhab.)

2016 (metropolitan regions)
2016 (Belgrade)
2017 (other cities)

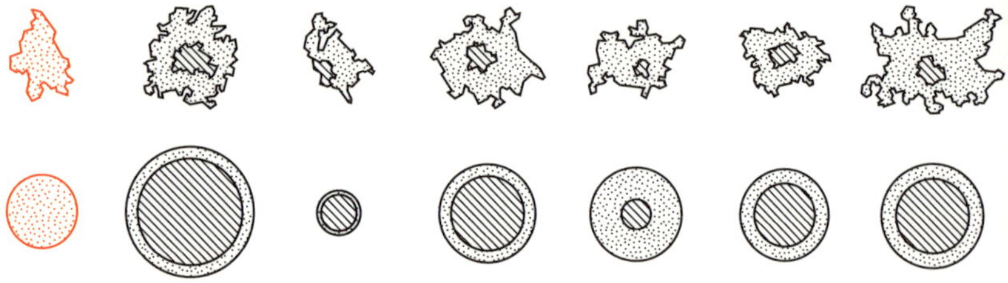

City

Metropolitan region

	Belgrade	Berlin	Bratislava	Budapest	Katowice	Prague	Warsaw
City		3.54	0.43	1.76	0.30	1.27	1.75
Metropolitan region	1.68	5.21	0.64	3.00	2.71	2.62	3.37

4.02

Built-up area footprint

City
2016
Total area: 3,234 km²
Population density:
521 inhab./km²

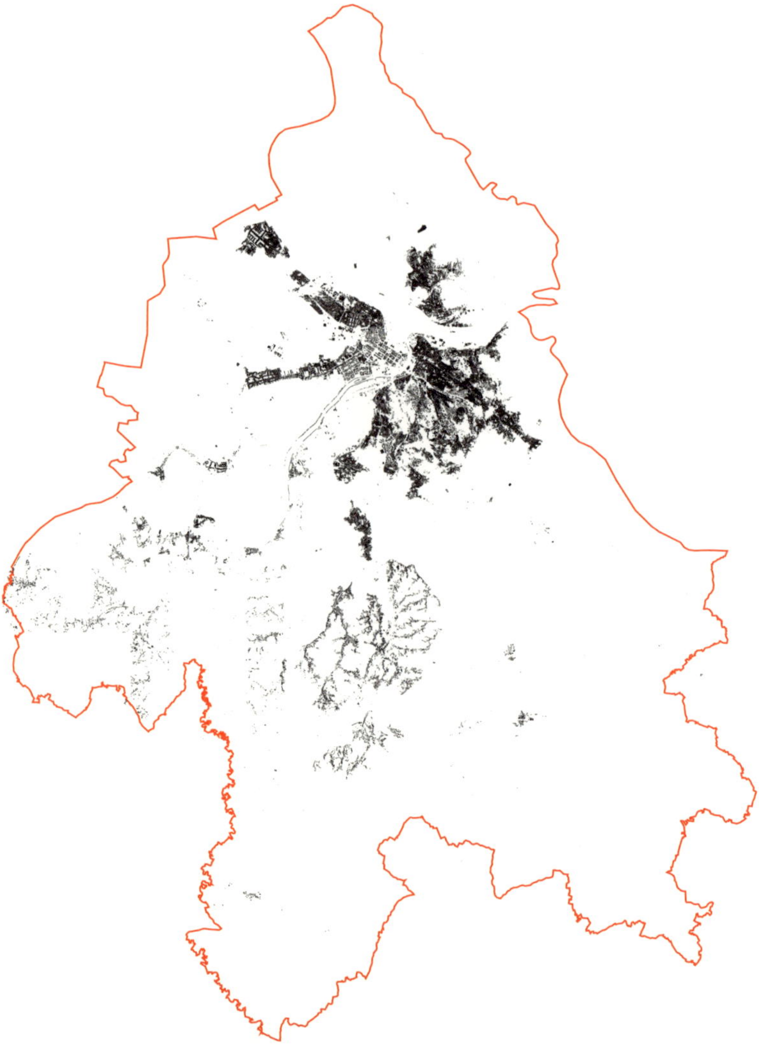

0 5 km

4.03

Transport modal split (per cent)

Cities
2016 (Prague)
2014 (Budapest)
2013 (Berlin)
2015 (other cities)

→ Mobility
Chart E.01, p. 26

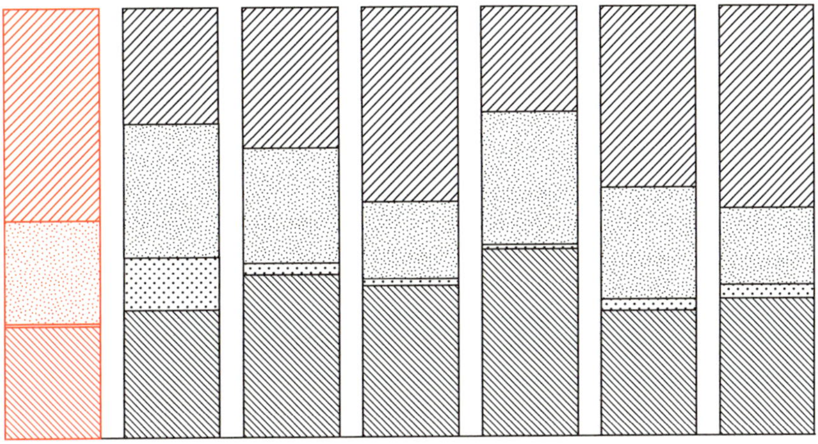

	Belgrade	Berlin	Bratislava	Budapest	Katowice	Prague	Warsaw
Public transport	49.0	26.9	32.6	45.0	24.5	42.0	46.8
Walk	24.0	31.0	26.7	18.0	30.8	26.0	17.9
Cycling and other	1.0	12.5	3.0	2.0	1.4	3.0	3.6
Car	26.0	29.6	37.7	35.0	43.3	29.0	31.7

4.04

Property price-to-income ratio

Cities
2018

→ Housing
Chart C.07, p. 21

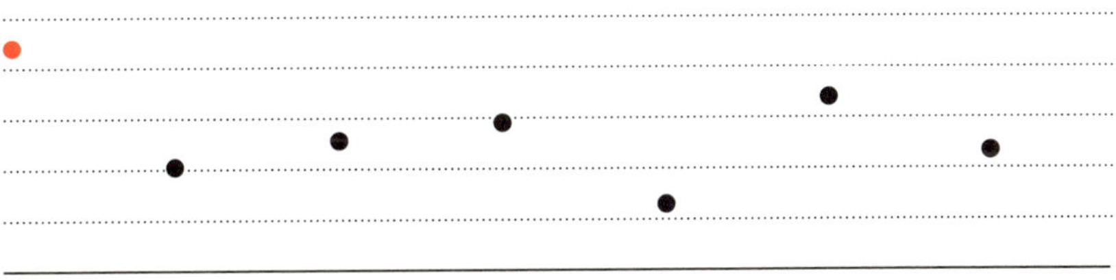

Belgrade	Berlin	Bratislava	Budapest	Katowice	Prague	Warsaw
21.71	10.12	12.62	14.32	6.45	16.74	11.58

4.05

Average area of living accommodation (m^2/inhab.)

City
2011

24.48

◆ = 5 m^2

4.06

Average monthly net salary (EUR)

City
2018

395.98

= 100 €

4.07

Registered passenger cars (cars/1,000 inhab.)

City
2016

314

■ = 20 cars

4.08

Tourists (number/year)

City
2016

913,150

= 1 million tourists

zepter

sky
Wellness

Urban Hub 1: Park Keep

Organization	Association of Belgrade Architects; Belgrade International Architecture Week – BINA
Address	Kneza Miloša 7a/III, 11000 Belgrade
Authors	Čuvari parka (Park Keepers)
Dates	1 February 2017 – 20 May 2018

Activities				
	Festivals	2	Discussion	1
	Conference	1	Publications	3
	Workshops	6	Neighbourhood Events	12
	Exhibitions	2		

rs

Urban Hubs. Infrastructure for Collaboration

Ivan Kucina

The twenty-first century has crossed the ethical boundaries between public well-being and austerity. Too many human trusts, especially cities, have already been sacrificed to corporations. In the last decades of the twentieth century, cities became the signifiers of their countries' identities and wealth. In an increasingly globalized and antagonistic world, a country's success is measured by its cities which compete for human, cultural, tourist, and financial capital and are often commodified in the process.

This model of urban development reflects the prevailing consumer culture governed by neoliberalism. Hence, its economic growth is measured by the growth of consumption, on the premise that urbanization leads to more prosperity for more people. Cities are the turf of consumer culture—literally and figuratively. This turf expands through privatizations, enclosures, segregations, real estate speculation, and the commodification of land and housing. This can be seen in the elaborate design of office buildings, designer architecture of urban landmarks, and the demand for oversized constructions. The spatialization of consumption has led to deregulated urbanization and unlimited use of resources. In short, the economic growth model along with consumer culture have amplified spatial and social disintegration.

The privatization of public spaces has spurred a series of new physical and mental divisions. City centres have been developed as competitive fields where each company fights for consumers by radiating the most seductive image to the public. As a result, public space has been turned into an illuminated scene for mass consumption. Shopping malls, luxury hotels, gated condominiums and office towers are seen as icons of progress. Urban spectacles have become the only common form of expression. However, behind all this extravaganza, the major part of urban territory has evaded the spotlight. The majority of urban dwellers live in neighbourhoods with crumbling façades, dirty streets, and deserted spaces. They no longer have faith in the public system which has failed them by implementing austerity in order to stimulate private business. Destroying public spaces is the most significant urban spectacle they can provide as counteraction.

Enduring Pledge

The transition from socialism to capitalism as defined by neoliberal shock therapy happens through privatization of resources and marginalization of public facilities. It has affected massive changes in social values in post-socialist countries in Central, East and Southeast Europe. Singularity has replaced collectivity. Highly competitive individual success is valued above ideals such as equality, solidarity, and unity. This new social order has materialized in cityscapes in the form of random sets of glass buildings in prime city spots and on the real estate market. They offer Western-inspired luxury instead of public services.

Architectural production in post-socialist countries is trapped in the process of adapting to rapidly changing economic and social conditions. The race for professional success does not leave room for critical engagement, especially in the disappearing public sphere. It seems that an alternative approach cannot be expected from architectural practices, but rather from self-organized civic groups. However, civic activism is not developed enough to effect major urban changes. Sharing experiences and learning from one another can give it the necessary boost.

Building Public Trusts

The building of public trusts is an evolving process that is central to the neglected neighbourhoods as it has the potential to adopt and transform public spaces. Public spaces need to become a political tool for citizen participation in urban reintegration. They should not serve as decorative assemblage for daily breaks, but provide the basis for gatherings and social exchange, for facilitating collaborative practices, for finding a common ground for different personal interests, and for mediating between citizens and public institutions.

This logic could also evolve towards resources that could be created by citizens, thus giving impetus to the rise of various new citizens' associations. Cities are fertile ground for the development of commoning practices that prioritize communities and collective production over privatization. Urban commons that emerge and thrive outside the dichotomy of public and private can give new meaning to the reorganization of cities.

Urban reintegration could also be supported with innovative forms of shared economy. As part of the efforts to transform the whole city into a productive ecosystem, local networks that directly connect entrepreneurs and users can have powerful impact on the ways citizens live, work, and interact. Public trusts foster curiosity, critical thinking, creativity, communication, and collaboration, motivating citizens towards a new ethos based on sharing. Sharing is about creating opportunities. Neglected public spaces are perfect for installing infrastructure for collaboration: urban hubs.

Urban Hubs

Urban hubs are places for citizens to meet, talk, and agree on what to do together to improve their neighbourhoods. They host discussions, workshops and other parts of the collaborative process. They initiate social exchange and create social energy that is orientated towards urban reintegration. An urban hubs network across neighbourhoods can influence the reconnection of the whole city. Urban hubs are defined by exchange rather than artifacts. They are a bare, raw, and modest set of things found on hand, repaired and reused. They are open-ended. Their high level of adaptability favours the freedom of provisional self-organized initiatives and networks.

The initial capital for urban hub startups lies in a proactive group of people ready to dedicate themselves to their development. Neighbours are invited to share their skills, making collaboration a key factor for the success of the project. Urban reintegration depends on multiple acts of collaboration that result in common proposals for the transformation of neglected local public spaces. In addition, citizens renew connections and mutual trust by transforming the spaces together. Collaboration shows how people can depend on one another, which can in turn boost connections within the community.

In Belgrade, two urban hubs have been developed by local partners, Park Keepers (*Čuvari parka*) and Schoolcity (*Škograd*), with support of the BINA team. Citizens' involvement in design, building and maintenance has revitalized relationships and increased the power of community. By helping citizens to reclaim their neighbourhood, these two urban hubs have been successfully testing Belgrade's social capacity to implement strategies for sustainable urban development that provides terms for a rightful, integrated, and shared city.

Park Keepers

Tatjana Vukosavljević

The 'Plato' urban hub is a participatory project designed to improve a shared public space based on collaboration with the community. 'Plato' is an open space between the skyscrapers on Mileševska Street in the central Belgrade municipality of Vračar. Built in the 1970s, it is a vast and slightly empty area, divided into several fields for playing and socializing. The urban hub is designed as a place of gathering and exchange, bringing together the community around shared interests. The project emphasizes the social role of civic initiatives in the improvement of modern cities. Its practical use is to develop citizens' and experts' existing proposals and suggestions, which have been formulated as a direct response to their current social and environmental needs.

> Playing around with our memories, our heritage, our imagination—with an eye to the future—brings us to our main meeting point: the table. The interviews we conducted with community members and regular passers-by clarified our need to understand 'Plato' as a space and our role in it; and encouraged us to meet, to talk, and to share. This is how the table became a key element of our work, and how it became the key element for the initiative going forward. Welcome to 'Plato'!
> Park Keepers (Čuvari parka)

The newly developed participatory planning methodology consists of four phases: conducting research and gathering data (interviews and surveys); analyzing and processing data (creation of datasets); working together (discussions, workshops, and exhibitions); building community (implementation of ideas developed together). The activities organized with the neighbourhood aimed to strengthen the sense of community and the culture of sharing, and included regular cleaning, swaps, charity events, and the reappropriation of cultural and artistic programmes from cultural and education institutions in the neighbourhood, and the creation of new ones. The ultimate goal of 'Plato' is to make the neighbourhood a more pleasant place to live. The true success of the project is the collaboration of so many different entities: City of Belgrade, Belgrade Land Development Public Agency (Beoland), Municipality of Vračar, Centre for Education and Culture 'Božidarac 1947', Kindergarten 'Mića and Aćim', a local bakery, local craftsmen, private companies and many others. The locals are the focus group and the most important partner and participant. Without them, a project like 'Urban Hub – Plato' would not have been possible.

1 Participatory Workshops
The Park Keepers (*Čuvari parka*) team and the BINA team created a new methodology and developed a model of participatory planning and intensive cooperation between the users of the space, experts, and competent institutions.

2 The Painting of Plato's Pavement
In a series of workshops, the local community including children chose the future look of the pavement. The Park Keepers' multidisciplinary team then created a design and realized it together with the BINA team and the locals.

3 The Community Table
The Park Keepers designed the community table as a result of yearlong participatory work with the community. The seating is mobile and can be changed to serve any occasion from open-air cinema, an outdoor kindergarten class, to just neighbours sitting down together for a cup of coffee together. The activities are supported by the community place and the Municipality of Vračar.

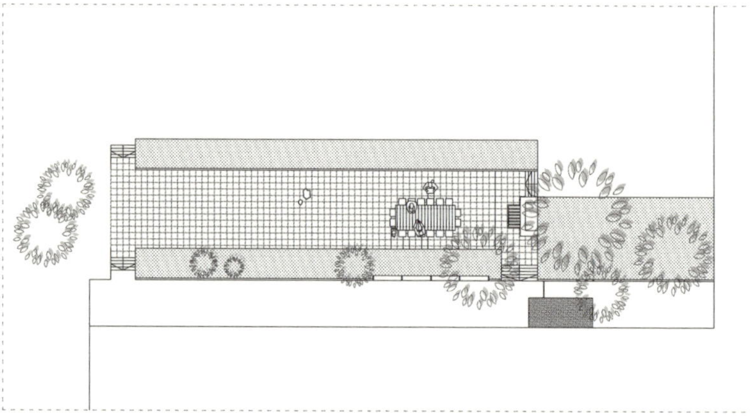

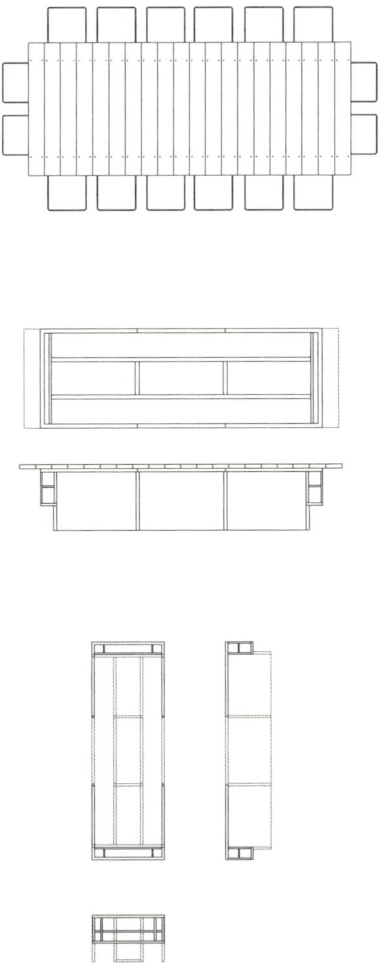

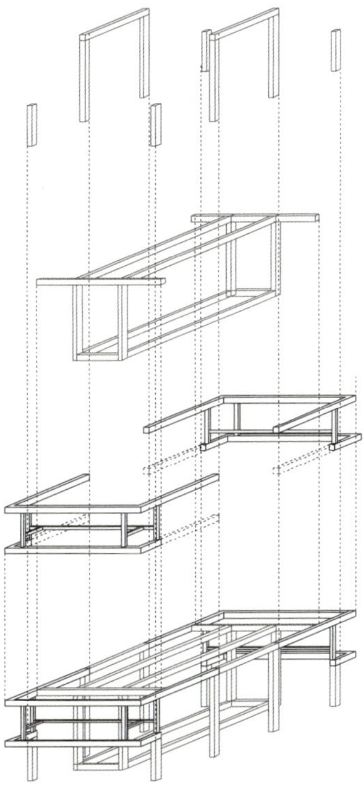

Belgrade Urban Activis Is Activism Female?

Lack of Participation in the Early 2000s

In former socialist countries all outdoor space was public by default, which left people unprepared for the future change modelled by the new political, economic, and social logic after 1989. Belgrade's public space has deteriorated due to poor maintenance, and at the same time, it has been commercialized, privatized, and adapted to the market economy. A representative study of Belgrade's population conducted in 2004 concluded that 'many citizens lack the motivation for public action because a widespread mistrust in public institutions leads them to believe that the prospects for meaningful participation in the decision making process on the local level are small or non-existent'.[1] 80 per cent of the participants believed they were not able to make any impact on urban development.

1 S.Vujović, M. Petrović, 'Belgrade's post-socialist urban evolution: Reflections by the actors in the development process', in Stanilov (ed.), *The Post-Socialist City* (Dordrecht: Springer, 2007), 361–384.

Chart 1
Channels of influence on the municipal level in Belgrade in 2004
Source: Vujović, Petrović 2007, 377

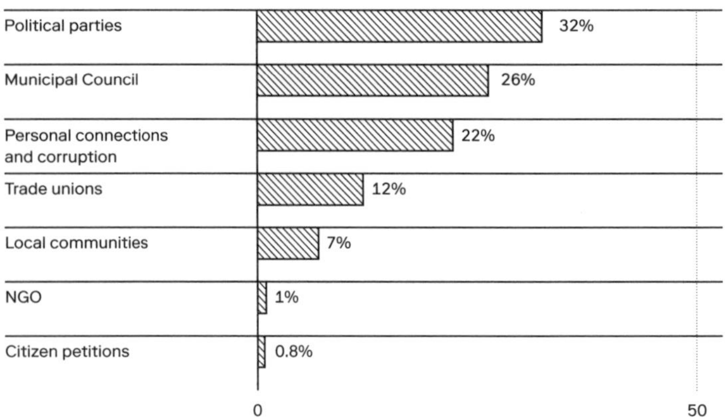

Scene.

Urban Activists Enter the Scene

In the past ten years, new and participatory initiatives for better living conditions and citizens' well-being in public space have emerged in Belgrade. Their aspirations are not primarily political but directed towards urban space, trying to achieve small, visible results and immediate improvement. Bottom-up urban activism impacts everyday life and the shared environment, from inner-block courtyards to entire neighbourhoods. Spontaneous, independent, citizen-initiated projects have popped up—in 2008 the playful punctual interventions in the district of Vračar called 'Urban Pockets', by the Students of Architecture and 'Peti park' civil initiative, municipality and the neighbourhood. Other projects included the modelling of a basketball and sports courtyard by the renowned basketball player Žarko Paspalj, the restoration of the Kalvarice stairs by the community in Zemun, or the 'Trash Hero' initiative for a cleaner and more sustainable Belgrade.

Who are the engaged citizens of Belgrade that are willing to take action to improve their shared living environment? A survey on urban activism conducted by BINA (Belgrade International Architecture Week) in cooperation with the 'Shared Cities: Creative Momentum' project researched the contemporary positions among BINA collaborators in 2018.

Chart 2
Does urban activism make a change?

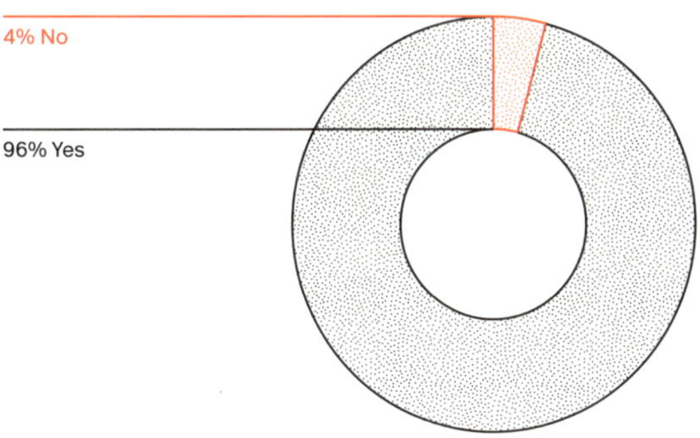

Who is an urban activist?

As the 2018 survey shows, urban activists strongly believe in making a difference (96 per cent). As architects and designers, they are professionally interested, driven by a vision of improvement and change, and are generally dissatisfied with the quality of urban space in Belgrade. The typical urban activist is between 25 and 44 years old, predominantly female. She or he works as an architect, in humanities or education. She or he is typically a university graduate. Most urban activists live in Belgrade's city centre, in the old town, and in the Vračar district (where the BINA Urban Hub project takes place).

Chart 3
Motivation of the respondents for activities in public space

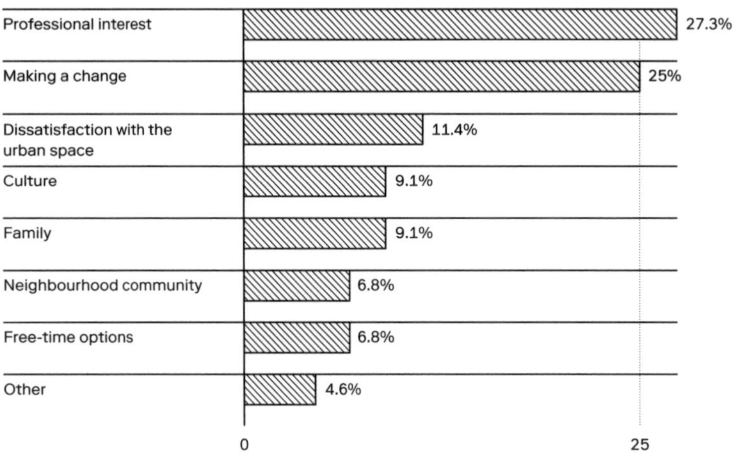

Chart 4
Respondent age

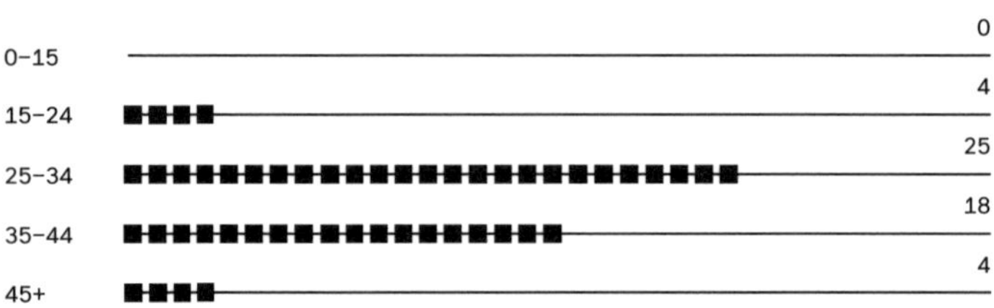

Chart 5
Respondent gender

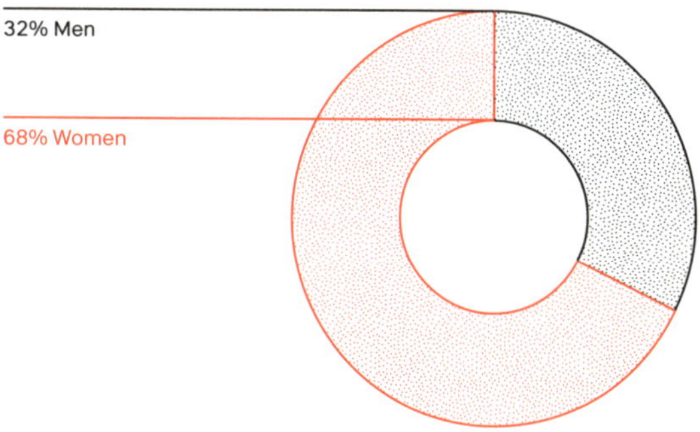

Chart 6
Highest education degree achieved

Chart 7
Active participation in BINA

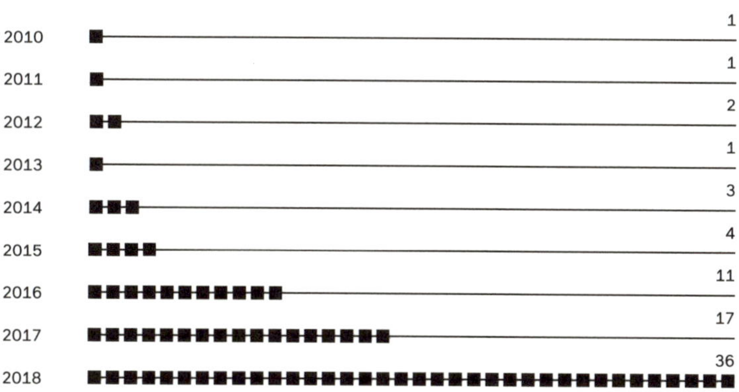

Chart 8
Professional background

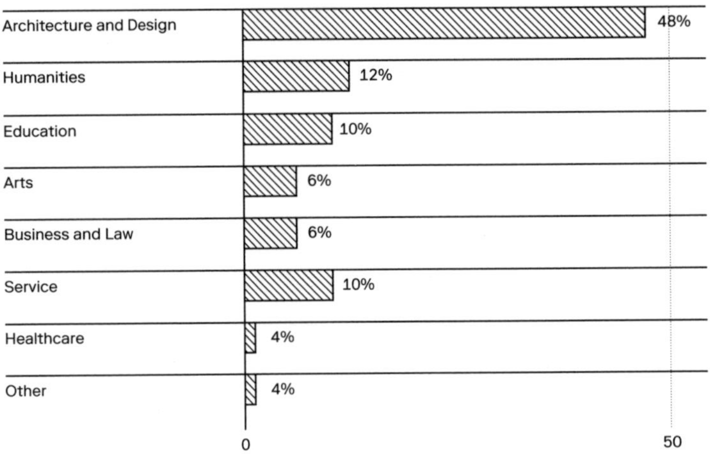

Chart 9
Respondent occupation (segments)

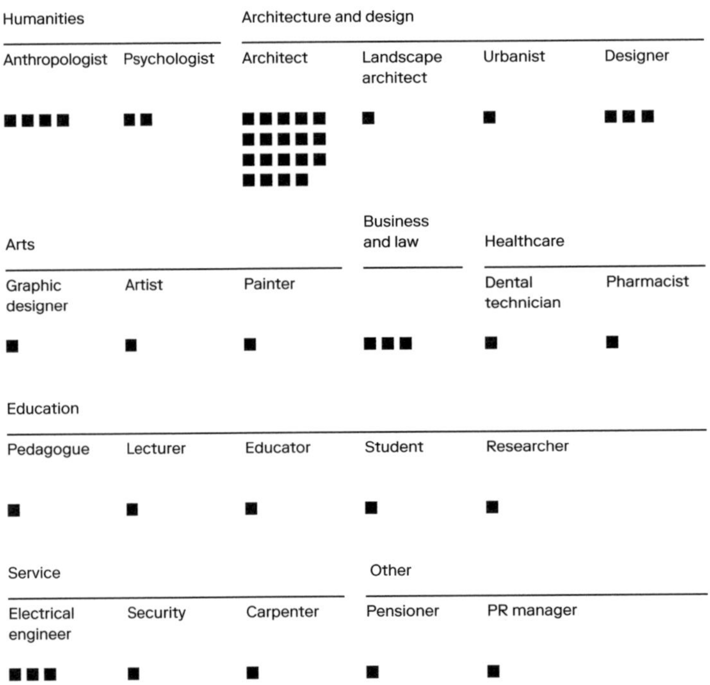

Chart 10
Place of residence in Belgrade (city district)
Source: Anketa BINA (Belgrade, 2018)

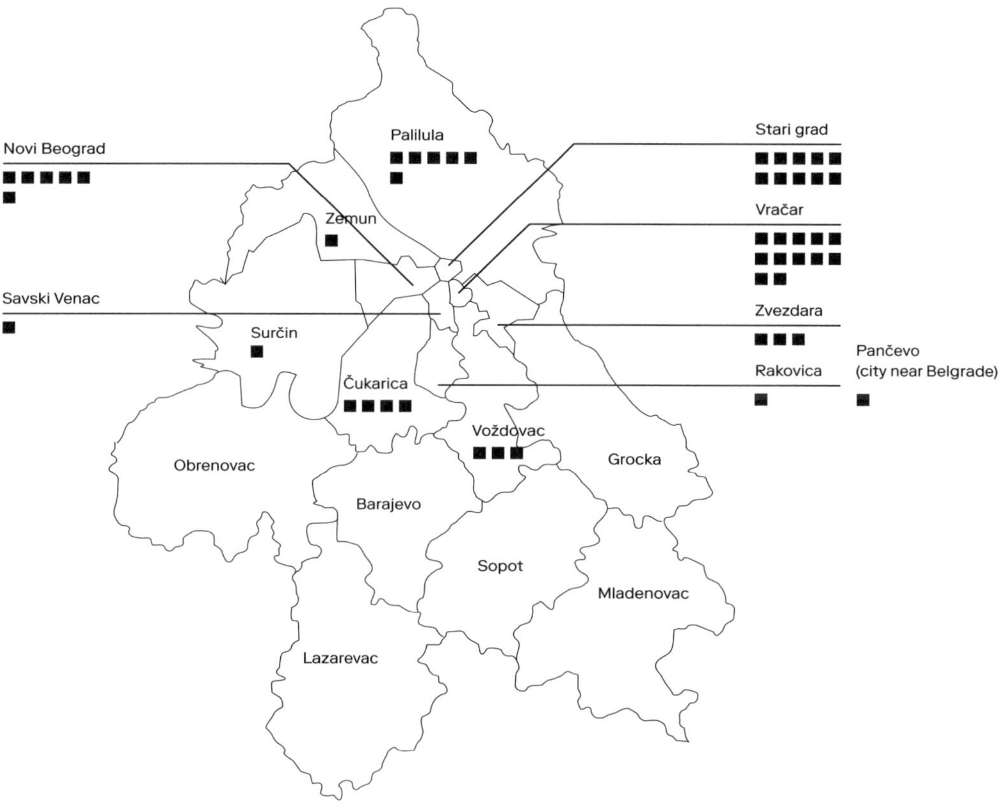

Women's Profiles in Serbia

One of the activism survey's main findings was the strong engagement of young women (68 per cent). Why is it so? Is urban activism female? The figure may be even more striking in light of the fact that there are more female than male graduates from the Belgrade faculty of architecture. Generally, women achieve the same levels of education, but traditional gender roles direct them towards different fields like culture and volunteering. Serbia scored low in all gender-equality domains of the EU Gender Equality Index except in the domain of power, as the country has adopted a 30 per cent quota of female representation in the National Assembly. A representative survey 'Women and Men in the Republic of Serbia' conducted by the Serbian Statistical Office in 2016 revealed differences in the distribution of paid and unpaid activities between men and women. Women tend to work longer hours, but they rank very high in terms of unpaid work. In other words, women spend more time doing non-profit activities and taking care of their households and children. The field of Belgrade culture is defined by women's activities, as several research studies showed. Women rank higher in outgoing, culture-oriented activities such as going to the theatre, cinema or gallery.

Chart 11
Women in decision-making positions in Serbia
Source: Women and Men in the Republic of Serbia (Belgrade, 2017), 222, 230

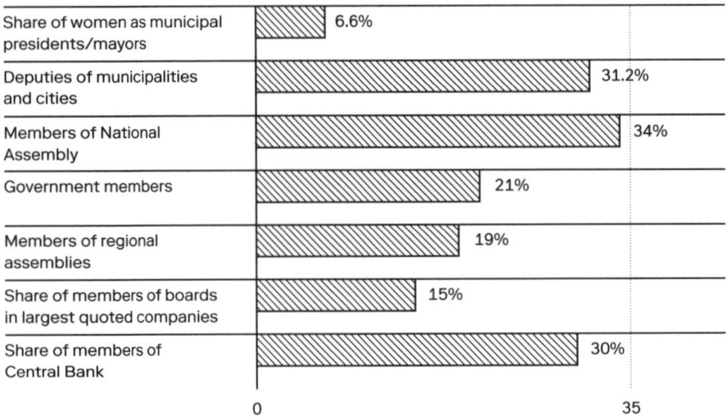

Chart 12
Gender ratio at architecture faculties, men/women graduates
Source: Visoko Obrazovanje 2016/2017 (Belgrade, 2017), 82

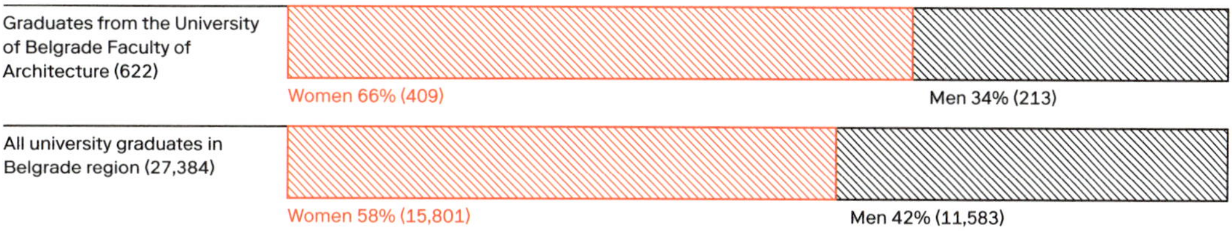

Chart 13
Affinity for individual activities according to gender and age structure of respondents (per cent)
Source: Cultural needs and habits of citizens of Serbia (Belgrade, 2016), 33

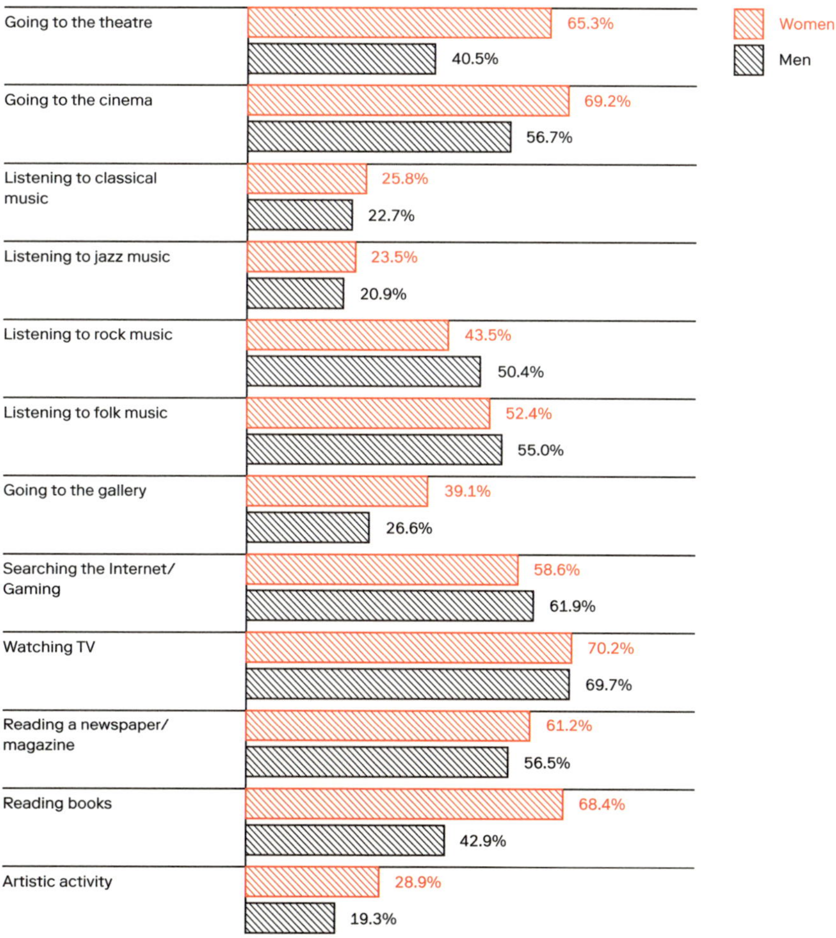

Chart 14
Distribution of paid and unpaid work

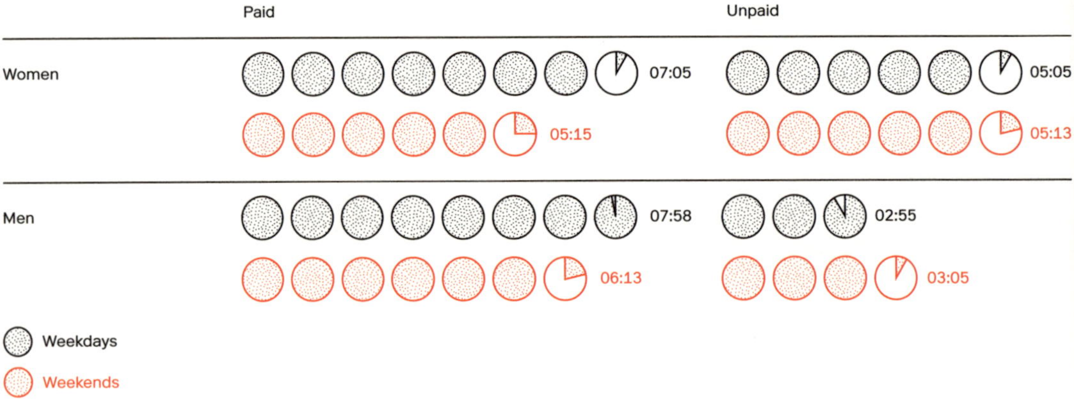

Chart 15
Types of unpaid activities
Source: Time Use in the Republic of Serbia, 2010 and 2015 (Belgrade, 2016), 119

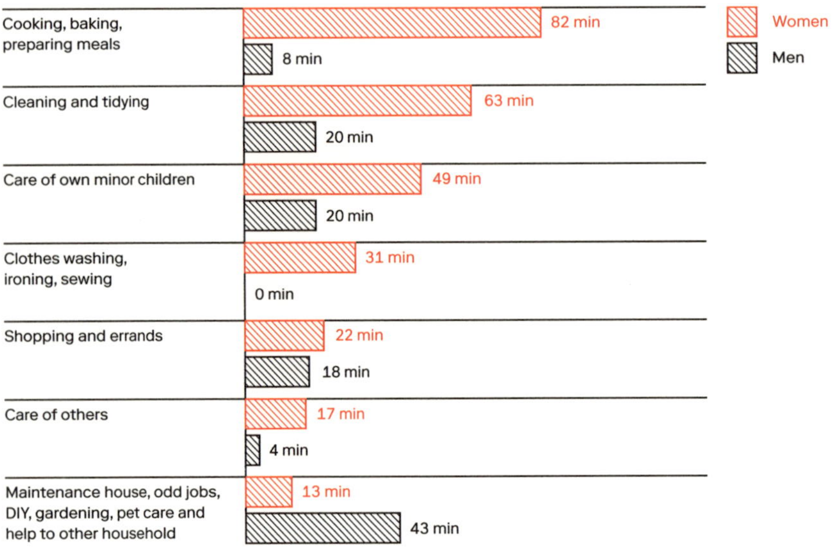

Female Activists and Public Space

The central energy behind urban space initiatives such as BINA or the Urban Hubs: Čuvari parka and Škograd is female. Professional interest becomes a community-oriented, activist attitude:

> 'The BINA team develops systems of activism that are recognized by institutions and politicians. Actors are mostly women (Ružica Sarić, Danica Jovović Prodanović, Tatjana Vukosavljević, Natalija Jovanović, Jelena Ivanović Vojvodić). The team's female members have a strong desire to help the development of architecture and activism both home and abroad.'[2]
> Jelena Ivanović Vojvodić, director and CEO, BINA, 13 December 2018

The public space shaped by women does not have a strictly feminized profile (sunbathing is less popular than sports). The caring approach brings a stronger emphasis on bottom-up, local cultural activities, and community events such as film screenings or urban games. Culture activities ranked higher than political engagement (discussion with municipalities, information distribution). Feminist activism is a multi-layered, long-term engagement that includes the willingness to create the neighbourhood's cultural programme, engage in discussion with local authorities through citizen workshops, and neighbourhood action.

2
Conversation w. Jelena Ivanović Vojvodić, director and CEO, BINA, 13 December 2018

Chart 16
Preferred shared activity in urban spaces
(multiple choice)

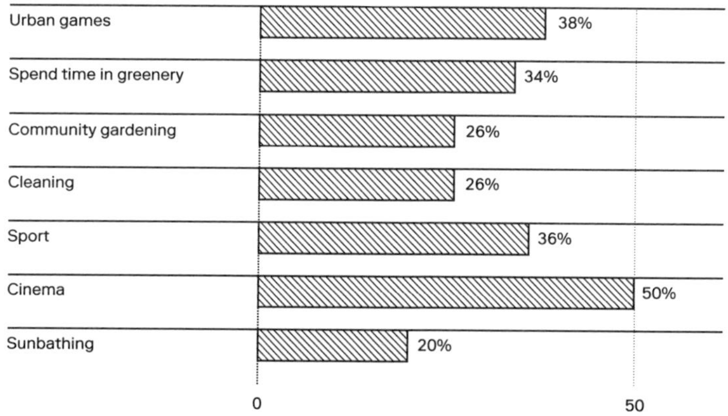

Chart 17
Fields of activities that need support and discussion of both citizens and administration to share the city in Belgrade (multiple choice)

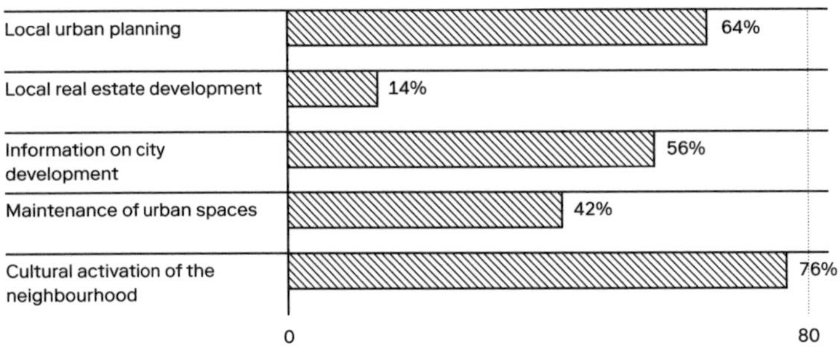

Chart 18
Preferred fields of action to get involved in (multiple choice)
Source: Anketa BINA (Belgrade, 2018)

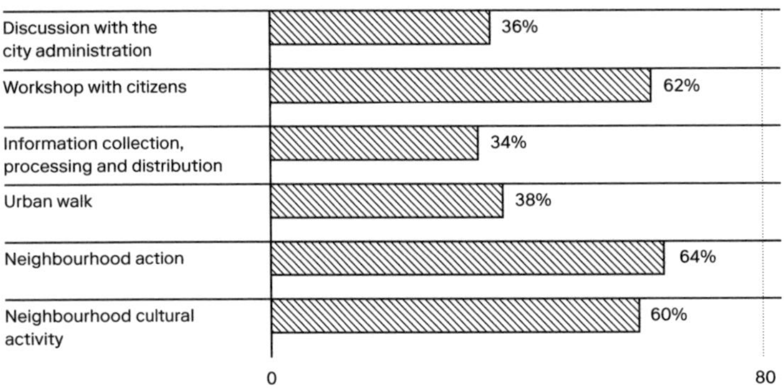

Sharing Dat
Knowledge

and

Katowice
Budapest
Warsaw

City as Interface. Self-generating Urban and the Question of La

For the better part of modern planning, city-making has been understood in terms of asset agglomeration and facilitation: that is to say, in terms of physical, economic, social and cultural value concentration and its further advancement aided by planning regulations and general legislation. Yet there is growing pressure from different ends of the political spectrum to rethink the well-trodden paths of urban development. While some argue that bureaucratic over-regulation has led to civic apathy and a sense of disenfranchisement among today's urban dwellers, others endorse the 'liberalization' of regulatory frameworks as a means of market stimulation. Incidentally, both inclinations draw on similar assumptions. Namely, that the active consideration of *users*' interests—what they need or want at a particular place and at a particular moment in time—as a decisive parameter in determining the production of goods and the provision of services will lead to a more efficient and effective outcome. Such assumptions alert us to two crucial aspects of intentional framing: first, with regard to the generalizing use of the term *users,* conflating the different demands of citizens, consumers, community organizations, and interest groups in the shape of a manageable recipient other; and second, with regard to the prevailing paradigm of efficiency of contemporary life. Taken in its usual meaning of performing a task with minimal waste of time and effort, an intensified exchange between service providers and users (e.g. knowledge sharing between municipal authorities and residents about what is needed, where and when for a smoother operation of urban infrastructures such as public transport or leisure facilities) might well allow for an accelerated and more purpose-driven urban metabolism, but it might also entail an element of mainstreaming and standardization when it comes to the kinds of urban life we can conceive of.

In this context, Henri Lefebvre's claim for a 'right to the city'[1] is to be seen as a critical framework for challenging the advance of capitalist forms of governance and the commodification of social interaction in cities. The resurgence of his idea in today's social and urban movements brings into focus urban space as a collective arena to (re)make ourselves and our cities. Grassroots initiatives around the world are struggling for fairer and more democratic forms of organization and governance with direct citizen involvement in decision-making. Their campaigns are often based on the idea that citizens know the actual needs of urban users better than governments or policy-makers ('people know best')

1
H. Lefebvre, *Le droit à la ville* (Paris: Éditions Anthropos, 1968).

vironments
our

and can provide more efficient knowledge about day-to-day requirements than bureaucratic institutions and their instruments of rule. Such reasoning consequently helps to avoid 'non-productive' forms of urban governance, in particular tendencies to ground development solely on principles of administrative abstraction and classification, which can never do justice to the multiplicity of individual needs and circumstances.

However, hitherto championed forms of bottom-up, citizen-led, smart governance also involve crucial processes of abstraction, when it comes to mining the knowledge produced on the spot and translating it into practical applications. Here, the development of data into a major infrastructural element of global interactions has profoundly changed every aspect of contemporary urban life. Yet it is not just technologies but people and their initiatives that have emerged as a key force driving this change. With urban habitats increasingly shaped by digital platforms, data generation, and analysis efforts, new questions have emerged around the complexities of ownership and access exacerbated by radically improving data processing capabilities. Demands have arisen for an improved, 'informational' right to the city that enables new forms of public beyond the techno-capitalist vision of an information society. These demands are strangely echoed in the widespread use of data mining expedited by platform companies and populist governments. While government agencies seek to befriend us, tech companies in search of the next market lure us into conversation with AI-enabled chatbots; maverick politicians ride on the emotional charge of popular internet memes; traditional sources of truth and belonging are being eclipsed by a new mode of public interaction shaped by the logics of interface technologies, instant consumption, and short-term alliances. What is it that is being shared between citizens in such unstable environments? How can sharing play a socially supportive role in emerging urban datascapes in which individual, commercial, and governmental agendas and actions are becoming increasingly blurred?

These questions are often raised by local initiatives and action groups in search of alternatives to coercive consumption promoted by corporate businesses in the digital creative and IT sector as individually made choices of collaboration. In the entrepreneurial ventures of the latter, sharing has become a byword for mastering shared assumptions about the value of a new product or service. In the new sharing economy, trust and confidence need to be maximized before a project can be realized.[2] But sharing also has a long tradition as an essential practice to counterbalance deprivation and inequality in urban cultures across the globe—as a mode of regulating the distribution of resources from the bottom up. Not long ago, this tradition started to play a vital role in many cities in Central Europe, for instance, when Warsaw's, Budapest's or Bratislava's well-established bottom-up sharing cultures took effect as an economic backstop for all members of society after the collapse of the socialist regimes in the former Soviet bloc. Warsaw's knowledge-sharing networks, in particular, have brought to the fore a persistent fabric of informality that does not only help strengthen livelihoods in economically deprived areas of the city but also reflects a set of common values that are fundamentally different from the values introduced by rampant free-market capitalism.[3] Such informal systems are constantly updated, and encompass the structuring of social relationships, the configuration of living environments and participation in political and social processes, as well as the generation of individual incomes and cultural production. In all these different sectors, urban informality is increasingly reliant on the digital realm for fostering new skills, crafts, and technologies that leverage the economic and social participation of a diverse set of actors on multiple levels.

Citizen initiatives engaged in crowd-sensing activities are part of such new movements evolving around demands for ecological, social, or institutional improvement. The Slovak crowd-sensing platform *Odkaz pre starostu* is just one example that demonstrates how municipalities and citizens can hold direct conversations about occurrences in urban areas that require remedial attention, be it unreported building activities, dirty paths, damaged benches, broken street lighting, or air pollution in a particular neighbourhood. Such initiatives to improve urban spaces allow citizens to express themselves more directly in the community and interact with institutional structures. As Jennifer Gabrys has argued, it is important to understand 'citizen sensing not as a practice synonymous with citizen science but as a modality of citizenship that concretizes through interaction with computational sensing technologies used for environmental monitoring and feedback.'[4] Traditional power apparatuses are now being confronted with citizens who are increasingly tasked with the self-servicing of the social, cultural, and infrastructural fabric of the societies they inhabit. Yet through their activities, citizens are not only providing environmental data, but also data about themselves, about their interests, attitudes, and values. Big data collection, analysis, and prediction are part of the ongoing transformation of urban life into new fabrics composed of algorithmic calculations, processes, and judgments.

In such data-driven environments, our personal data are not only mined and exploited for use by platform industries and

2 M. Feher, *Rated Agency: Investee Politics in a Speculative Age* (New York: Zone Books, 2018), 191.

3 See M. Zakowska (ed.), 'Shared Cities: Mapping the Post-Communist Status Quo', *Cities Magazine* (2017) vol. 1, online, available HTTP: https://www.sharedcities.eu/material/shared-cities-magazine-117/ (accessed 28 February 2019).

4 J. Gabrys, *Program Earth: Environmental Sensing Technology and the Making of a Computational Planet* (Minneapolis: University of Minnesota Press, 2016), 187.

5 E. Morozov, 'The Case for Publicly Enforced Online Rights', *Financial Times* (28 September 2018), 11.

6 B. Bratton, *The Stack: On Software and Sovereignty* (Cambridge, MA: MIT Press, 2016), 8–13.

governance institutions: a key aspect of this development is the constant valorization of our individual performances as human subjects. What matters under the aegis of data-optimized operations in the urban realm is the maximization of efficiency, productivity, and profitability, and hence real-time information is key to avoid idle time. That way, urban life in the present becomes subordinate to an economy of future options. Access to these new cities is no longer only a question of individual wealth (or class) but of individual collateral based on reputation, and consequently these cities will not be open to all. If our social graph is not up to scratch, access to these brave new worlds may be denied. This is why Evgeny Morozov, in a commentary for the *Financial Times*,[5] has pointed out that in our digital era claiming one's right to the city needs to include demands for our right to data. And this is a conversation that we will need to engage in when thinking about ways in which the capacity of urban spaces to materialize and signify the production of value can be enlisted in endeavours to create more equitable cityscapes.

Trading Values

Corporate digital platforms such as Facebook, Twitter, Instagram, Uber, Lyft, or Airbnb are first and foremost economic and technological constructs. But they are also a broader force that includes extra-economic components such as trust, shared assumptions, values, belief systems, social bonds, well-being and emotional attachment—components that all depend on architecture and design to realize their full potential. That way, technology-enabled platforms are key to how we are all enrolled in embracing the new imperative of being good and productive digital citizens. Cloud-based software, social media, and mobile applications enable us to be part of the game. And, indeed, at first glance everything may seem fine with this democratization of involvement. But once this kind of digital participation is connected to the urban realm, what comes into focus is the production of new infrastructural space that amounts to more than just the instrumental use of new technologies *in* the urban realm—something that we often see reflected in the Smart City concept and its promise of generating more efficient cities. What emerges is a phenomenon that may be termed 'platform urbanism', an entirely new paradigm of social organization anchored in beliefs around peer-to-peer interaction and new forms of sharing and entrepreneurship for which urban space has become a key technology. In his book *The Stack*, Benjamin Bratton has aptly argued that what we are witnessing here is not a preconceived plan set in motion by new technology, but what he calls an 'accidental mega-structure'[6] that is responding to the neoliberal imperative of city *as* platform.

To engage with this growing conundrum about the future of urban civic participation and knowledge production, we need to consider the changing role of the urban environment in the data economy, as the city increasingly becomes the latter's generating interface: through our movements and actions in urban space, from our commute to work to how we spend our leisure time in public spaces, urban infrastructure serves as a recording device. This raises crucial questions about the balance of power between different stakeholders involved in the creation of future cityscapes. For this reason, we need to take a closer look at the changing relationship between the city and its *users*, examining the kind of labour citizens provide in urban interactions. The informational labour of urban users, such as unwittingly evaluating urban demand and user behaviour, is not paid with monetary means but incentivized by promises of improved urban experience, from the simple promise of pleasure and comfort to the reassurance of belonging. While the spread of new digital technologies that allow not only for the recording of data but also for numerous other ways of accessing, processing, transmitting, and sharing data has the potential to provide ground-breaking opportunities for citizen engagement with their urban environments, it will be essential to critically observe the actual trade-offs involved in these deals.

A case in point for this new spatial paradigm is the rise of urban innovation hubs that promise a kind of vibrant, holistic and sustainable form of urban regeneration, all based on the collaborative spirit of people involved in these place-led efforts. Such entrepreneurial initiatives tend to occupy retrofitted iconic buildings including museums, warehouses, railway yards, hospitals and prisons, in parts of cities ripe for gentrification. These architectural icons act as a fixer-upper canvas for clusters of start-up businesses that thrive on the urban potential of these locations. They provide the conditions for both global venture capital to localize its investments and local initiatives to scale up their operations. That way, business and culture are combined under one roof, suggesting creative synergies that serve both ends, as is expected to be the case with aspirations to brand Budapest's Csepel Island as a creative hub for local businesses. Exploring the potential of such a strategic development, the Hungarian Contemporary Architecture Centre (KÉK) has embarked on a series of workshops and presentations that examine the possibilities of a more coordinated approach to repurposing the largest industrial complex in Hungary, which is currently occupied by several hundred small and medium-sized companies. How to integrate the cultural heritage of Csepel Works in a more future-oriented vision for the site? How can existing businesses benefit from pooling resources and from a better understanding of their common values?

Thorough data analysis and the use of infographics as a modeling method can help stakeholders get a better idea of the

7 See https://dataforculture.eu/en/ (accessed 28 February 2019).

mechanisms governing a site: ownership structure, management, labour, productivity, value chains, regulatory approaches and all the other elements that contribute to a particular sense of sharing. In this way, policy makers, businesses and community-based initiatives alike have begun to acknowledge cultures of sharing in urban development and to propose frameworks for reaping the benefits of these practices. The 'Data for Culture' project in Katowice[7] is another example that aims to study the use of data visualization around cultural institutions and events—composition of audiences, use of social media, motivations for participation, public concerns, etc.—as a means to reappraise our judgement of the cultural life of a city. It raises important questions about the need to fundamentally rethink the categories we have hitherto relied on to describe the exchange economies that keep the urban metabolism alive. Above all, how to redefine labour and value creation in an era of knowledge economies driven by a sharing ethics? If it is a new kind of infrastructure, created and provided by turning the city into a network of digital interfaces, how can we guarantee equal access for all to this new sphere? If the convenience of urban populations is advanced by turning bus stops into data hubs, how can we ensure community control over this digital infrastructure?

Today, open source and open data are critical platforms to enable urban collaboration and interactive communities. They have become central to concepts of citizen participation in government and the imagination of the civic in general. What is lacking is proper recognition of the role of immaterial labour involved in these processes of valorization and of the possibilities that lie beyond the current focus on infrastructural innovation. Some of the data collecting urban projects and citizen-driven initiatives mentioned in this text have not only triggered widespread attention, they are also important sites to reimagine and negotiate a shared future. One of the most valid outcomes of their efforts is therefore how they offer invaluable material for reflection. But beyond that, as a proactive step to counter the exploitative tendencies of a rapidly expanding conversational economy, we might consider recapturing the productive force of 'making' in the etymological core of our modern conception of 'efficiency' (from Lat. *facere* = to make). Here, the principles and values of open-source movements can provide some meaningful insights. Open-source projects, too, are based on the notion of sharing, but they emphasize sharing in a two-way direction. Opening up access to various types of goods (from entertainment to infrastructure, and from knowledge to data) is the first critical step on the path to more efficient forms of production. But it is the subsequent step of allowing users to actively participate in and *share* the rewriting, recoding, and reshaping of the open source itself (whether it is a product, service or platform), that is essential for fairer and more efficient outcomes for all.

Katowice

5.01

Population
(millions of inhab.)

2016 (metropolitan regions)
2016 (Belgrade)
2017 (other cities)

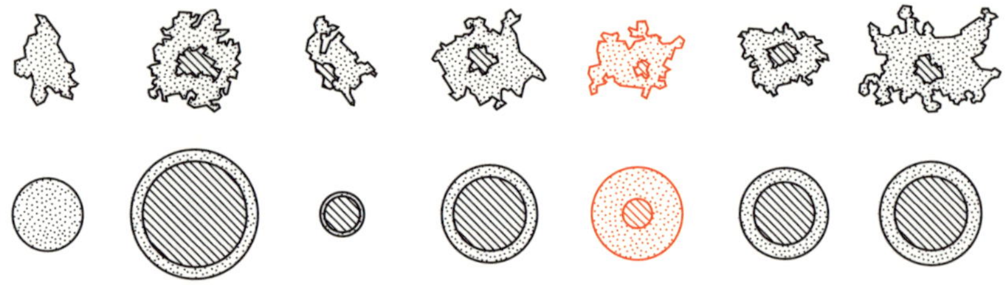

	Belgrade	Berlin	Bratislava	Budapest	Katowice	Prague	Warsaw
City		3.54	0.43	1.76	0.30	1.27	1.75
Metropolitan region	1.68	5.21	0.64	3.00	2.71	2.62	3.37

5.02

Built-up area footprint

City
2016

Total area: 165 km²
Population density:
1811 inhab./km²

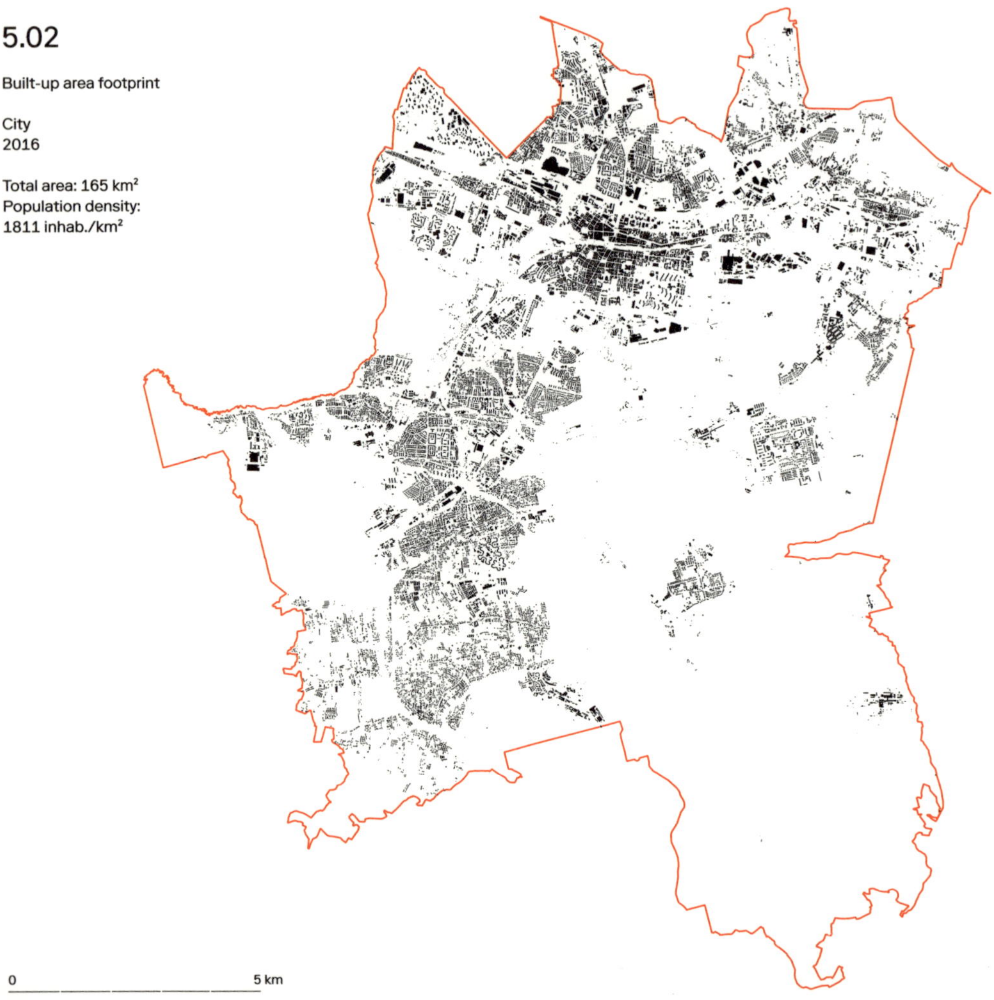

5.03

Students

Cities
2017 (Katowice, Warsaw)
2016 (other cities)

→ Society
Chart B.10, p. 18

(students/100 inhab.)	Belgrade	Berlin	Bratislava	Budapest	Katowice	Prague	Warsaw
	8.2	5.1	12.8	5.9	17.5	8.3	13.7

5.04

Old-age-dependency projection
(number of working age people [15–64]/one post-working age person [65+])

Metropolitan regions
2016–2040 (Belgrade)
2016–2050 (other cities)

→ Population
Chart B.05, p. 17

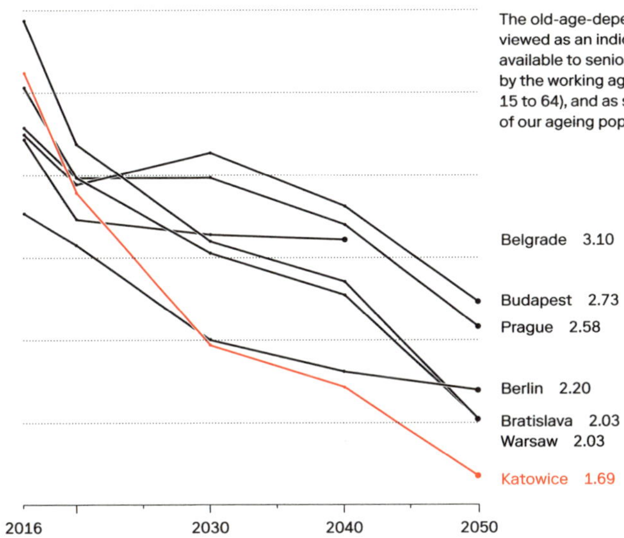

The old-age-dependency ratio is traditionally viewed as an indication of the level of support available to seniors (those aged 65 or over) by the working age population (those aged 15 to 64), and as such is a useful barometer of our ageing populations.

5.05

Average area of living accommodation (m²/inhab.)

City
2011

26.60

◆ = 5 m²

5.06

Average monthly net salary (EUR)

City
2018

708.62

▨ = 100 €

5.07

Registered passenger cars (cars/1,000 inhab.)

City
2016

668

■ = 20 cars

5.08

Tourists (number/year)

City
2016

379,823

= 1 million tourists

KATOWICE
Pyszne.pl
App Store
Google Play

CROPP
MOHITO
sinsay
Massimo Dutti
OYSHO

Data (for) Culture

Organization	Katowice City of Gardens
Address	Plac Sejmu Śląskiego 2, 40–032 Katowice
Authors	Medialab Katowice Team
Graphic design	Medialab Katowice Team
Partners	Muzeum Śląskie, Regionalny Instytut Kultury w Katowicach
Dates	9 January 2016 – 31 December 2018

Activities				
	Workshops	69	Discussions	17
	Exhibition	1	Lectures	17
	Publication	1	Surveys	3633

Data (for) Culture. The City-Making Role of Cultural Events

Karol Piekarski, Medialab Katowice Team

Only a few years ago, the link between Katowice and culture would have been far from obvious. This changed in 2015, when a massive investment effort into cultural infrastructure and cultural events catapulted Katowice into the grand international league of the UNESCO Creative Cities Network. Has the city undergone a true cultural revolution? Is it just a fad or could it herald major changes in the city centre? In order to find out, Medialab Katowice teamed up with cultural researchers, designers, programmers, and analysts to study responses given by 3633 participants in over a dozen local events, and to process tens of thousands of posts published on social media and online information services.

Cultural institutions and event operators rarely use solid data to back their management and decisions. Is there anything they can learn from their business counterparts, such as in how far culture drives city growth? The lack of reliable data on cultural life is not a problem just for our city. The methods of monitoring cultural activity fail to keep pace with mainly web-induced, rapidly changing patterns of participation. If the internet has revolutionized culture, why do we still gauge data on cultural participation using such antique statistical tools as the *per capita* numbers of library loans or cinema seats?

At the same time, we are still hesitant to trust online data, and somewhat rightly so, as cultural activity does not end with 'likes' on social media. In our study, we try to combine traditional repositories and research methods with online data, as social media is where we think people of all ages go for information, discussions, and event recommendations.

The web is also a knowledge vault and a record of locals' opinions, events, and initiatives. It is not an alternate reality, but rather a digital enhancement to the physical environment. As such, a shared city should be seen as a commonly accessible space: a hybrid of physical and online space.

The study by Medialab Katowice focused on a single aspect of this hybrid space: cultural events and their role in enlivening the city centre. The reason for this was that some of the key initiatives for the city's identity and development emerged in this particular sphere, including important discussions, new ideas, and creative activities.

Naturally, we wanted to find out how accessible culture is to the locals. How has the landscape of urban culture changed in the last few years? Who are the initiators and organizers of cultural events? How has the web aided the organization and promotion of fringe events with little media coverage? And how do their participants use the physical public space—where do they travel from, what transport do they use, and what is it that they do there once they arrive in central Katowice? Above all, we were curious to find online traces of these cultural activities and their participants.

Traditional studies of cultural events are based on data sourced from various data-collecting institutions, e.g. state and local government units, universities, research institutes on the one hand, and, on the other, from the event participants and residents surveyed as part of the study.

We are inundated by allegedly huge amounts of available data, but do communities really have free access to these resources (the digital commons)? There is also the problem of how to embrace with traditional methods the massive volume of activities, meetings, and events dotted around the city space, and what they can tell us about the people who take part.

This is the central challenge of sharing in hybrid spaces: authorities collect more and more data, but do not make it widely available in practice. This is not so much about institutional transparency, which still presents a difficulty to most Central European city authorities, but about the convenient option of using such content freely in computer-friendly formats, without having to go through tedious red tape and time-consuming data cleaning.

Our project cannot reasonably be expected to settle all doubts about culturally-led city development, nor do we dare formulate firm recommendations (although the idea of replacing speculation with solid data definitely has its appeals). Instead, we intend to provide data and research tools that will stimulate discussion and informed decision-making. In many cases, our findings merely indicate problem areas, serving as a starting point for further in-depth studies of cultural life in the city.

We have set out to create and provide open access to a digital archive of knowledge about cultural events in Katowice, which can be used by event organizers, researchers, local administration officials and cultural policy makers. In doing so, we would like to show the practical aspects of sharing data in contemporary cities where the physical public sphere is infused with the ambient, digital overlay of communication and knowledge.

1 Activities of the participants in the city alongside taking part in the event

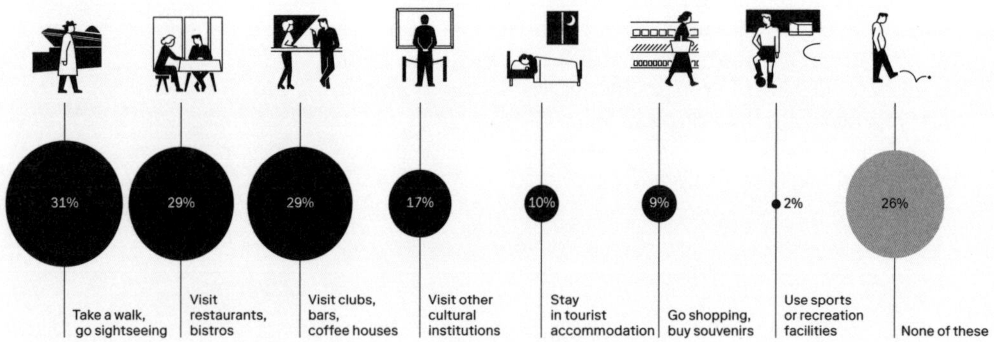

2 What do the participants of particular events do? Culture tends to attract people to public spaces in the city centre. The surveyed participants came specifically to take part in the event. The decision to participate is primarily influenced by an interesting topic, an opportunity to socialize, or a habit. Can a greater offer of cultural events help enliven the city centre by attracting residents and visitors from other cities?

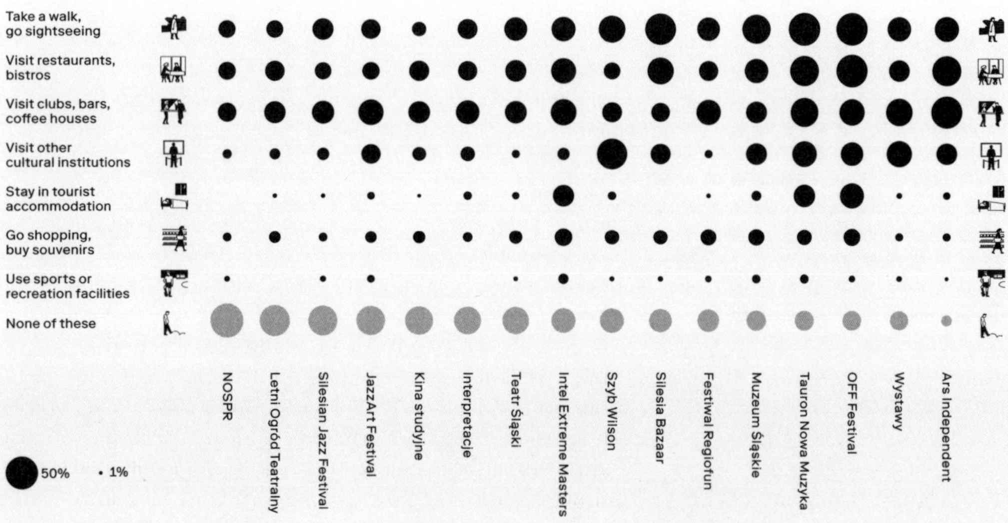

3 Which cultural events attract audiences with similar interests? Where do you go to find new audiences for your activities? A question asked by many cultural event organizers. As conducting city-wide surveys would be a difficult and costly task, we have opted for existing data from social media. By studying the statements of Facebook users who are interested or taking part in particular events, we were able to find links between their organizers.

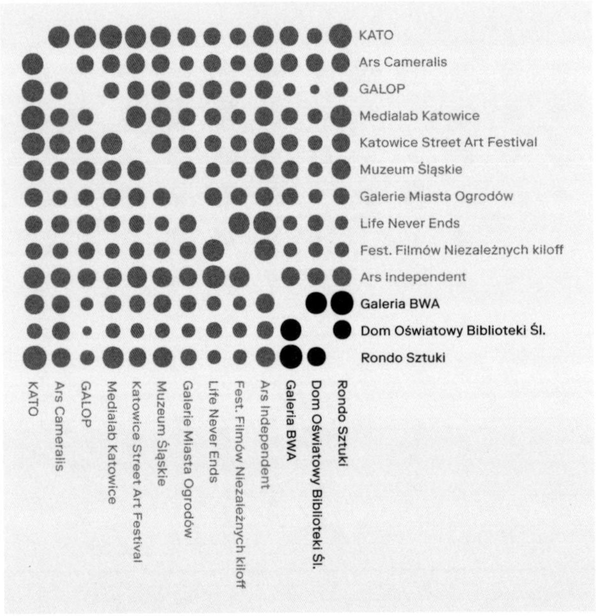

Sztauwajery
Kontener Coolturу
Mary Komasa
Prepar
Jazz Club Hipnoza
Festiwal Tauron Nowa Muzyka
Stowarzyszenie Moje Miasto
Dwie Lewe Ręce
Zabawa taneczna
Biuro Dźwięku Katowice
Kinoteatr Rialto
Kino Światowid
CSF / Kino Kosmos
Kontenery Kultury
Katowice Miasto Ogrodów
GALERIA NEGATYW
Drzwi Zwane Koniem
KATO
Ars Cameralis
GALOP
Medialab Katowice
Katowice Street Art Festival
Muzeum Śląskie
Galerie Miasta Ogrodów
Life Never Ends
Fest. Filmów Niezależnych kiloff
Ars Independent
Galeria BWA w Katowicach
Dom Oświatowy Biblioteki Śl.
Rondo Sztuki
Teatr Korez
Dagma Art
Fundacja Giesche
Fabryka Porcelany
Fest. Sztuki Reżys. Interpretacje
Centrum Zimbardo w Nikiszowcu
The Bisquits
Lennie Boycott
Michał Kapuściński
A<24
Wudec
BAZAR
Women in Technology
Vinted
Max Bravura
Dzielnica Brzmi Dobrze
?SC
Ulice i place Katowic
Szlak Zabytków Techniki
Silesian Jazz Festival
Małe Wielkie Projekty M.Ogrodów
Warszawskie Targi Książki
Jarmarki Śląskie
Kocham Katowice
Katowice – oficjalny profil miasta
Orkiestra Dęta Katowice
MBP Filia Bogucice
Stand-up w Hipnozie
FOOD FEST
Międzynarodowy Festiwal Seriali
Bookszpan Katowice
Pracownia plakatu ASP Katowice
Centrum Promocji Młodych
Rawa Blues Festival
Katofonia jazz&blues club
Swing City Katowice
La Clave
MDK Szopienice – Giszowiec
Miasto Muzyki UNESCO
MDK Bogucice – Zawodzie
Stow. Music Everywhere
Polska Noc Kabaretowa
Katowicki Dzień Psiaka
Strefa Chwały Festiwal
Chór Kameralny Akademii Muz.
P.W. Events – koncerty
Automatik
Katowice – koncerty, spektakle
Good Taste Production
Silesia Wedding Day
Międzynarod. Centrum Kongres.
Miejski Dom Kultury Koszutka
Spodek
SILESIA BAZAAR
Jarmark Na Nikiszu
Rozkręcamy Katowice
Zespół Pieśni i Tańca „Silesianie" UE
Studencki Zespół Pieśni i Tańca UŚ
Chór Uniwersytetu Ekonomicznego
GOSPEL SOUND – Chór Gospel
4M Band
OFF Festival
Metal Mind Productions
AlterArtShow
MegaClub

4 Event-goers from outside of Katowice and the metropolitan area

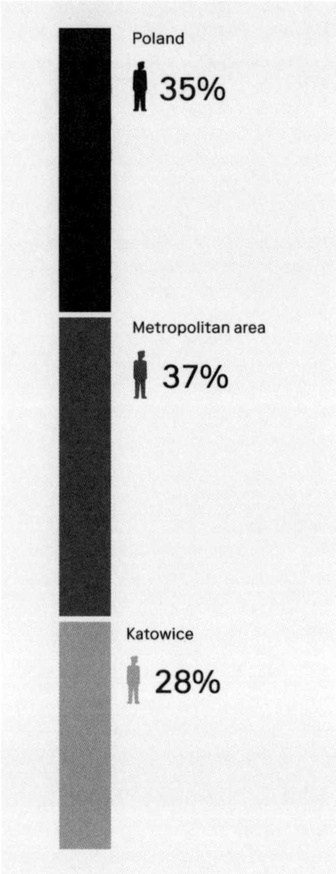

5 Towns/cities in Poland, from which people came to attend the events

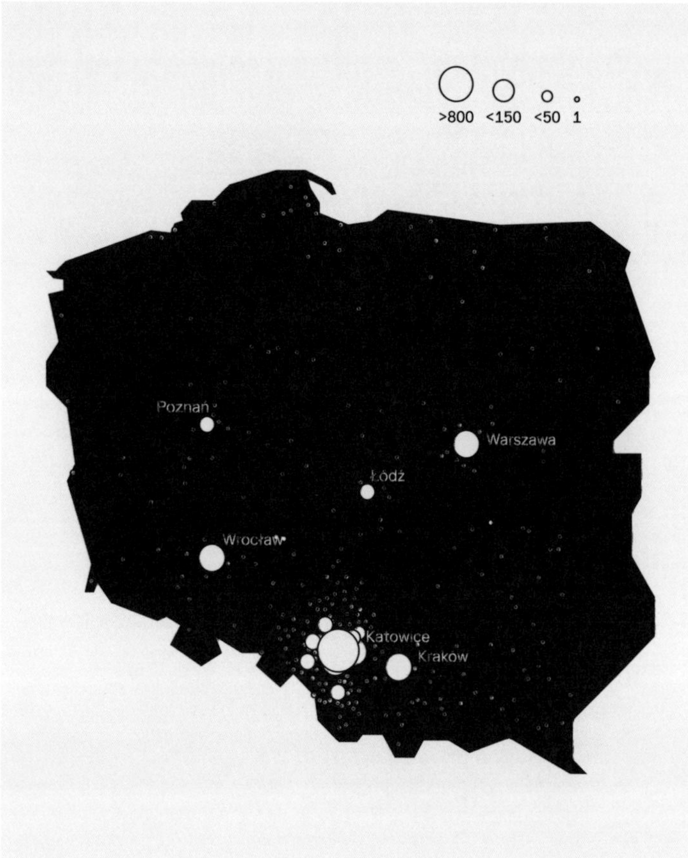

6 Age distribution of event participants

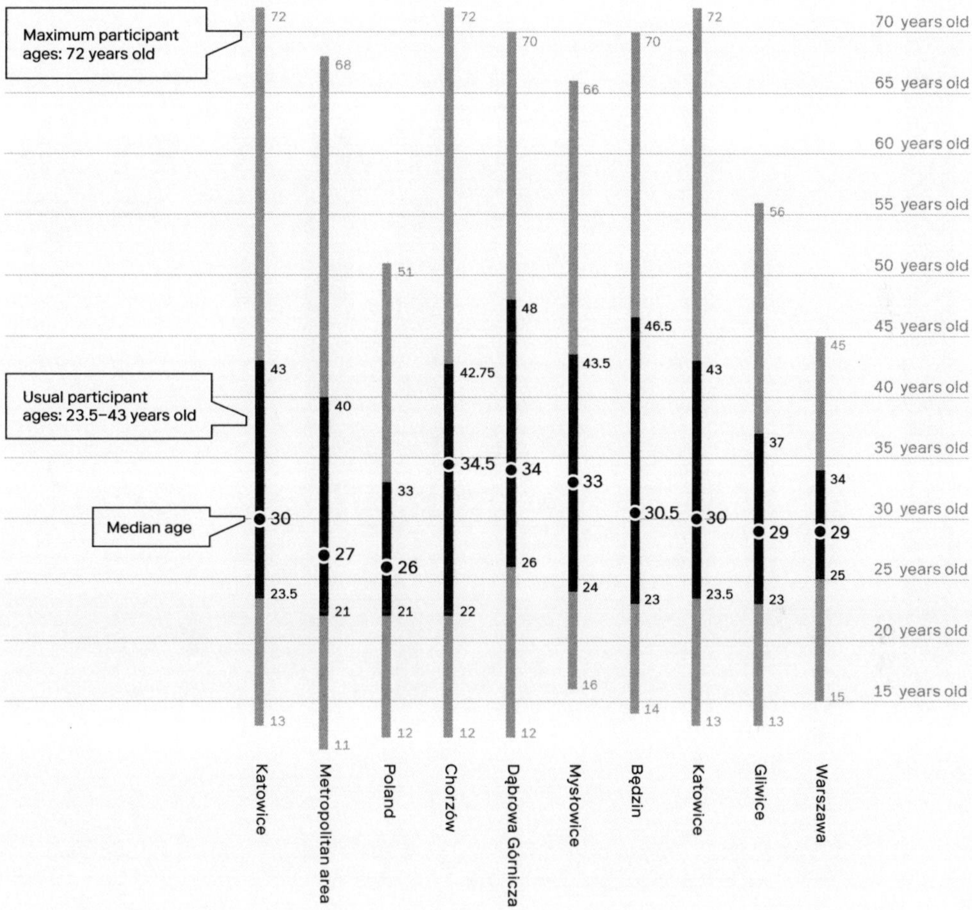

7 What do we know about the audiences of large Katowice festivals?

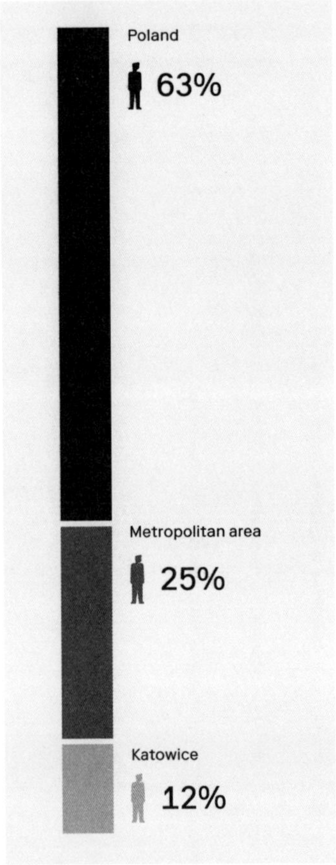

8 Who are the participants accompanied by?

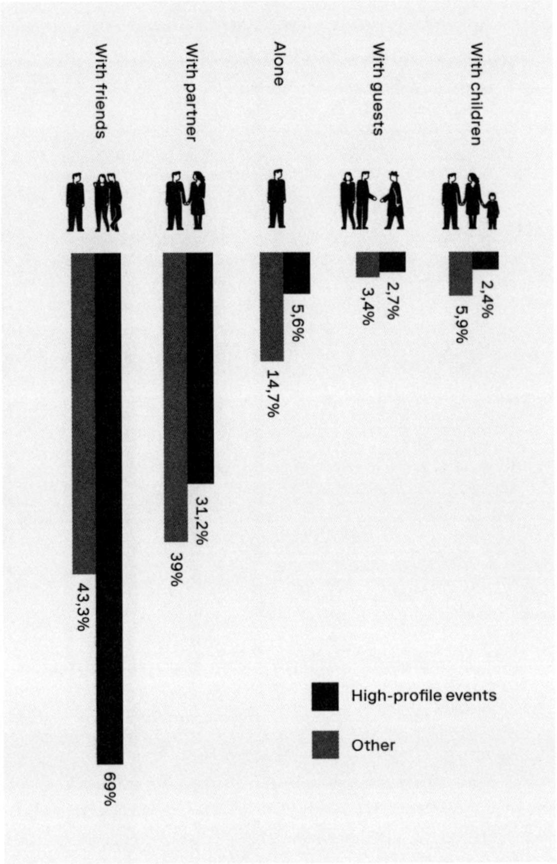

9 Why do festival visitors spend more?
Those attending high-profile events are more likely to spend time and money in the city centre than regular event participants. They take advantage of other cultural events, visit pubs and restaurants, go shopping and sightseeing, or use hotel accommodation.

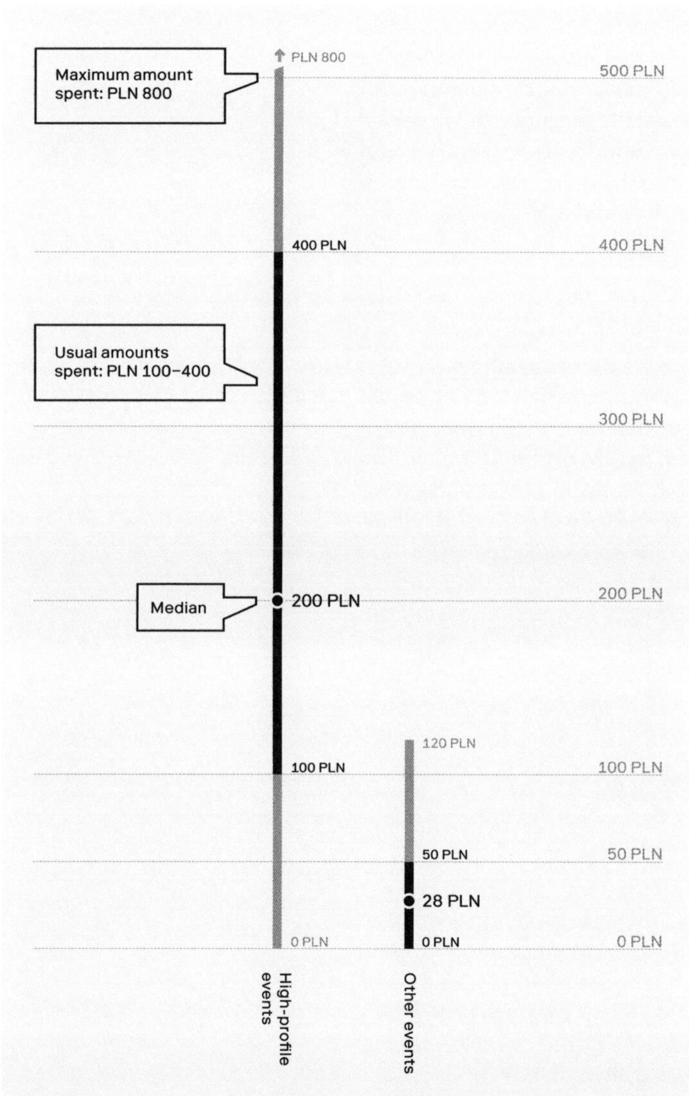

(In)accessible Culture. W Is Affected by Limited F

Online Public Space

What does the growth of internet networks, databases, or artificial intelligence have to do with a city's cultural life? It hardly needs to be pointed out that our cities' public spaces are not limited to actual streets, squares, or parks. An equally important element of the public sphere is the Web and our online activity—how we look up information, how we recommend events to each other and how, smartphone in hand, we navigate the urban space in search of all those must-see tourist attractions and architectural gems.

Point of Departure

We carried out two case studies to demonstrate how cultural researchers can use digital tools and data analysis to gain an understanding of how the city's cultural landscape changes in our data- and network-augmented, hybrid urban space. In the study of public transport access to cultural venues, the data we sourced from a partner institution was checked against the findings of our own survey. Then the results were scaled up to include the whole city thanks to the calculations made using Google's Distance Matrix API. Our second strategy was to draw data from the Web, including social media, to create a universal database of tens of thousands cultural events held in Katowice, for which task we relied heavily on the benefits of machine learning algorithms, among other things.

Culture Zone

Katowice's Culture Zone is a new cultural infrastructure project located on the site of a former coal mine, comprising a number of landmark venues, such as the Silesian Museum, the NOSPR Concert Hall and the International Congress Centre. Despite its convenient central location, the zone is cut off from Katowice's inner-city centre by a busy, multi-lane arterial road, leading to repeated complaints of tricky access from residents and visitors.

hose Participation blic Transport Access?

Chart 1.1
Proportion of residents of different Katowice districts who visited the Silesian Museum (per cent, September 2017)
Source: Silesian Museum

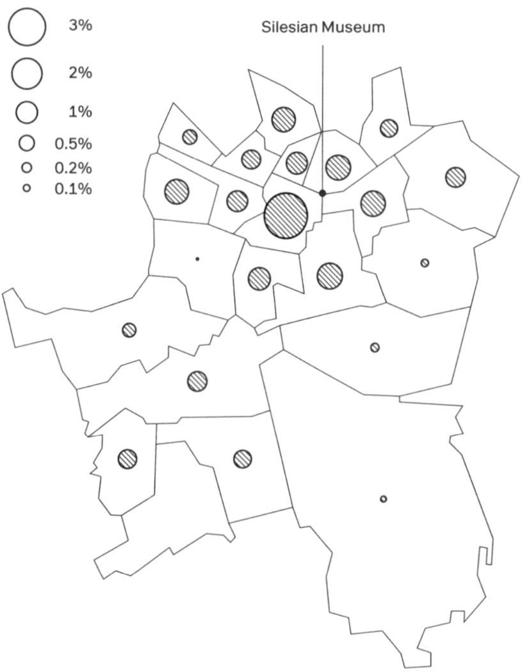

Chart 1.2
Proportion of participants of other events (Data for Culture, 2016–2017)
Source: Medialab Katowice

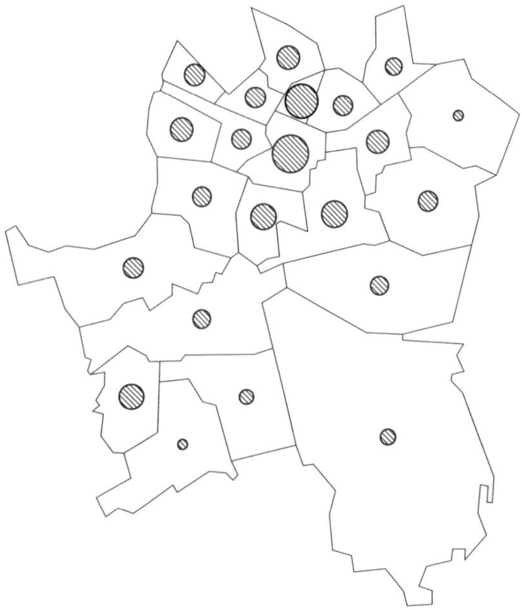

The Silesian Museum

Thanks to the data provided by the Silesian Museum, we were able to find out where its visitors travel from to attend the exhibitions and events.[1] By dividing the number of visitors from particular districts by the total number of residents, we learned how popular the museum's events are among residents of different Katowice districts. People living in the city centre and the neighbouring districts are more likely to visit the Museum (even though some of these, e.g. Bogucice and Załęże, are former working-class districts). These figures coincide with the results of our study of other events held in the centre of Katowice. We were thus led to suspect that cultural participation is related to the accessibility by public transport of cultural venues from various parts of the city.

1
'Is the Katowice Culture Zone an isolated cultural island?', in: Data for Culture, online, available http: https://dataforculture.eu/en/is-the-katowice-culture-zone-an-isolated-cultural-island/ (accessed 21 November 2018).

Chart 2
Public transport travel times to the Silesian Museum from selected locations
Source: Google Maps

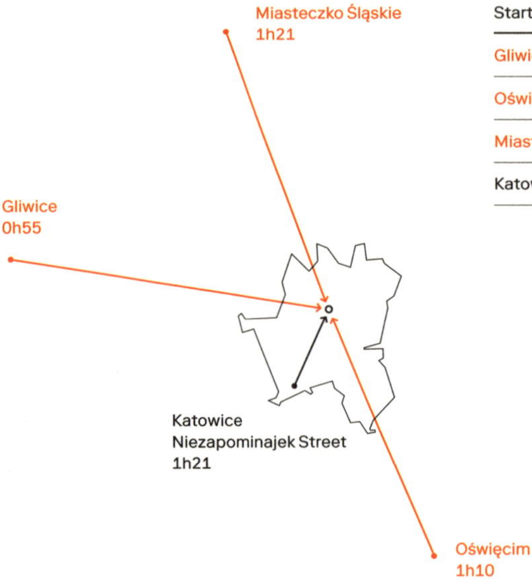

Starting point	Distance	Travel time
Gliwice	30 km	0h55
Oświęcim	35 km	1h10
Miasteczko Śląskie	35 km	1h21
Katowice, Niezapominajek St.	15 km	1h21

Chart 3
Mode of transport to get to the event venue (per cent)

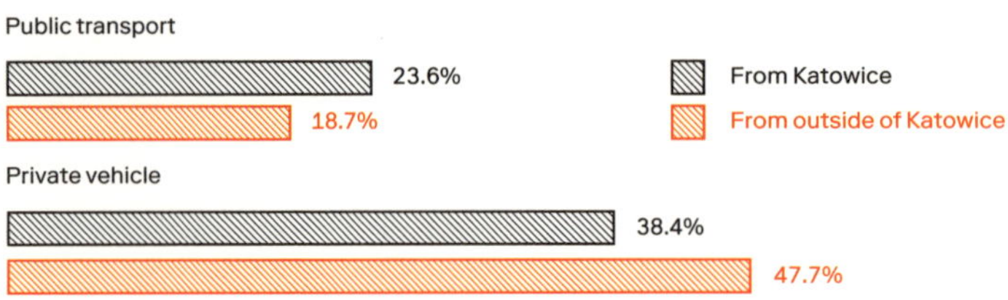

We then used Google's Distance Matrix API to study journey times to the Museum from all address points across the city, to find out which districts suffer from problematic transport access to the city centre. The initial results made us wonder how these figures relate to the actual resident travel experience—in other words, is a 30-minute bus ride acceptable or too much to bother? In order to answer this question, we reviewed the results of our survey, in which several hundred event participants told us from where exactly they travelled to the event[2]. Interestingly, only 23.6 per cent of the interviewed Katowice residents used public transport.

2
'Data for culture, a study of Katowice cultural events', online, available http: https://dataforculture.eu/en/about/ (accessed 21 November 2018).

Then, also courtesy of the Google Distance Matrix API, we studied how long it took each of the examined people to travel to the event. Among all the surveyed public transport users, 25 per cent reached the event in less than 17 minutes, another 50 per cent travelled no more than 37 minutes, while the remainder took up to 58 minutes.

Based on these calculations, we have created a model of travel convenience.

- Convenient – journey times of up to 17 minutes is convenient and not a cause of major concern.
- Standard – travel times between 18 and 37 minutes are the most typical for participants.
- Demanding – journey times over 37 minutes are acceptable.
- Difficult – an hour or more seems to be so inconvenient as to discourage people from taking part in events.

Chart 4.1
Average travel times to the Silesian Museum from all address points in the city

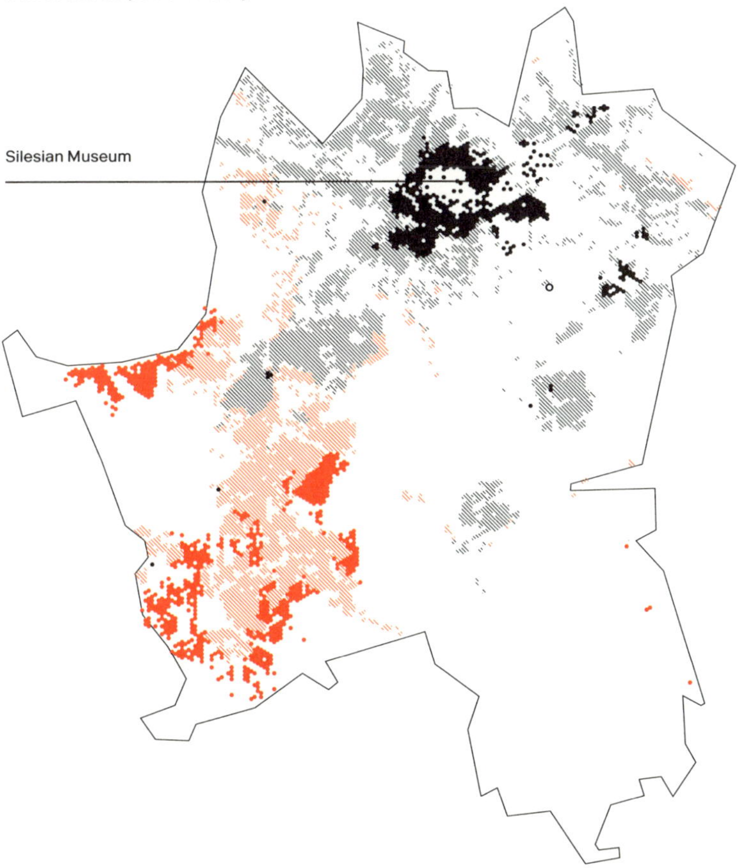

Chart 4.2
Average travel times to cultural events in Katowice

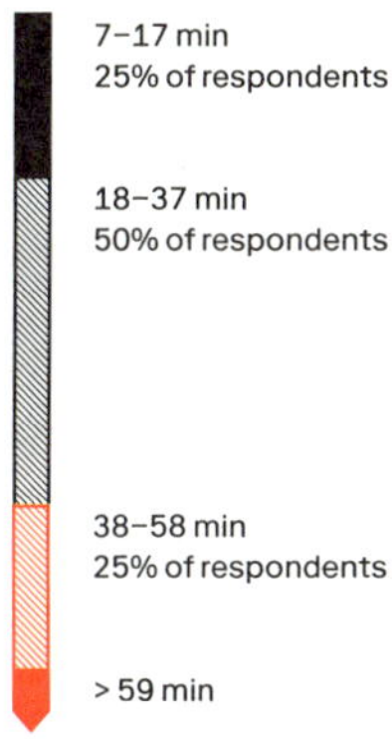

Knowing the real time of travel to events in Katowice, we checked the accessibility of 14 cultural venue locations in the city centre from all address points across the city. The results show that the Culture Zone's Silesian Museum is slightly more difficult to access by residents than other locations in the city centre. As many as 13.3 per cent of addresses in the city are over an hour away from the Museum by public transport.

Chart 5
Percentage of Katowice address points within specific time zones for the institutions studied

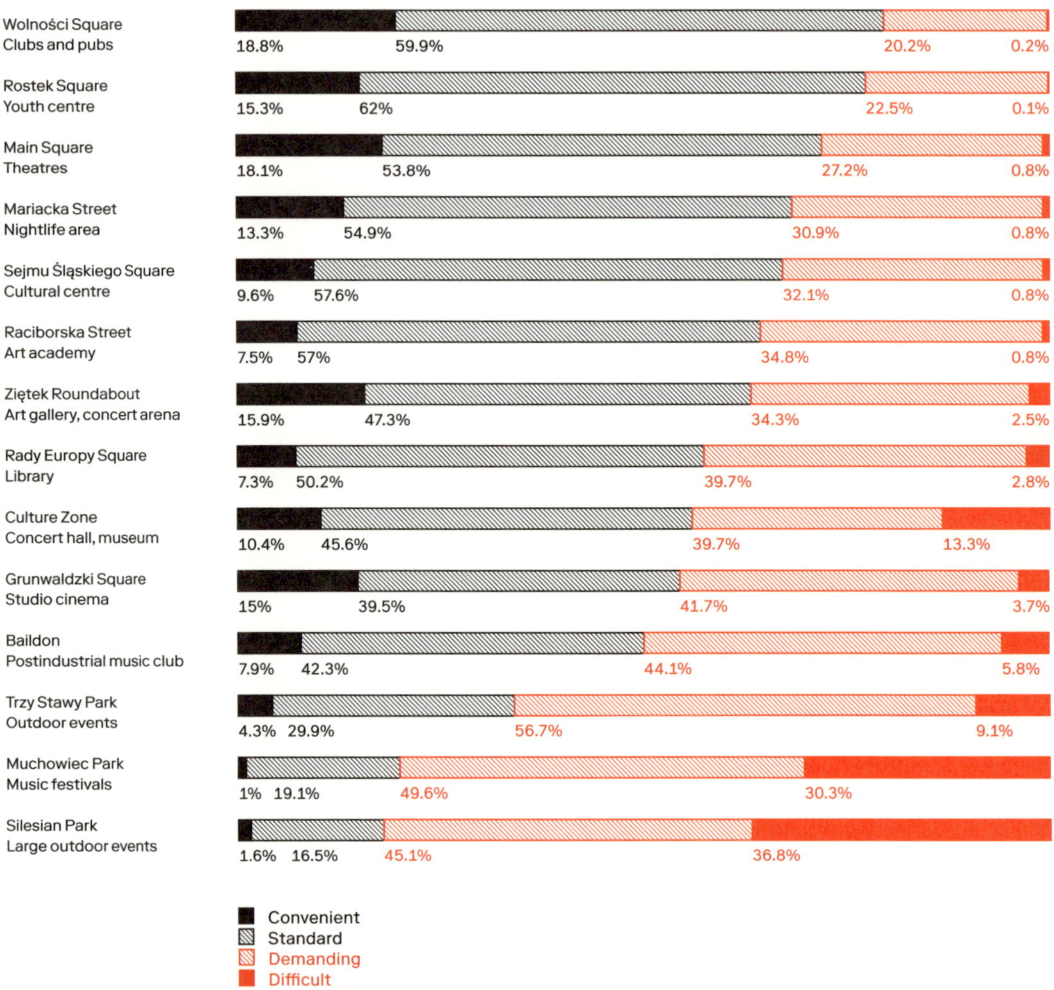

Of course, we cannot be sure that public transport inconveniences are a decisive factor in making residents from the city's southern districts less likely to participate in cultural events. In order to verify this, we intend to turn to traditional research methods in 2019 and run a series of studies in different Katowice districts with an objective to gain insight into the residents' motivations and needs. Nonetheless, the use of the data-driven approach allowed us to simulate potential resident behaviour and indicate the areas where action should be taken first.

> 'Data-driven approaches are often particularly good at raising new questions, which may need to be answered with different methods.'
> Karin van Es[3]

3
Ł. Mirocha, interview with Karin van Es, 'Data-driven approaches are often particularly good at raising new questions, which may need to be answered with different methods' (9 February 2018), online, available HTTP: https://blog.medialabkatowice.eu/en/karin-van-es-data-driven-approaches-are-often-particularly-good-at-raising-new-questions-which-may-need-to-be-answered-with-different-methods/ (accessed 10 November 2018).

Budapest

6.01

Population
(millions of inhab.)

2016 (metropolitan regions)
2016 (Belgrade)
2017 (other cities)

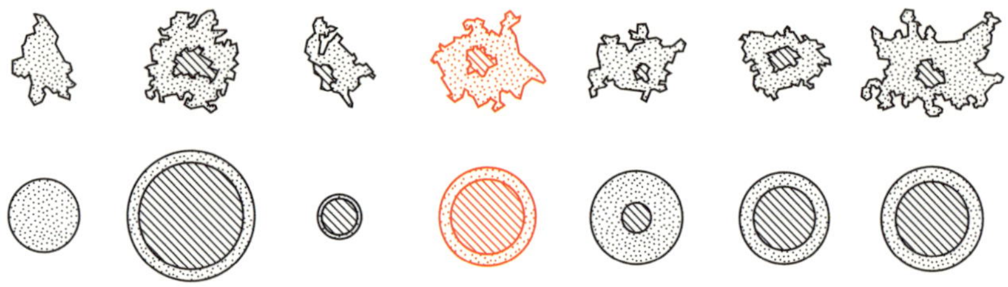

	Belgrade	Berlin	Bratislava	Budapest	Katowice	Prague	Warsaw
City	1.68	3.54	0.43	1.76	0.30	1.27	1.75
Metropolitan region		5.21	0.64	3.00	2.71	2.62	3.37

6.02

Built-up area footprint

City
2016
Total area: 525 km²
Population density:
3,350 inhab./km²

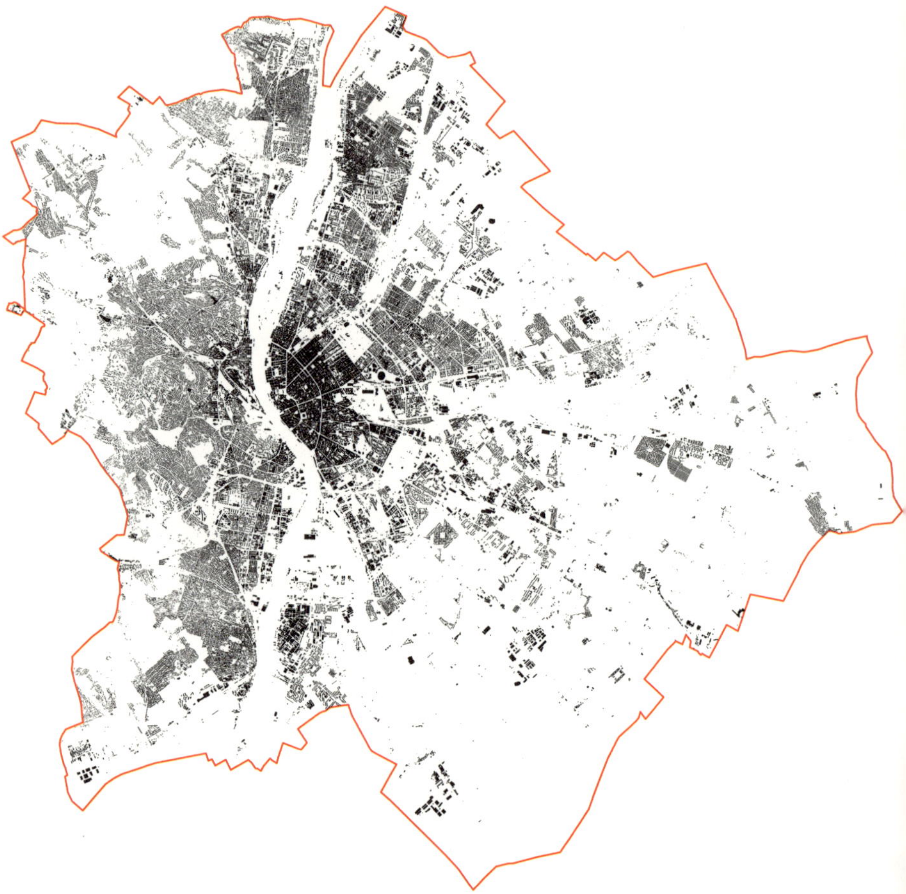

0 5 km

6.03

Theatres

Cities
2018 (Katowice)
2017 (Prague)
2015 (Budapest)
2016 (other cities)

→ Society
Chart B.13, p. 19

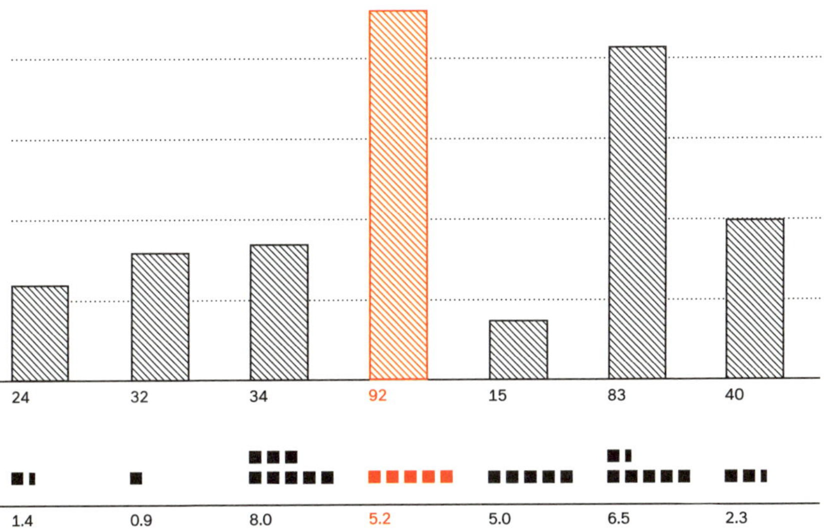

6.04

Population as a share of national population (per cent)

Metropolitan regions
2017

→ Population
Chart B.02, p. 16

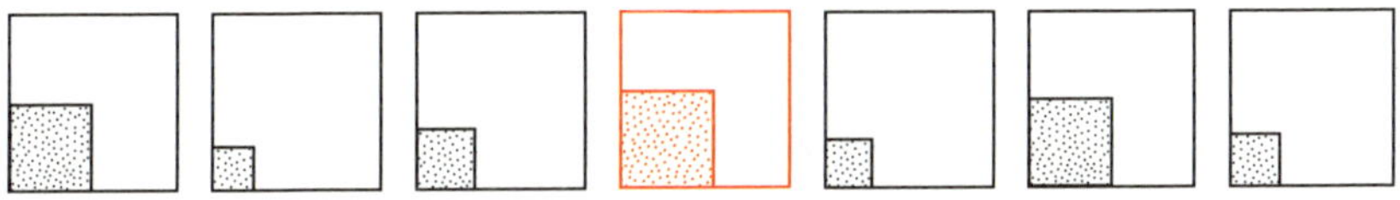

6.05

Average area of living accommodation (m²/inhab.)

City
2011

34.55

◆ = 5 m²

6.06

Average monthly net salary (EUR)

City
2018

638.33

▨ = 100 €

6.07

Registered passenger cars (cars/1,000 inhab.)

City
2016

362

■ = 20 cars

6.08

Tourists (number/year)

City
2016

4,085,178

= 1 million tourists

KELETI PÁLYAUDVAR

HOTEL BUDAPEST

M 2 Széll Kálmán tér
M 2 Széll Kálmán tér

BEAUTY SALON

DÉLI PÁLYAUDVAR

GOLDWIN SÖRÖZŐ

LG OLED TV 4K

NAGYBAN HIRDETSZ.
MERT A MERET
SZAMIT!

Csepel Works

Organization	Hungarian Contemporary Architecture Centre – KÉK
Address	Bartók Béla út 10–12, 1111 Budapest
Authors	Bálint Horváth, Julianna Libárdi, Samu Szemerey
Graphic design	Panni Bodonyi, Zoltán Szmolka
Partners	Association of Csepel Industrialists and Employers, ELTE University – Department of Social And Earth Sciences
Dates	1 September 2016 – 1 September 2019

Activities				
	Workshops	10	Discussions	10
	Exhibitions	2	Web-platform	1
	Publication	1	Festival	1

Shared Future: Reactivating Stakeholder Networks in the Former Csepel Plant

Bálint Horváth, edited by Samu Szemerey

A 'forgotten' area in Budapest, Csepel Works is one of the oldest industrial sites in Hungary with a rich cultural and architectural heritage. Its location, the twenty-first district in South Budapest, has the largest percentage of brownfield areas in the city and 19 per cent of all brownfield sites in the capital. Stretching out along the Danube riverbank, Csepel Works occupies an area of 240 hectares comprised of hundreds of factory, storage, and office buildings, and hosts over 400 active businesses without a central organizing authority. Logistics, retail, and services are gaining more importance at Csepel Works as heavy industry is being moved out of the city centre. The changing uses of properties and surrounding spaces bring new interests and visions for the future of the area, which do not always coincide with established business models.

The story of the once largest contiguous industrial entity in Hungary dates back to 1882, when Manfréd Weiss and his brother Bertold founded the First Hungarian Canned Goods Factory, producing canned fruits and vegetables primarily for the army. War proved to be a loyal customer, especially at the turbulent turn of the century. The small factory rapidly began making ammunition and grew into an industrial behemoth by the middle of the twentieth century, producing virtually everything 'from pins to airplanes'. Purposely developed from the beginning with workers' and officers' housing quarters, a hospital, cultural halls, casino, sports and other facilities, Csepel Works was like a city within a city.

Socialist industrialization put increased space pressure on the area, adding new buildings and expanding older ones. On the other hand, it was also characterized by a pragmatic rationalization process, narrowing production down to 10 specialized units. Due to a lack of investment and the weakened Eastern Bloc economy, most of the production became inefficient and uncompetitive, which resulted in the gradual degradation of physical assets, infrastructure, and profitability within the plant. In 1983, Csepel Works was officially shut down as an organically functioning, centrally managed plant, although several factories and production units remained in operation, some to this day.

The number of Csepel Works employees has always been directly proportional to its population growth. In its heyday in the 1940s, over 40,000 people worked in the factories. Culture houses, theatres, cinemas, and sports clubs opened in Csepel as more and more people came to work there. Though employment began to decrease in the 1950s, the real turning point came in the 1980s when the shared Eastern Bloc market began to crumble. Today, an estimated 6–8000 people work there. Ownership is a key question of the plant. Most of the area, including roads, buildings, and land is now in private hands as undivided common property. The municipality owns only a few roads. Before the mid-1990s, over a thousand companies were registered at Csepel under one lot and one address. Many were ghost companies evading banks, lenders or authorities. The former Csepel Plant boasted the title of the largest 'company cemetery' in the history of Hungary. The area has since been divided into over 220 lots and addresses, which has helped to uncover businesses and to achieve a clearer ownership structure.

Hundreds of businesses now share the premises of the once largest industrial plant in Hungary, along with its unique physical infrastructure and cultural and architectural heritage. There is a fence that separates the 200-hectare area from the city on all sides, suggesting that it is being managed from the inside, where work-oriented spaces are even separated from housing and leisure. But the fence also invites nostalgic fantasies about the plant and its workers. Legendary products such as the Csepel Bike and Motorcycle date back to a time when three-generation families worked at the plant all at the same time. On the other hand, in the absence of central management and help from the municipality, the businesses are left to solve issues on their own, and to coordinate their efforts towards a concise, shared vision for the future of the area.

Since 2016, KÉK Hungarian Contemporary Architecture Centre has conducted meetings, discussions, and interviews with the municipality, urban planners, local businesses, local cultural actors, and other stakeholders in order to evaluate the potential and challenges of the area. In the summer of 2017, with the help of geography students from ELTE University, KÉK compiled a highly accurate database of buildings, roads and businesses, registering their estimated physical condition, age, and use as well as current business activities. To supplement the research, a data mining expert created a complete database of companies registered in the plant area. KÉK also surveyed the use of public space, carried out a pedestrian and a traffic count, as well as a building façade analysis in selected street sections. These three research methods were used for the very first time to study the brownfields at Csepel Works. The results provide unique guidance for discussions about future improvement and development possibilities of the plant area. The findings, conclusions, and research questions were exhibited in October 2018 at KÉK Hungarian Contemporary Architecture Centre.

1 Travel times to the Csepel plant

8:00	Distance	Public transport	Car	Bicycle
Keleti railway station	10,5 km	37'	20–45'	40–50'
Nyugati raiway station	9,9 km	32'	15–45'	30–40'
South railway Station	10,6 km	44'	16–40'	45–55'
Deák Ferenc square	8,7 km	35'	14–35'	40–50'
Széll Kálmán square	11,2 km	48'	16–40'	45–55'
Batthyány square	10,8 km	45'	14–28'	30–40'
Kőbánya Kispest station	8,6 km	37'	12–26'	30–40'
Liszt Ferenc Airport	20,9 km	70'	26–45'	

Szent Imre tér, Csepel

2 The partition of the giant parcel: from 1 parcel to 223 parcels

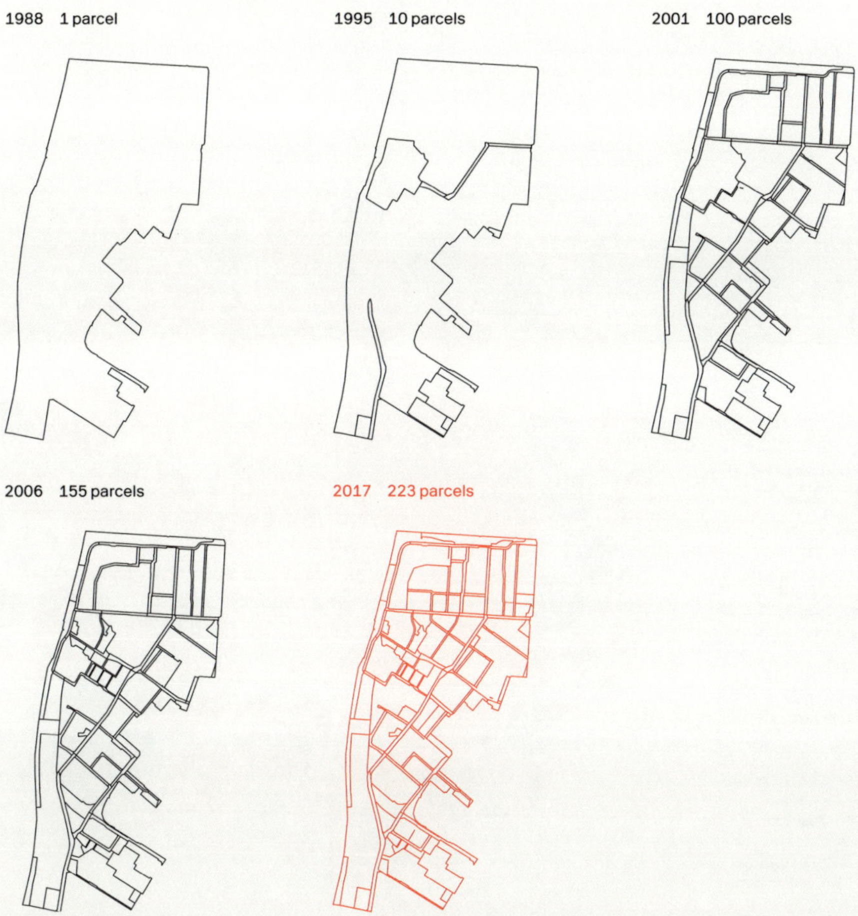

3 Clusters of companies based on primary activities

Total number of registered companies:

869

Submitted annual financial report in 2017

29

Submitted annual financial report in 2016

312

Service
171 companies
(+94 disfunctional)

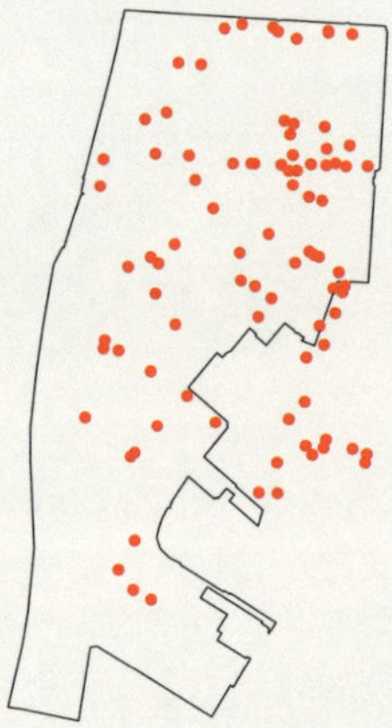

Manufacturing, processing
97 companies
(+26 disfunctional)

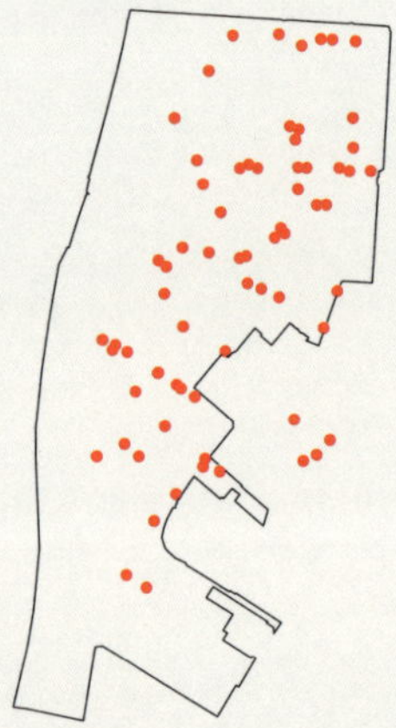

Sum of the turnover of all companies in 2017:

109 billion HUF
(EUR 35 million)

Average turnover of all companies in 2017:

321 million HUF
(EUR 1 million)

Median income of all companies in 2017:

40 million HUF
(EUR 130,000)

- Companies with net turnover of more than HUF 1 billion (EUR 3,2 million): 20 companies
- Companies with net turnover of HUF 500–1000 million (EUR 1,55–3,2 million): 20 companies
- Companies with net turnover of HUF 250–500 million (EUR 0,75–1,55 million): 71 companies
- Companies with net turnover of HUF 100–250 million (EUR 300,000–750,000)
- Companies with net turnover of less than HUF 100 million (EUR 300,000)

Trade
78 companies
(+57 disfunctional)
Storage, logistics
9 companies
(+6 disfunctional)
Primary sector
1 company
(+1 disfunctional)

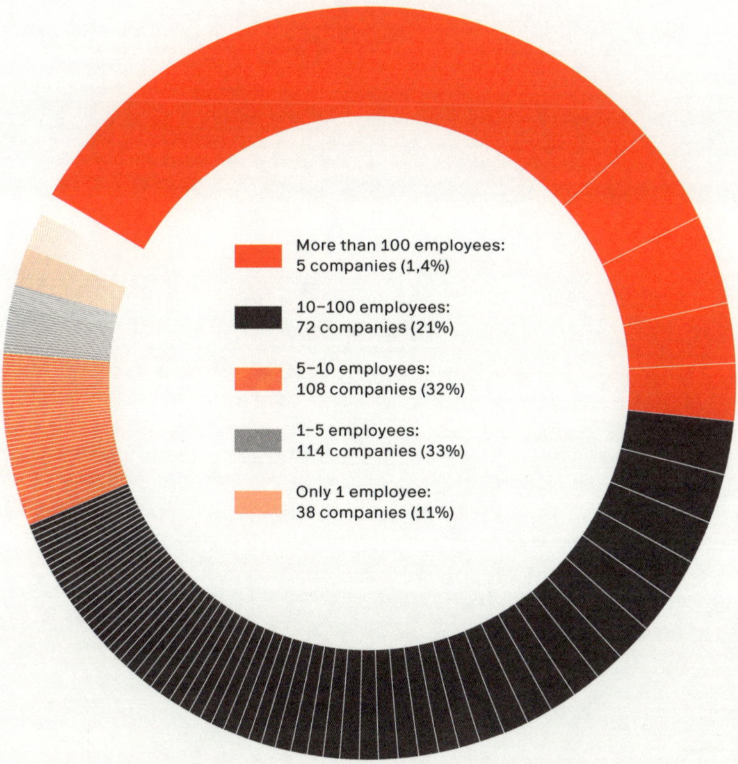
More than 100 employees:
5 companies (1,4%)
10–100 employees:
72 companies (21%)
5–10 employees:
108 companies (32%)
1–5 employees:
114 companies (33%)
Only 1 employee:
38 companies (11%)

4 Condition of buildings

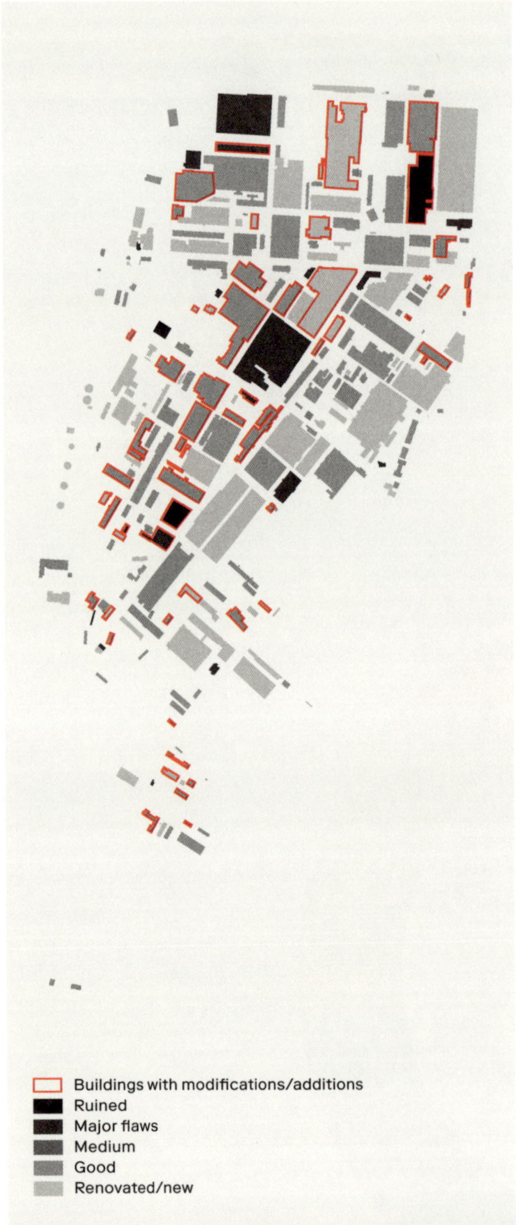

5 Age of buildings

6 Properties for sale

7 Road infrastructure

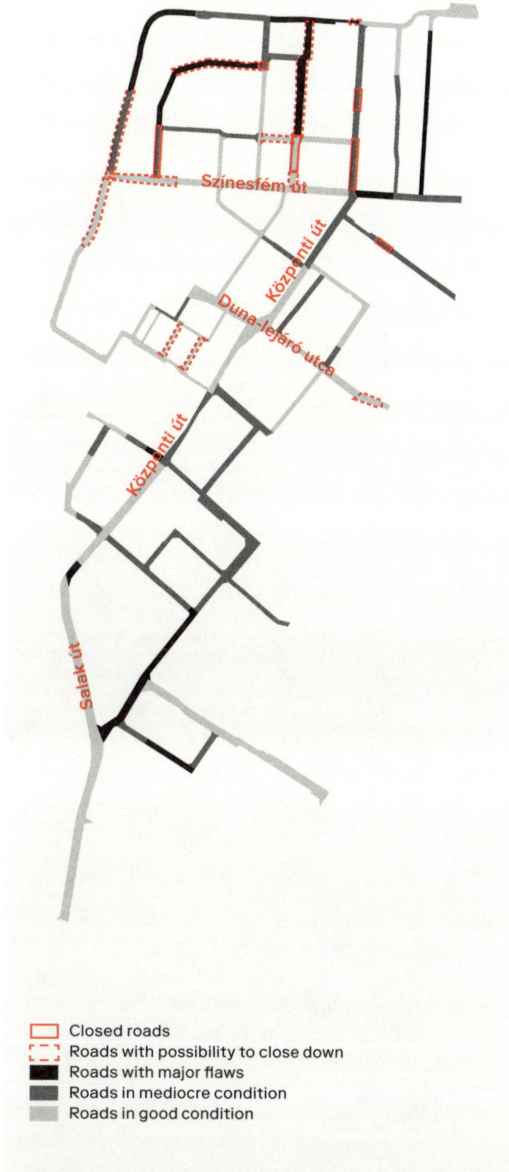

8 Use of public space, building façades, incoming and outgoing traffic

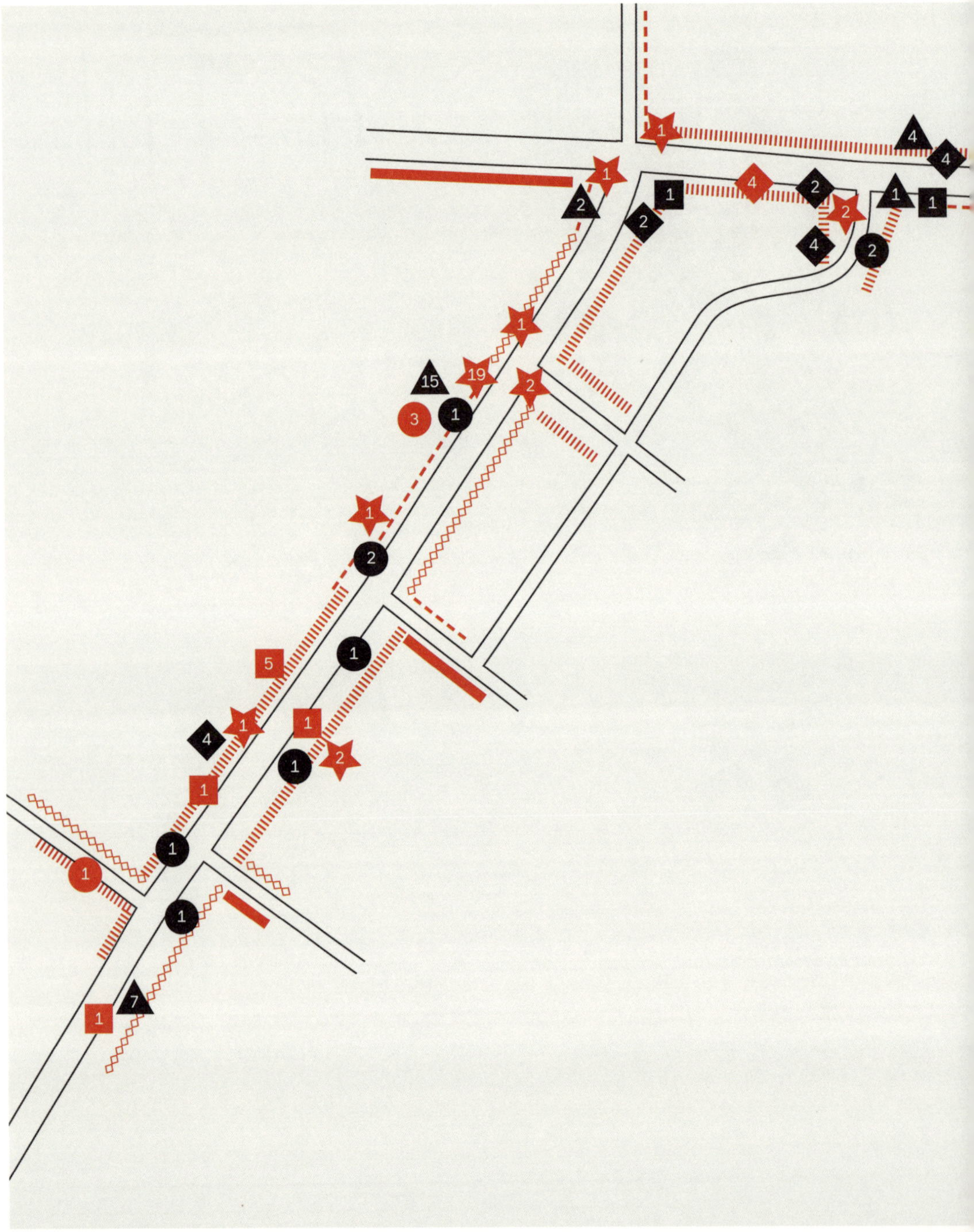

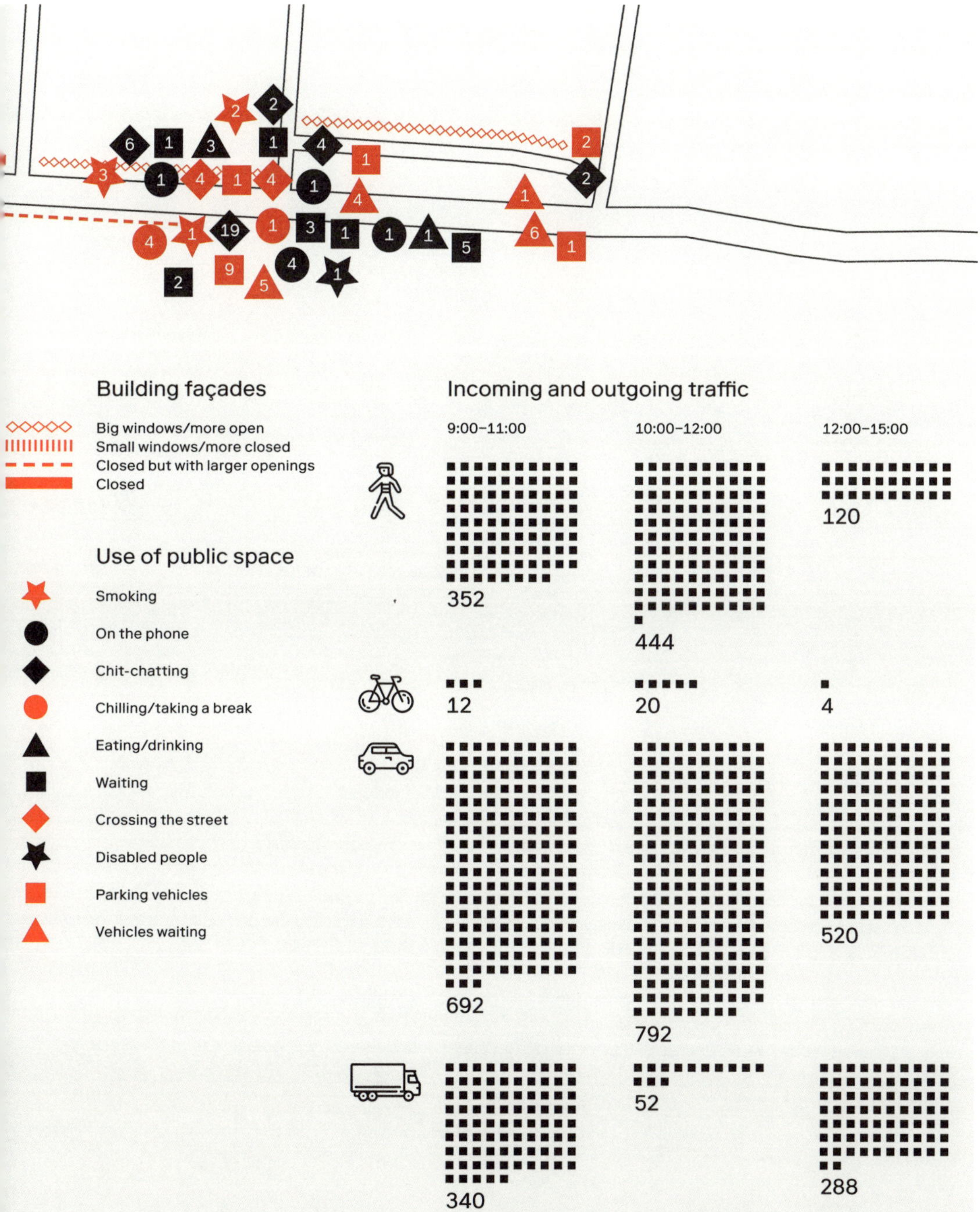
Building façades
Big windows/more open
Small windows/more closed
Closed but with larger openings
Closed
Use of public space
Smoking
On the phone
Chit-chatting
Chilling/taking a break
Eating/drinking
Waiting
Crossing the street
Disabled people
Parking vehicles
Vehicles waiting
Incoming and outgoing traffic
9:00–11:00
10:00–12:00
12:00–15:00
352
444
120
12
20
4
692
792
520
340
52
288

9 Change of population of the city of Csepel
Change of employment numbers in the Csepel Plant 1890

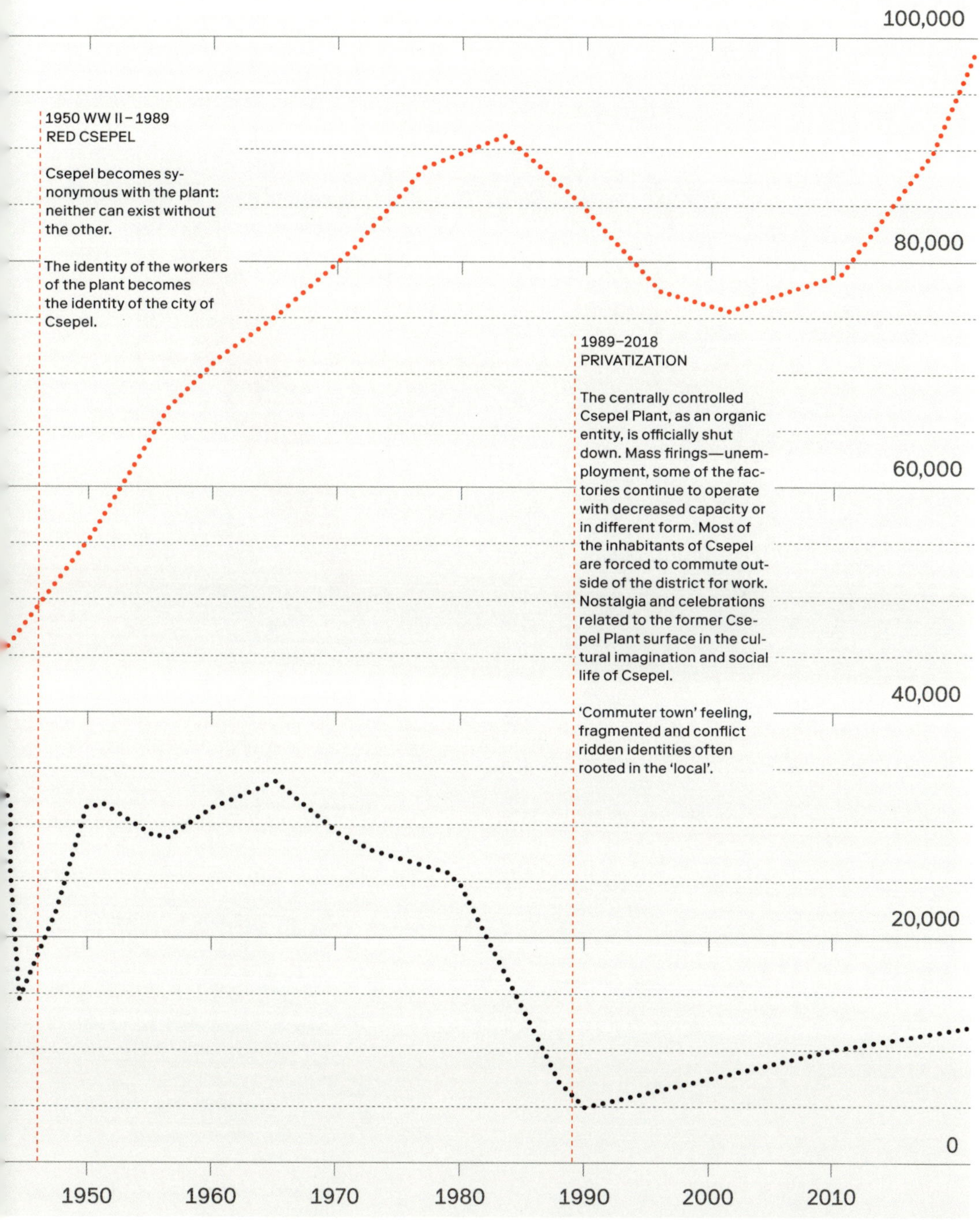
100,000
80,000
60,000
40,000
20,000
0
1950 WW II – 1989
RED CSEPEL
Csepel becomes synonymous with the plant: neither can exist without the other.
The identity of the workers of the plant becomes the identity of the city of Csepel.
1989–2018
PRIVATIZATION
The centrally controlled Csepel Plant, as an organic entity, is officially shut down. Mass firings—unemployment, some of the factories continue to operate with decreased capacity or in different form. Most of the inhabitants of Csepel are forced to commute outside of the district for work. Nostalgia and celebrations related to the former Csepel Plant surface in the cultural imagination and social life of Csepel.
'Commuter town' feeling, fragmented and conflict ridden identities often rooted in the 'local'.
1950
1960
1970
1980
1990
2000
2010

Milota Sidorová with Samu Szemerey, Bálint Horváth (KÉK), Zoltán Erdős

Népsziget. The Forgott

Map 1
The island in the context of Budapest districts

1
D. Szigetek, 'Lehorgonyzott Népsziget' (28 December 2012), online, available HTTP: https://dunaiszigetek.blogspot.com/2012/12/lehorgonyzott-nepsziget.html (accessed 21 December 2018).

2
K. Klaudt, 'Hungary after the Revolution: Privatization, Economic Ideology and the False Promise of the Free Market', in *Law & Inequality: A Journal of Theory and Practice* 2 (1995) vol. 13, online, available HTTP: https://scholarship.law.umn.edu/cgi/viewcontent.cgi?article=1495&context=lawineq (accessed 3 January 2018).

3
City of Budapest, 'Baseline study for Népsziget Island' (October 2017).

Island

People's Island: A Brief History

Népsziget, or People's Island, is a long-forgotten recreational island in the northern part of central Budapest. Its bay is a winter shipyard at the industrial belt's riverfront. Over the course of its history, the island has gone through multiple transformations from industry to recreation. It was the planned site for the 1928 Olympic games[1] and although they did not happen, boathouses and sports facilities made it a popular destination for workers. During communism, workers' holiday homes were built alongside their factories, a practice historically found in other European cities (Baťa's residential workers' areas in Zlín, Czech Republic, or Hidropark, a public sports facility on an island in Dnepr, Kyiv, Ukraine). On the island's western side, there used to be a riverfront beach where many companies built holiday homes for their employees, competing with the nearby Római Part. After 1989, the island was partly abandoned, and most factories closed as well. Although it is just across Óbudai sziget, the home of the popular Sziget festival, and is serviced by two metro stops, it is still a hidden gem where locals go for their weekend walks and other free-time activities.

Transformation and Defragmentation of the Land Ownership

Budapest's property ownership structure has changed significantly over the past decades. Unlike in the Czech Republic and slightly differently than in Slovakia, restitution in the 1990s happened via voucher privatisation.[2] The state offered people coupons in exchange for their former property, which they could use to buy land and property. Land titles and transformed buildings were not consolidated, and properties were often sold to tenants at below-market prices. Privatization vouchers rapidly turned into an inflated secondary market. As a result, few owners acquired their former properties, and the market became highly fragmented. In the case of Népsziget, ownership changed and many new buildings appeared on the few cadastral units. As subsequent uses did not correspond with the shared land titles, it became highly difficult to sustain them while managing the land. Roads are officially joint property and listed as part of the shared land rather than separate infrastructure. Many holiday homes were neglected or abandoned; some live on, some boathouses are still running, others have been rented out as homeless shelters. Some buildings and land now belong to foreign investors who planned to build housing here, but zoning prohibits that. The island is now co-regulated by two districts and Budapest City Hall in two sections, further complicating its management. The districts only own a few small properties.[3]

Map 2
Népsziget cadastre units and ownership

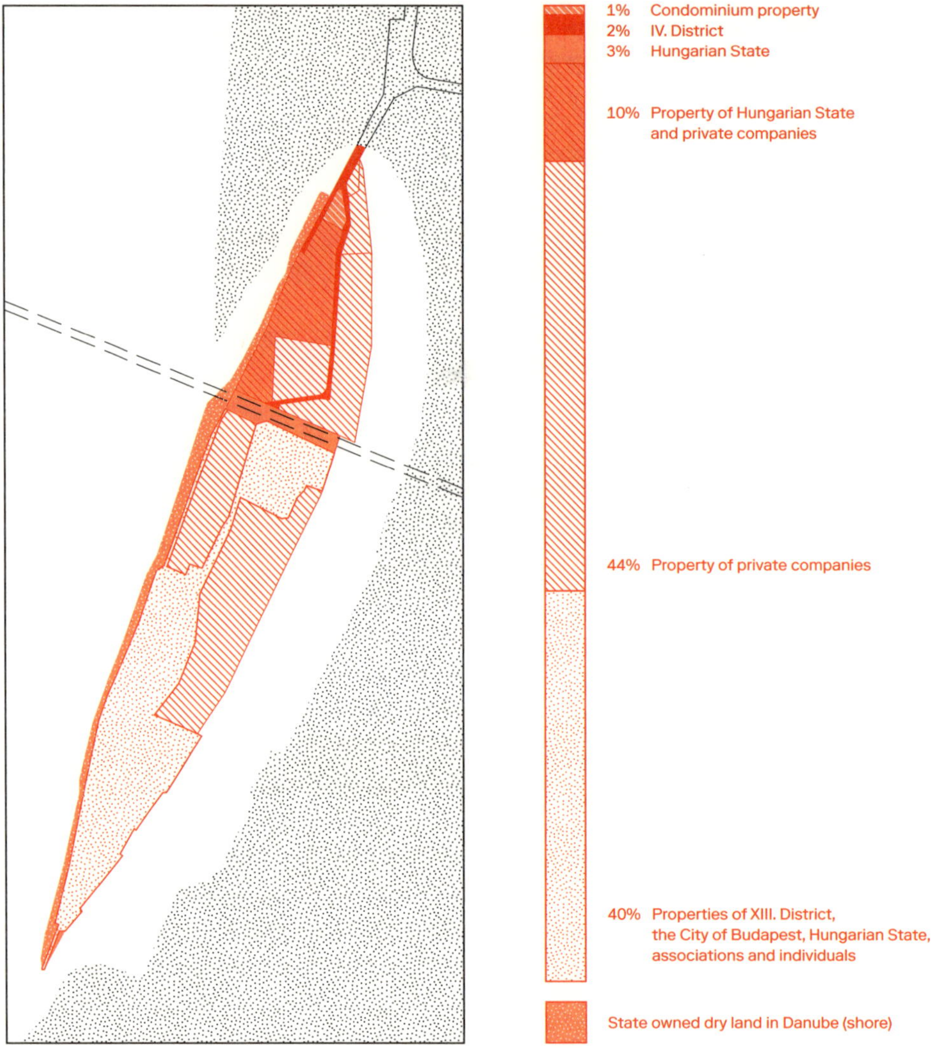

Map 3
The ownership of Népsziget (plot 25992/1)

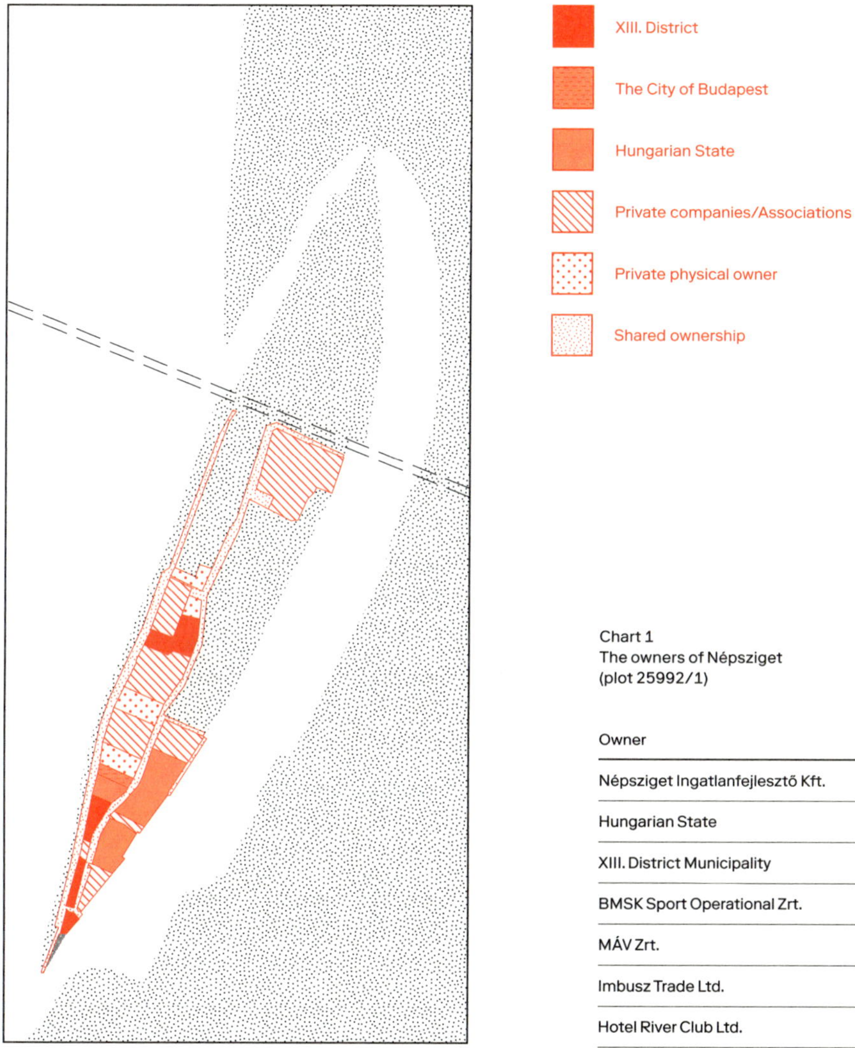

Chart 1
The owners of Népsziget
(plot 25992/1)

Owner	Area (m²)	Share (%)
Népsziget Ingatlanfejlesztő Kft.	639,100	37.96
Hungarian State	295,190	17.53
XIII. District Municipality	149,430	8.88
BMSK Sport Operational Zrt.	144,700	8.60
MÁV Zrt.	70,650	4.20
Imbusz Trade Ltd.	68,970	4.10
Hotel River Club Ltd.	65,830	3.91
BKV Zrt.	24,300	1.44
Budapest Rowing Association	23,544	1.40
Municipality of Budapest	20,750	1.23
Hungarian Rowing Association	15,696	0.93
GE Hungary Kft.	10,540	0.63
Evangelical Gerontology Association	6,720	0.40
7 private owners	148,030	8.79
All together	1,683,450	100

Map 4
Facilities on Népsziget

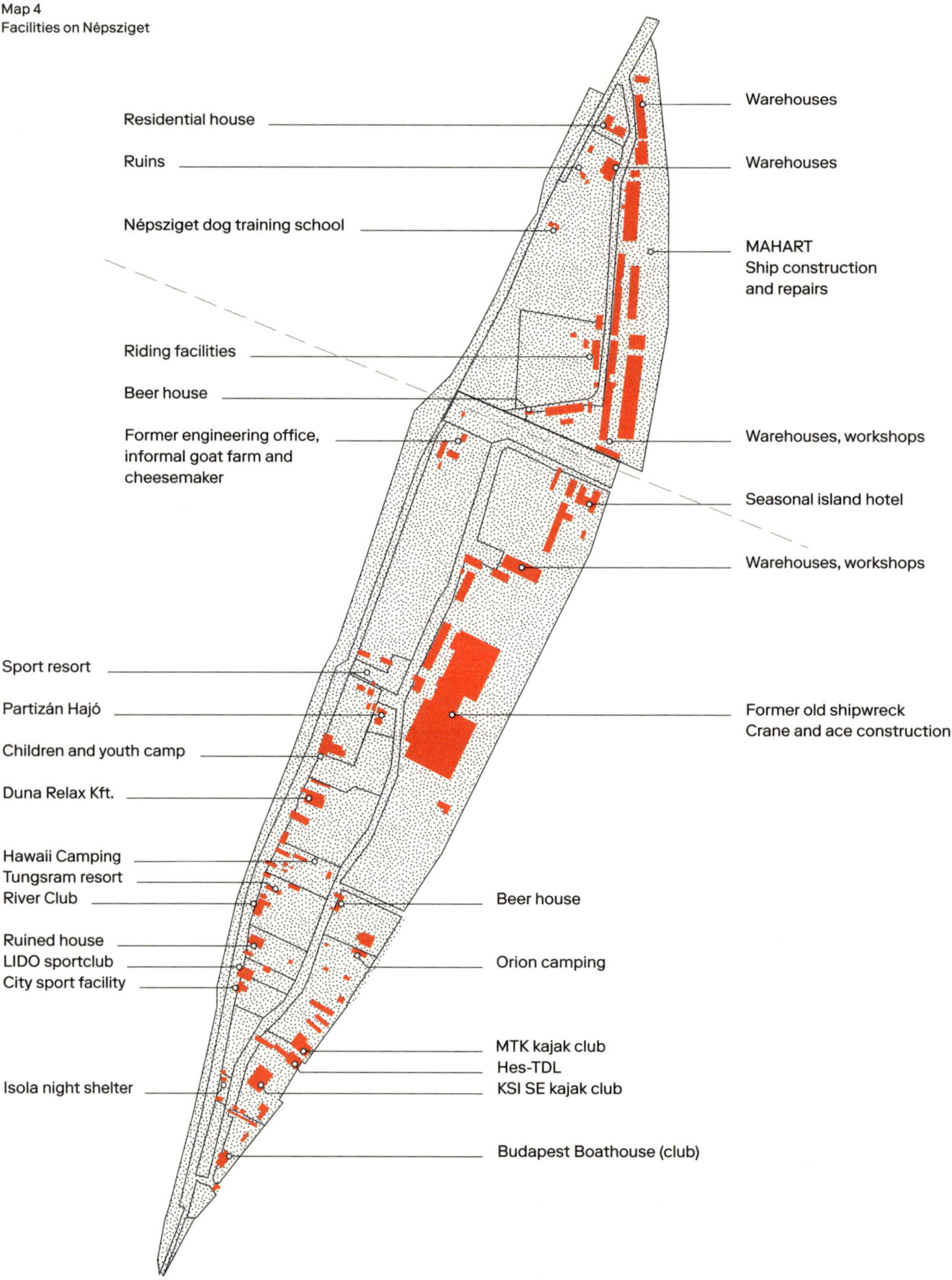

Public Amenities

The island's decay and isolation provide a natural shelter for the homeless. Still, Népsziget became popular among locals and visitors as a place for picnics, running, biking, water sports or walks along the Danube. A riding hall, a dog-training school, and even a goat farm can be found here.[4] Factory buildings are used mostly by car repair shops, with a few vintage shops and cafés appearing in the last two years. Several informal activities exist all over the island from goat farms to fish stands, temporary and permanent homes, and camping. Most of these are seasonal with the exception of homeless shelters, some workshops (car tyres) on the northern tip, and possibly the goat farm/petting zoo at the railway bridge.[5]

Future Prospects

According to a public survey conducted in 2016 by the Hungarian Urban Knowledge Centre, people want to keep the island as a low-key, local recreational area. Zoning plans and municipalities have the same intention, although protected green recreational areas with limited building prospects rarely attract investors. Some activity could come from the current owners of abandoned properties, both recreational and industrial. After all, this part of Budapest has continuously seen more residents and new development investments than any other.[6] In fact, in the neighbouring areas, concrete large-scale developments rose up from the ground in a relatively short time. Due to the emerging housing market, this kind of luxury housing will continue to appear at a high rate: this is also one of the city's most expensive areas, as it is a unique, bay-side part.[7] Some areas, except those for public recreation, have been enclosed by fences. Road surfaces have deteriorated as a result of prioritizing conflicting owners' interests. The most problematic ownership situation in the XIII. district is that of Népsziget plot 25992/1. This may be an obstacle to further developments because it makes it difficult to access financial resources (such as loans), and can serve as a permanent source of conflict. The effectiveness of cooperation between owners and investors under the complicated conditions of fragmented ownership will frame the future of the island. Solutions are expected to come from the local government as rehabilitation is badly needed, but much depends on the framework of the changes. In the meantime, small changes are coming from bottom-up projects and initiatives: the community.

4
B. Dezse. 'Go Beyond in Budapest: the islet of Népsziget' (2016), online, available HTTP: https://welovebudapest.com/en/2016/08/25/go-beyond-in-budapest-the-islet-of-nepsziget/ (accessed 21 December 2018).

5
City of Budapest, 'Baseline study for Népsziget Island' (October 2017).

6
Housing stock in municipal districts of Budapest, 2005, 2010, 2015, ArcData statistical database of Hungary, (2005), online, available HTTP: http://www.geoindex.hu/analysis-topics/purchasing-power/whats-livable-districts-budapest/ (accessed 21 December 2018).

7
'Periculum in mora – Vision of the People's Island', *Örökségfigyelő* (28 August 2018), online, available HTTP: https://oroksegfigyelo.blog.hu/2018/08/28/periculum_in_mora_jovokep_a_nepszigeten (accessed 21 December 2018).

Chart 2
Demographic change among districts of Budapest 2005–2015

Population change

500–1,460
250–500
100–250
50–100
0–50
-430–0

Chart 3
Real estate development in districts of Budapest 2005–2015

Dwellings built

1,000+
500–1,000
100–500
50–100
25–50
0–25

2005

2010

2015

recepco

MST

Warsaw

7.01

Population
(millions of inhab.)

2016 (metropolitan regions)
2016 (Belgrade)
2017 (other cities)

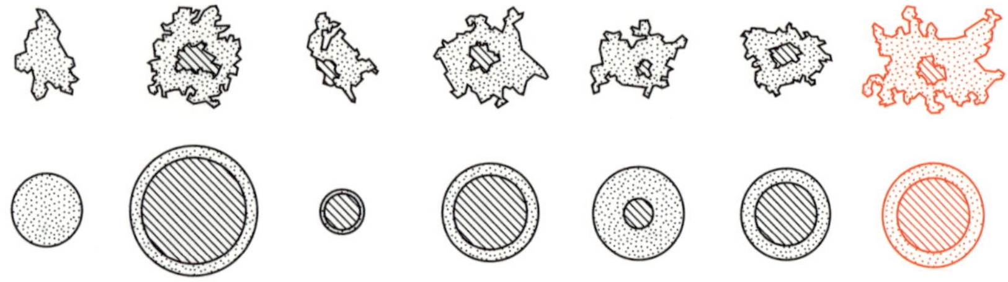

	Belgrade	Berlin	Bratislava	Budapest	Katowice	Prague	Warsaw
City	1.68	3.54	0.43	1.76	0.30	1.27	1.75
Metropolitan region		5.21	0.64	3.00	2.71	2.62	3.37

7.02

Built-up area footprint

City
2016
Total area: 517 km²
Population density:
3,391 inhab./km²

7.03

Unemployment (per cent)

Cities
2016

→ Economy
Chart D.06, p. 25

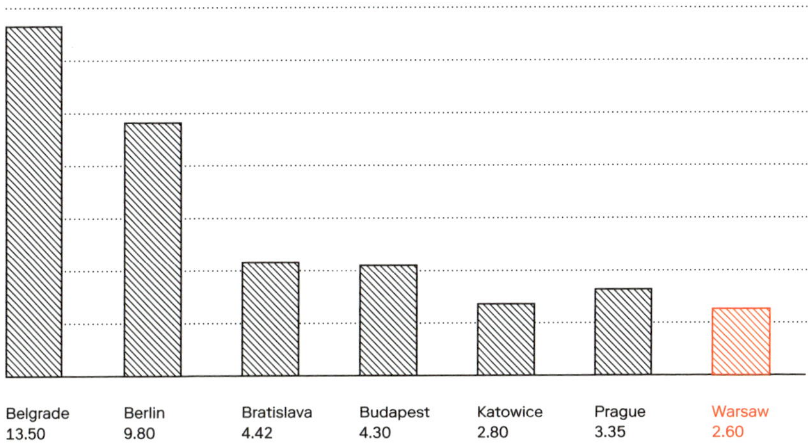

7.04

Sprawl index

Metropolitan regions
2012

→ Spatial Development
Chart E.07, p. 25

The sprawl index measures city growth (over the periods 2000–2006 and 2000–2012) in built-up areas against local population growth. The index is higher (lower) than zero when built-up area growth is greater (smaller) than population growth, leading to an increase (decrease) in city density.

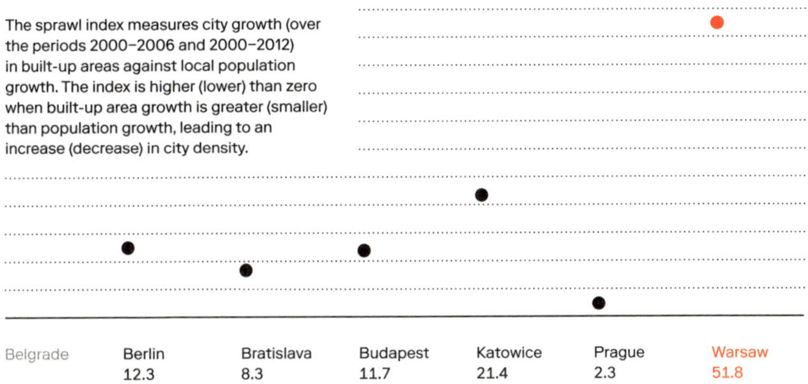

7.05

Average area of living accommodation (m^2/inhab.)

City
2011

29.40

◆ = 5 m^2

7.06

Average monthly net salary (EUR)

City
2018

885.68

▧ = 100 €

7.07

Registered passenger cars (cars/1,000 inhab.)

City
2016

673

■ = 20 cars

7.08

Tourists (number/year)

City
2016

3,315,531

= 1 million tourists

TEATR D

PASAŻ HANDLOWY
BOHEMIAN RHAPSODY
APTEKA

QUERCUS
Bank Pekao

Česká
NOVOTEL
express
C&A

WARSZAWA BERLIN

ZTE

KIA MOTORS
WARSZAWA

WPEK: Shared Cultural

Culture. A Populist View

Perhaps it is the lack of clarity and awareness about the dynamics and impact of seed-funded creativity and culture that contribute to the widespread populist idea that they are of a lesser significance to society. Sometimes portrayed as a greedy recipient of public funds, culture ought instead to be seen as a flow heater that ignites, fosters, and streamlines creative energy. It generates financial profit too, but most importantly it generates education and well-being among the diverse groups that participate in its creation and reception.

Culture. A Societal View

The primary objective of culture should be cultural education and active youth participation, according to extensive research of City DNA, conducted by ResPublica in the 100 biggest Polish cities (2016).[1] This notion of culture is very different from the rather simplistic efforts of municipalities we have seen so far, to spend more and more on large cultural infrastructure projects, which are supposed to be drivers of urban development: iconic landmarks enhancing the image and attractiveness of the city for private investments, but also platforms for the 'new creative class' and incentives for social integration through self-reflection and cultural inclusion.

Varsovians. A Cultural Profile

The dynamic, rapidly developing capital of Poland is known for its strong art and cultural scene, accommodating a diverse public. There are music clubs, bars, massive museum or concert infrastructures that attract visitors from both home and abroad. A traditional 'high' culture exists next to the independent scene. But what has been articulated through discussions and surveys among artists, cultural animators, and cultural officers, is a community-oriented culture and cultural education aimed at young people and citizens, and not just those in vibrant, culturally rich districts.

1
Res Publica, 'City DNA. Urban Cultural Policies' (2016), online, available HTTP: https://www.culturepartnership.eu/en/article/report-on-cultural-policy-in-poland (accessed 3 August 2018).

etwork

Chart 1
Changing notion of the objectives of culture
(per cent)

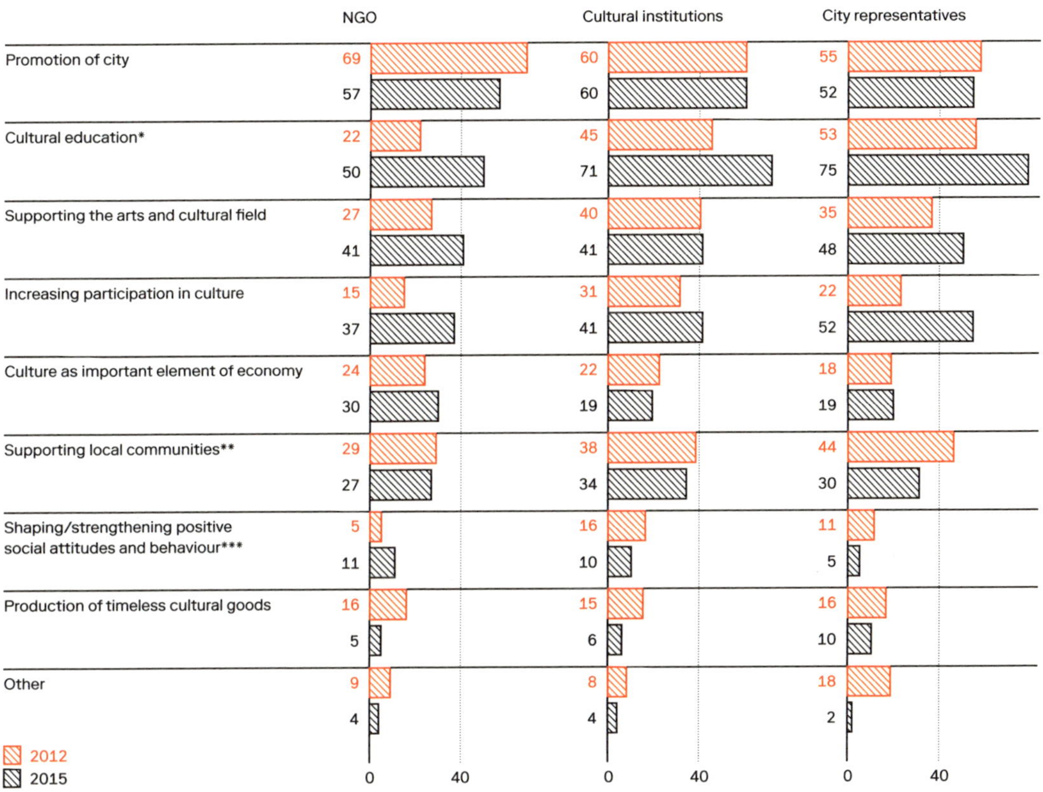

Several possible options for answer (in 2012)

* Promoting culture among young people
** Strengthening social relations of citizens through participation in culture
*** Promoting particular lifestyle and values

Chart 2
How do Varsovians spend their free time?

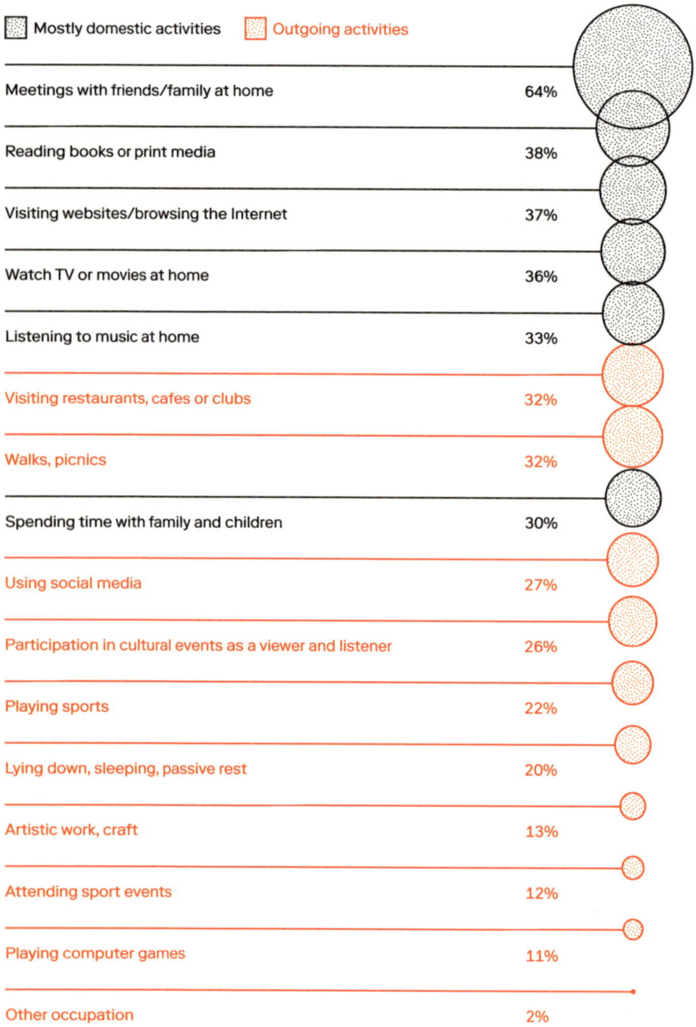

According to a survey of audiences in Warsaw, participation in cultural events ranked relatively high, listed as a preferred leisure activity by every fourth respondent.[2] 13 per cent of the participants were willing to become active cultural producers pursuing their own artistic work or craft. The report points to a rather high cultural potential of Varsovians.

2
K. M. Brown, 'Audience survey report from Warsaw's cultural institutions' (2016), online, available HTP: https://www.nck.pl/badania/raporty/raport-z-badania-publicznosci-warszawskich-instytucji-kultury (accessed 29 October 2018).

Chart 3
Attendance of cultural events in municipal districts of Warsaw in 2015

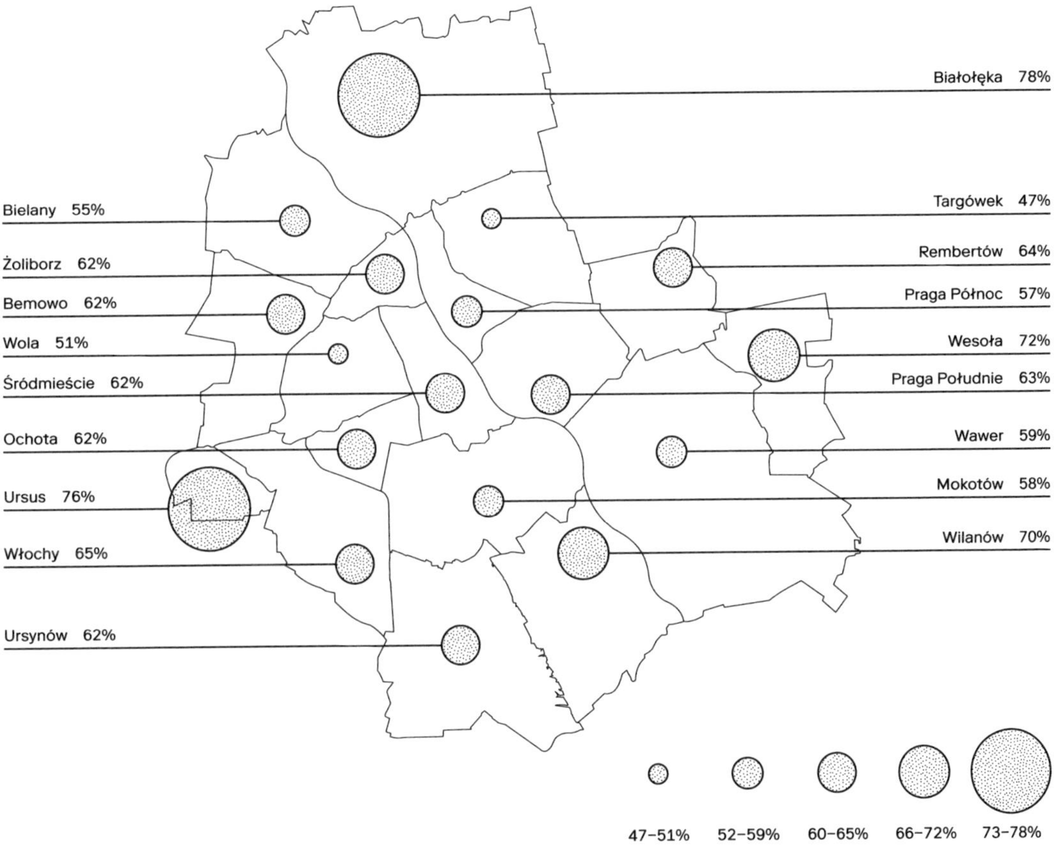

Chart 4
Warsaw cultural audience split

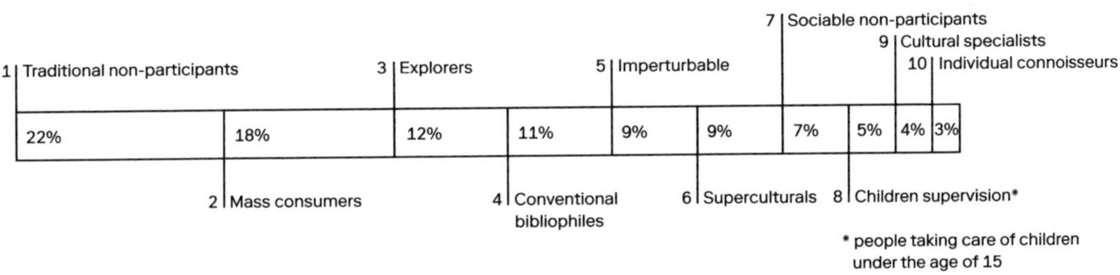

WPEK. A Network Culture

The mission of Warsaw's Cultural Education Programme (WPEK)[3] is to develop tools for conscious and active participation in culture, and to increase the cultural competences of Warsaw's residents. It integrates spaces involved in cultural education: institutional, educational, non-governmental, and informal. The programme interconnects the resources of theatres, museums, galleries, music and film institutions, cultural centres, libraries, associations, foundations, and enterprises, responding to the needs and expectations of residents. WPEK creates a knowledge base for cultural education and its makers, information on publications, studies, good practice.

Chart 5
Institutional context of WPEK

2006/2007

- Discussion about a different understanding of culture in Warsaw
- Survey among cultural animators, artists, officers
- Strategies suggested by the report were not useful (practical enough) for the city administration—and were not implemented

2012

- Warsaw municipality participates in the international contest European City of Culture 2016. Thanks to this, a new cultural strategy is adopted by the City Council.
  Part of the strategy aimed at education
- Warsaw Cultural Educational Program – Warszawski Program Edukacji Kulturalnej (WPEK) established by the City of Warsaw

Chart 6
WPEK: participating stakeholders
(per cent and absolute numbers)

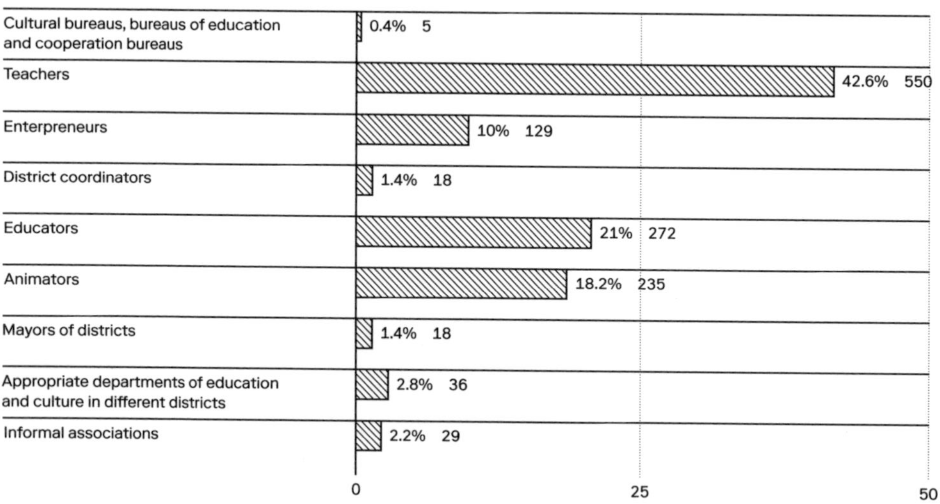

Chart 7
WPEK: venue diagram
(per cent and absolute numbers)

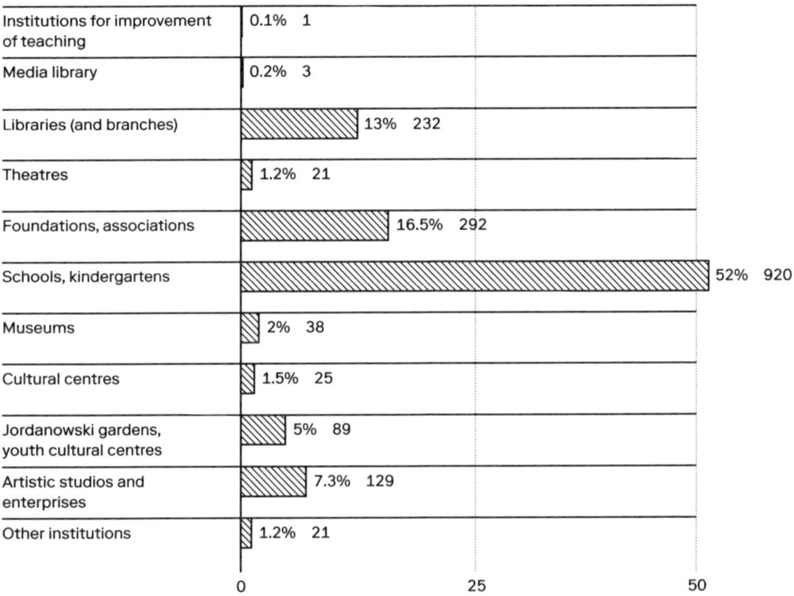

> 'The culture and education community lived side by side eight years ago, they were even competing with each other. This project certainly changed that—they stopped competing and they know each other, they are in a shared network and sometimes even cooperate. In short, what we have done is support networking, partnerships, investments in culture, information and promotion.'
> Anna Michalak Pawłowska, founder and main coordinator, WPEK[4]

3 Warszawski Program Edukacji Kulturalnej, online, available HTTP: http://www.wpek.pl/wpek,3,265.html?locale=pl_PL (accessed 3 August 2018).

4 Interview with Anna Michalak Pawłowska, 3 November 2018.

Chart 8
WPEK: activity analysis
(per cent and absolute numbers)

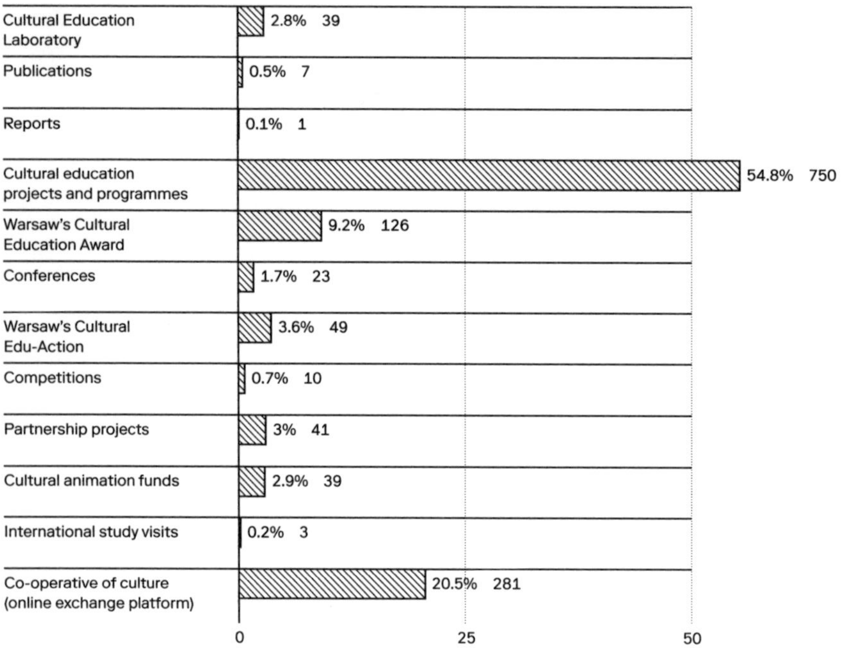

When it comes to funding for culture, the situation is very dynamic in each city. Poland's 10 biggest cities spend the majority of the country's culture budget.[5] According to Anna Michalak Pawłowska. the programme started with a budget of around 200,000 PLN / 47,000 EUR and in six years it grew almost 20 times to approximately 4,000,000 PLN / 935,000 EUR.[6] Compared to the city's cultural budget, WPEK is still far from the major spenders, but its results have outperformed its investment costs.

5
Res Publica, 'City DNA. Urban Cultural Policies' (2016), online, available HTTP: https://www.culturepartnership.eu/en/article/report-on-cultural-policy-in-poland (accessed 3 August 2018).

6
Interview with Anna Michalak Pawłowska, 3 November 2018.

7
Ibid.

Chart 9
Leaders in public expenditure on culture

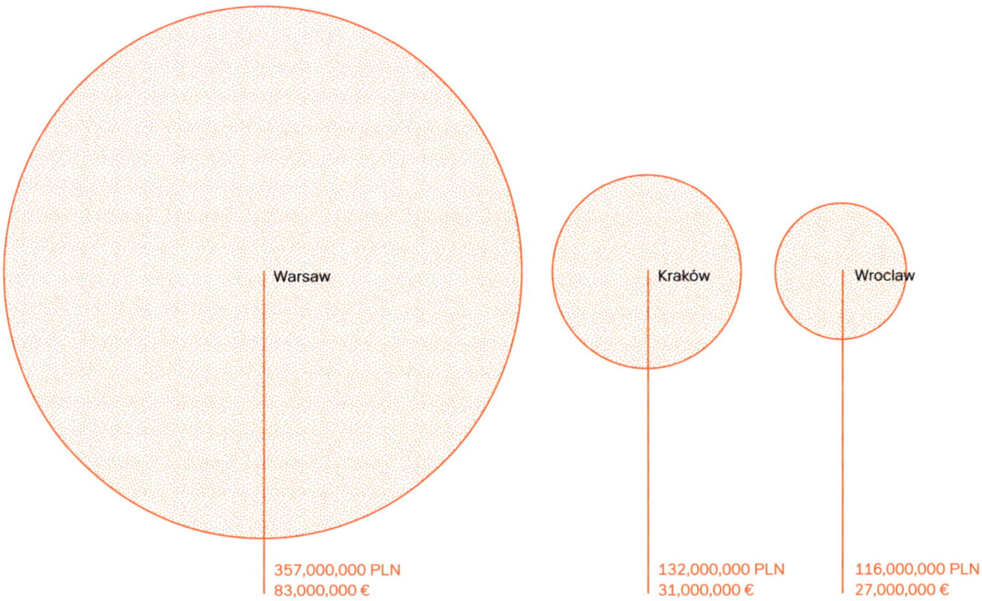

Impacts of Cultural Education

Anna Michalak Pawłowska describes a change in the behaviour of Varsovians, who started to use and enjoy community centres (Pol. *dom kultury*)—former places of centralized cultural programmes during communism that went out of use and fashion in the 1990s. Through the activities of the Cultural Education Laboratory, their offer significantly changed in quality and became relevant for the 21st century, but also for the needs of the local community.

'The employees of cultural centres and directors were taught the trends of the 21st century in the animation of culture. A Warsaw resident can also feel that today in his or her immediate neighbourhood, the school, non-governmental organization, activists and community centres—they all work together and offer something, which was not the case eight years ago, before this project.'[7]

WPEK has created a network of cultural actors. The programme should keep going. Let's hope that the new, rather progressive Warsaw leadership will award the project with appropriate funding as cultural education really fosters profound values: it changes the locals' attitude towards a warm and creative relationship with their city, something of which the economy is hardly truly indicative.

Shared Cities: Creative Momentum

6 Countries, 7 Cities, 11 60+ SCCM Members, 45

Activities

Total: 386

Activities	Belgrade	Berlin	Bratislava	Budapest	Katowice	Prague	Warsaw
Workshops 185	25	5	27	41	64	23	0
Public debates (discussions) 82	9	3	11	37	9	13	0
Film screening 61	0	53	1	0	1	6	0
Market 27	0	25	1	1	0	0	0
Urban games 9	5	0	0	4	0	0	0
Cultural pop-up space 8	4	0	0	4	0	0	0
Study trips 5	1	1	1	1	1	0	0
Residency 4	0	4	0	0	0	0	0
Research and evaluation 5	0	0	0	2	1	2	0

artner Organizations, Months, 492 Activities

Outcomes

Total: 106

Outcomes	Total	Belgrade	Berlin	Bratislava	Budapest	Katowice	Prague	Warsaw
Video documentaries/Interviews	46	0	0	0	0	0	46	0
Exhibitions	20	1	1	9	6	1	2	0
Publications	15	0	1	2	0	2	7	3
Festivals	10	3	0	0	6	1	0	0
Conferences	7	1	1	0	0	1	4	0
Web-platforms	7	0	1	1	3	1	1	0
Performance	1	0	0	0	0	0	1	0

Note 1
The Activity and Outcome numbers correspond with the entire project period 2016–2020 and include overall outcomes of the project.

Note 2
The particular activities for each case study (working sessions, research surveys, etc.) are included in the detailed activity overview of each case study separately.

Prague, Goethe-Institut

Heublein, Stefanie; Ráček, Jakob
Čermáková, Zuzana
Hudcová, Barbora
Krucká, Jitka
Moravec, Tomáš
Pavelka, Kamil
Peachment Brehmer, Martina
Sidorová, Milota
Tscholakidi, Sofia

Prague, Czech Centres

Pela, Přemysl; Koblerová, Monika
Černá, Ivana
Higgs, Michael
Jungwirthová, Petra
Karacsony, Sandra
Štolba, Josef

Prague, reSITE

Barry, Martin J.
Cienfuegos, Gil
Hasmanová, Ludmila
Nováková, Markéta
Okamura, Osamu
Ondráčková, Radka
Sýkorová, Tereza

in collaboration with
Doudová, Helena

Belgrade, Association of Belgrade Architects – Belgrade International Architecture Week

Vukosavljević, Tatjana
Đokić, Ana
Galassi, Barbara
Glavički, Ana
Ivanović Vojvodić, Jelena
Ivković, Vera
Jovanović, Natalija
Jovović Prodanović, Danica
Kucina, Ivan
Marković, Aleksandra
Milunović, Milica
Rapp, Tatijana
Sarić, Ružica
Vračar, Miloš
Vukoje, Vladimir

Berlin, KUNSTrePUBLIK

Einhoff, Matthias
Enne, Lena
Horst, Philip
Kuč, Miodrag
Lindenau, Dennis
Metz, Sylvia
Sachs, Harry

Bratislava, Academy of Fine Arts and Design in Bratislava

Halada, Vít
Brádňanský, Benjamín
de Gelder, Nina
Hájek, Petr
Holocsy, Zoltán
Niczová, Alexandra
Pastorková, Alexandra
Pišteková, Danica
Rypáková, Kristína
Stec, Peter
Studený, Ján
Trubiniová, Soňa

Bratislava, Old Market Hall Alliance

Mazúr, Ján
Bindics, Gábor
Chylová, Denisa
Hliničanová, Veronika
Hurný, Juraj

Košťál, Ctibor
Lényi, Peter & 2021 Architects
Marcinov, Michal & team Labak
Neupauer, Martin
Prachárová, Veronika

Budapest, Hungarian Contemporary Architecture Centre – KÉK

Szemerey, Samu
Horváth, Bálint
Huszár, Daniella
Jeczkó, Mercédesz
Libárdi, Julianna
Simon, Vera
Szakál, Anna

Budapest, Mindspace

Zsargó, Szilvia; Kobrizsa, Ádám
Bánfi, Norbert
Bezsenyi, Tamás
Böszörményi, Edina
Czobor, Szabolcs
Elek, Zsófi
Gunther, Dóri
Kenessey, Tamás
Madácsi, Flóra
Major, Réka
Nánási, Emese
Pignitzky, Ágota
Pusztai, Lola
Sipos, Balázs
Sipos, Márti
Somló, Dávid
Varga, Cili
Vida, Vera

Katowice, Katowice City of Gardens

Piekarski, Karol
Adamus, Oskar
Badera, Matylda
Chmiel, Magdalena
Górny, Dawid
Kostrzewska, Hanna
Pampuch, Krzysztof
Urbańska, Paulina
Węgrzyn, Waldemar

Warsaw, Magazyn Miasta: Cities Magazine / Res Publica

Żakowska, Marta; Celiński, Artur
Burszta, Jędrzej
Dall, Galan
Dorda, Katarzyna
Gradziuk, Jakub
Grądzka, Joanna
Kiedrzyńska, Anna
Kubecka, Magdalena
Obarska, Martyna
Penza Gabler, Zofia
Sęk, Michal

Special thanks to

Anděl, Jaroslav; Dieterle, Jule; Favero, Irene; Foerster-Baldenius, Benjamin; Feireiss, Lukas; Hilscher, Teresa; Hoidn, Barbara; Koolhaas, Charlie; Kopecký, Jakub; König, Anne; Kratochvíl, Kryštof; Mocek, Jan; Oldewarris, Hans; Sankotová Morávková, Zuzana; Schad, Anke; Storm, Wolf Arne; Švehlová, Táňa; Raabová, Tereza;

the teams of achtQuark; Akademie der Künste Berlin; Creative Europe Desk Czech Republic; Divadlo Archa; Economic impacT; Filmová Manufaktura; IPR Praha & CAMP; PINK & Loom on the Moon; Side2; Studio NAND.

Prague, Goethe-Institut

The Goethe-Institut is the Federal Republic of Germany's cultural institute, active worldwide. It promotes and encourages international cultural exchange. With 159 branches of the Goethe-Institut around the world, Goethe Centres, cultural societies, reading rooms, libraries, and exam and language learning centres, it has played a central role in the cultural and educational policies of Germany for over 60 years. The Goethe-Institut's projects strengthen the development of structures in civil society and foster worldwide mobility as well as exchange of best practices.

Prague, Czech Centres

The Czech Centres are a contributory organization network of the Ministry of Foreign Affairs of the Czech Republic. They were established to promote the Czech Republic's history, culture, language, tourism, and trade abroad. Considered an active instrument of foreign policy of the Czech Republic, the network consists of centres in over 20 countries across three continents. The Czech Centres participate in *Shared Cities: Creative Momentum* to engage with the *Iconic Ruins* exhibition, and to promote discussion about postwar architecture in socialist regimes in the V4 countries. The Czech Centres network is also involved in the preparation of a study on the economic impact of project implementation on the participating countries.

Prague, reSITE

reSITE is a global non-profit action to improve the urban environment, dedicated to creating livable and lovable cities. Since its founding in late 2011, reSITE has become a leading voice in Europe in the field of rethinking urban planning, architecture, and urban development, attracting political leaders of inspirational cities to its flagship events. A bottom-up start-up, reSITE connects leaders across disciplines and brings a multitude of side events, debates, film screenings, exhibitions, and bike rides for the general public. reSITE is also the initiator of Manifesto Market, a temporary gastro and culture market in Prague that revived a derelict area in the city center. reSITE is the Curatorial Lead of Shared Cities: Creative Momentum.

Belgrade, Association of Belgrade Architects – Belgrade International Architecture Week

Since its foundation in 1960, ABA has been dedicated to promoting and increasing the knowledge, skills, and proficiency of its members to serve and protect the public interest. ABA organizes the Belgrade International Week of Architecture (BINA). Founded in 2006, BINA encourages intercultural dialogue, trans-national cooperation and mobility. The festival brings together experts from Serbia and other European countries and the Americas, enabling an exchange of ideas and experiences and providing a link between the international and the local creative scene in Serbia.

Berlin, KUNSTrePUBLIK

KUNSTrePUBLIK is a registered non-profit organisation and artist collective founded in 2006. Since its establishment, the group has conceived and realized many site-specific exhibitions and has engaged in other community-based activities including education, urban planning, artmaking, and curation. KUNSTrePUBLIK is the organization behind ZK/U – Centre for Arts and Urbanistics – exploring urban communication structures and implementing experiments to foster the conversation between diverse stakeholders in the urban arena.

Bratislava, Academy of Fine Arts and Design in Bratislava

Despite being rather small in size, the Department of Architecture is an influential school of architecture, where students benefit from an intensive contact with their lecturers. This individual approach enhances the development of innovative technical aspects of design. Presentations of student works take place in front of invited critics, while lectures by prominent guest speakers as well as various exhibitions encourage inspiring interactions and critical thinking.

Bratislava, Old Market Hall Alliance

The Old Market Hall alliance is a civic association founded in 2012. Its main aim is to revitalize the long-abandoned and closed historical building of The Old Market Hall in Bratislava. The association has been in charge of the building since September 2013 and has gradually turned it into a modern urban centre providing space for conferences, markets, and cultural events. Old Market Hall's activities catalyze progress in the whole neighbourhood.

Budapest, Hungarian Contemporary Architecture Centre – KÉK

KÉK is an independent architectural cultural centre located in Budapest. Operated by young Hungarian architects, artists, and civilians, the centre shows the way to new perspectives in architectural and urban thinking in Hungary using fresh, provocative, and focused programs. KÉK regularly organizes conferences, workshops, roundtable discussions, festivals, movie nights, exhibitions, urban walks, and community gardening programmes, which remain professional in their content while encouraging the wider public to participate in the shared production of visions and concrete plans for today's cities.

Budapest, Mindspace

Mindspace is a non-profit organization, founded in 2011. The team manages cultural urban projects, with a focus on livable cities and consciousness through participation and engagement. Mindspace's main projects are neighbourhood development in the VIII. district of Budapest with a special focus on Rákoczi square Market Hall.

Katowice, Katowice City of Gardens

Katowice City of Gardens focuses on cultural, publishing and educational activities as well as on organizing artistic events such as the Katowice JazzArt Festival, the Gardens of Sounds, Katowice Street Art Festival, Independent Arts Festival and the Interpretacje Festival of Theatre Directorial Art. Additionally, Katowice City of Gardens supports non-governmental artistic projects on education and cultural animation such as Medialab Katowice. In 2015, Katowice became a UNESCO City of Music as a part of the UNESCO Creative Cities Network.

Warsaw, Magazyn Miasta: Cities Magazine / Res Publica

Magazyn Miasta is the first publication in Poland covering urban issues as diverse as sustainable urban culture, green spaces, mobility, social participation, smart cities, and innovation in administration. Set up in 2014 by Marta Żakowska, its editor-in-chief, and the Warsaw Institute for Public Space Research, it is the only Polish interdisciplinary magazine on urban issues. *Magazyn Miasta* is dedicated to anyone interested in topics affecting cities today, reaching out to not only local governments and city councils, but also to architects, activists, and scientists.

Berlin
KUNSTrePUBLIK
Germany
Creative Centre:
Goethe-Institut
Czech Centres
reSITE
Prague
Czech Repu
Academy of Fine Arts and Design in Bratislava
Old Market Hall Alliance
Share your ideas with us:
sharedcities.eu
#SharedCities
#SCCM2020
1:1000

Res Publica – Cities Magazine
Warsaw
Poland
Katowice City of Gardens
Slovakia
Bratislava
Budapest
Hungarian Contemporary Architecture Centre – KÉK
Mindspace
Hungary
Association of Belgrade Architects
Belgrade
Serbia

SHARED CITIES: CREATIVE MOMENTUM

Shared Cities: Creative Momentum (SCCM) is a four-year long cultural project that brings together eleven partners from **seven major European cities: Belgrade, Berlin, Bratislava, Budapest, Katowice, Prague, and Warsaw.** Shared Cities establishes an international network for a creative discourse at the intersection of architecture, art, urbanism, and the sharing economy to contribute to the transformation of urban spaces. **From 2016 to 2020 more than 300 activities take place**—festivals, films, exhibitions, artist residencies, or case studies. The project's ambition is to improve the quality of life in European cities and to show urban citizens that their role in creating a pleasant and valuable urban environment is essential. Co-funded by the Creative Europe Programme of the European Union.

sharedcities.eu
#SCCM2020 #SharedCities

David Crowley
is Head of the School of Visual Culture at National College of Art and Design in Dublin, Ireland. He has a specialist interest in the art and design histories of Eastern Europe under socialist rule.

Helena Doudová
is an author and art historian based in Berlin and Prague. She is a curator of the architecture collection of the National Gallery Prague.

Elke Krasny
is a cultural theorist, urban researcher, and curator. She is a professor at the Academy of Fine Arts Vienna.

Ivan Kucina
is a professor at Dessau International School of Architecture, Anhalt University of Applied Sciences. His academic research focuses on sustainable architecture and urban development with concepts based on informal building strategies and participatory practices.

Medialab Katowice
is an experimental project combining creative, research, and education activities at the intersection of art, design, and digital media.

Monika Mitášová
is an architecture theorist. She lectures at the Faculty of Philosophy and Arts at Trnava University. Her research focuses on contemporary architecture theories and architecture interpretation.

Peter Mörtenböck and Helge Mooshammer
are cultural theorists and architects based at Vienna University of Technology and Goldsmiths College, University of London. Mörtenböck and Mooshammer's joint work is concerned with new forms of spatial production vis-à-vis current processes of planetary change and the dynamics that inform them.

Karol Piekarski
is a freelance researcher interested in data science and data-driven urban studies. He is the programme director at Medialab Katowice.

Milota Sidorová
is a moderator, planner, networker, feminist, and walker in service of more inclusive cities, currently residing in Bratislava.

Olja Triaška Stefanović
was born in former Yugoslavia. Currently based in Bratislava (SK), she is a photographer and visual artist with a special interest in the space and architecture of Eastern Europe. She finished her PhD at the Academy of Fine Arts and Design in Bratislava, where she works as an Assistant Professor.

Marian Zervan
is an art and architecture historian and theorist. He is a member of the Department of Theory and History of Art at the Academy of Fine Arts and Design in Bratislava. He also works at the Faculty of Philosophy and Arts at Trnava University. His research is focused on art and architecture theory, methods of interpretation and sacral iconography.

Lila Athanasiadou
is a freelance writer and researcher with a background in architecture whose work explores feminist and queer pedagogical practices and intersections of digital data with human and territorial bodies.

Markus Ambach
is an artist, author, and initiator of various art projects and exhibitions focusing on public space. He studied at the Düsseldorf Art Academy and in 2002 founded the project platform MAP.

Anastasia Eggers and Ottonie von Roeder
are a design duo working in the field of speculative and critical design, graphic design and cultural education.

ifau – institute for applied urbanism
is a Berlin-based collective of architects with a focus on interrelated, interdisciplinary projects in the field of architecture and urban design. ifau was founded in 1998 by Susanne Heiss, Christoph Heinemann, and Christoph Schmidt.

Lydia Karagiannaki
is formally trained in architecture and has engaged in design, editorial, and research projects centered around community engagement and cultural critique.

raumlaborberlin
is a collective based in Berlin working at the intersection of architecture, city planning, art, and urban intervention, using the term urban practice for its hybrid working process. raumlaborberlin are Francesco Apuzzo, Markus Bader, Benjamin Foerster-Baldenius, Frauke Gerstenberg, Andrea Hofmann, Jan Liesegang, Axel Timm, Christof Mayer, Florian Stirnemann, Mathias Rick († 2012).

umschichten
was founded in 2008 by architects Lukasz Lendzinski and Peter Weigand. The artist-architecture-collective works as a build and design praxis.

Unless otherwise stated, the data used in the charts comes mainly from: Eurostat, OECD databases, statistical databases and statistical yearbooks of individual countries and cities, and the Numbeo online database.

The full database used in the project along with detailed sources is available at:
https://github.com/medialabkato/sccm-atlas-statistical-data/blob/master/dataset.csv

General Overview

A.01 Statistical Yearbook of the Republic of Serbia 2017;
Eurostat
A.02 Municipalities and regions in the Republic of Serbia 2017;
Berlin. Statistisches Jahrbuch 2017;
Regional Statistical Yearbook of Slovakia 2017;
Hungarian Central Statistical Office;
Statistical Office in Katowice;
Statistical Yearbook of Prague 2017;
Statistical Yearbook of Warsaw 2017
A.03 Statistical Yearbook of the Republic of Serbia 2017;
Eurostat
A.04 Natural Earth;
OECD;
OpenStreetMap

Population and Society

B.01 Municipalities and regions in the Republic of Serbia 2017;
Berlin. Statistisches Jahrbuch 2017;
Regional Statistical Yearbook of Slovakia 2017;
Hungarian Central Statistical Office;
Statistical Office in Katowice;
Statistical Yearbook of Prague 2017;
Statistical Yearbook of Warsaw 2017;
Statistical Yearbook of the Republic of Serbia 2017;
Eurostat
B.02 Statistical Yearbook of the Republic of Serbia 2017;
Eurostat
B.03 Population projections of the Republic of Serbia 2011–2041;
Eurostat
B.04 Population projections of the Republic of Serbia 2011–2041;
Eurostat
B.05 Population projections of the Republic of Serbia 2011–2041;
Eurostat
B.06 Municipalities and regions in the Republic of Serbia 2017;
Berlin. Statistisches Jahrbuch 2017;
Štatistická ročenka hlavného mesta SR Bratislavy 2017;
Hungarian Central Statistical Office;
Statistical Office in Katowice;
Statistical Yearbook of Prague 2015;
Statistical Office in Warsaw
B.07 Municipalities and regions in the Republic of Serbia 2017;
Berlin. Statistisches Jahrbuch 2017;
Regional Statistical Yearbook of Slovakia 2017;
Hungarian Central Statistical Office;
Statistical Office in Katowice;
Statistical Yearbook of Prague 2017;
Statistical Yearbook of Warsaw 2017
B.08 Municipalities and regions in the Republic of Serbia 2017;
Berlin. Statistisches Jahrbuch 2017;
Štatistická ročenka hlavného mesta SR Bratislavy 2017;
Hungarian Central Statistical Office;
Statistical Yearbook of Prague 2016
B.09 Statistical Office of the Slovak Republic;
Hungarian Central Statistical Office;
Państwowa Komisja Wyborcza;
Statistical Yearbook of Prague 2014;
Municipalities and regions in the Republic of Serbia 2017;
Kleine Berlin Statistik 2017 (in English)
B.10 Municipalities and regions in the Republic of Serbia 2017;
Berlin. Statistisches Jahrbuch 2017;
Štatistická ročenka hlavného mesta SR Bratislavy 2017;
Hungarian Central Statistical Office;
Statistical Yearbook of Prague 2017;
Statistical Office in Katowice;
Statistical Office in Warsaw
B.11 Municipalities and regions in the Republic of Serbia 2017;
Štatistická ročenka hlavného mesta SR Bratislavy 2017;
Berlin. Statistisches Jahrbuch 2017;
www.teir.hu;
Statistical Yearbook of Prague 2017;
Statistical Office in Katowice;
Statistical Office in Warsaw
B.12 Berlin. Statistisches Jahrbuch 2017;
Statistical Yearbook of Budapest 2015;
Statistical Office of the Republic of Serbia;
Štatistická ročenka hlavného mesta SR Bratislavy 2017;
Statistical Yearbook of Prague 2017;
Statistical Yearbook of Warsaw 2017;
Katowice City Hall, Department of Culture
B.13 Statistical Yearbook of Budapest 2015;
Statistical Office of the Republic of Serbia;
Berlin. Statistisches Jahrbuch 2017;
Štatistická ročenka hlavného mesta SR Bratislavy 2017;
Statistical Yearbook of Warsaw 2017;
Database of cultural facilities, IPR Prague;
Katowice City Hall, Department of Culture
B.14 Municipalities and regions in the Republic of Serbia 2017;
Berlin. Statistisches Jahrbuch 2017;
Štatistická ročenka hlavného mesta SR Bratislavy 2017;
Hungarian Central Statistical Office;
Statistical Office in Katowice;
Statistical Yearbook of Prague 2017;
Statistical Yearbook of Warsaw 2017;
Statistical Office of the Republic of Serbia

Housing and Cost of Living

C.01 Statistical Yearbook of Belgrade 2016;
Eurostat
C.02 2011 Census of Population, Households and Dwellings in the Republic of Serbia;
Eurostat
C.03 Statistical Yearbook of Belgrade 2016;
Eurostat
C.04 Municipalities and regions in the Republic of Serbia 2017;
Kleine Berlin Statistik 2017 (in English);
Regional Statistical Yearbook of Slovakia 2017;
Hungarian Central Statistical Office;
Statistical Office in Katowice;
Statistical Yearbook of Prague 2017;
Statistical Office in Warsaw
C.05 Numbeo, www.numbeo.com
C.06 Numbeo, www.numbeo.com
C.07 Numbeo, www.numbeo.com
C.08 Numbeo, www.numbeo.com
C.09 Numbeo, www.numbeo.com

C.10 Numbeo, www.numbeo.com
C.11 Numbeo, www.numbeo.com
C.12 Numbeo, www.numbeo.com
C.13 Numbeo, www.numbeo.com

Economy

D.01 OECD
D.02 OECD;
Statistical Office of the Republic of Serbia
D.03 The Cultural and Creative Cities Monitor
D.04 The Cultural and Creative Cities Monitor
D.05 Eurostat;
Municipalities and regions in the Republic of Serbia 2017
D.06 Statistical Yearbook of Belgrade 2016;
Kleine Berlin Statistik 2017 (in English);
Štatistická ročenka hlavného mesta SR Bratislavy 2017;
Hungarian Central Statistical Office;
Statistical Office in Katowice;
Statistical Yearbook of Prague 2017;
Statistical Office in Warsaw
D.07 Municipalities and regions in the Republic of Serbia 2017;
Berlin. Statistisches Jahrbuch 2017;
Štatistická ročenka hlavného mesta SR Bratislavy 2017;
Hungarian Central Statistical Office;
Statistical Office in Katowice;
Statistical Yearbook of Prague 2017;
Statistical Office in Warsaw

Mobility and Spatial Development

E.01 Tabellenbericht zum Forschungsprojekt „Mobilität in Städten – SrV 2013" in Berlin;
Balázs Mór Plan 2014–2030, Budapest Mobility Plan, Volume I: Objectives and Measures;
TEMS – The EPOMM Modal Split Tool;
Územný generel dopravy hl. mesta SR Bratislavy;
Wieloletni plan rozwoju zintegrowanego systemu transportowego miasta Katowice 2015;
Warszawskie Badanie Ruchu 2015;
Prague Transportation Yearbook 2016
E.02 Berlin Traffic in Figures 2013;
Strategija razvoja bicklistickog saobracaja Grad Beograd;
Statistical Yearbook of Warsaw 2017;
Prague Transportation Yearbook 2016;
City of Bratislava (direct request);
www.teir.hu;
Katowice City Council (direct request)
E.03 Numbeo, www.numbeo.com
E.04 Územný generel dopravy hl. mesta SR Bratislavy
Municipalities and regions in the Republic of Serbia 2017;
Berlin. Statistisches Jahrbuch 2017;
Statistical Yearbook of Warsaw 2017;
Statistical Office in Katowice;
Prague Transportation Yearbook 2016;
Hungarian Central Statistical Office
E.05 Eurostat
E.06 Eurostat
E.07 OECD
E.08 Municipalities and regions in the Republic of Serbia 2017;
Kleine Berlin Statistik 2017 (in English);
Regional Statistical Yearbook of Slovakia 2017;
Hungarian Central Statistical Office;
Statistical Office in Katowice;
Statistical Yearbook of Prague 2017;
Statistical Yearbook of Warsaw 2017
E.09 Eurostat;
Municipalities and regions in the Republic of Serbia 2017
E.10 OECD
E.11 OpenStreetMap

International Benchmarking

F.01 Eurostat;
Statistical Yearbook of the Republic of Serbia 2017;
Municipalities and regions in the Republic of Serbia 2017;
Berlin. Statistisches Jahrbuch 2017;
Regional Statistical Yearbook of Slovakia 2017;
Hungarian Central Statistical Office;
Statistical Office in Katowice;
Statistical Yearbook of Prague 2017;
Statistical Yearbook of Warsaw 2017;
Stadsdelen in cijfers 2017
F.02 OECD
F.03 Statistical Yearbook of Belgrade 2016;
Eurostat
F.04 Berlin. Statistisches Jahrbuch 2017;
Statistical Yearbook of Budapest 2015;
Statistical Office of the Republic of Serbia;
Štatistická ročenka hlavného mesta SR Bratislavy 2017;
Statistical Yearbook of Prague 2017;
Statistical Yearbook of Warsaw 2017;
Katowice City Hall, Department of Culture;
Athens in numbers – Athens website;
World Cities Culture Forum
F.05 Numbeo, www.numbeo.com
F.06 Numbeo, www.numbeo.com
F.07 Numbeo, www.numbeo.com
F.08 Numbeo, www.numbeo.com
F.09 Numbeo, www.numbeo.com

Bratislava

1.01 Regional Statistical Yearbook of Slovakia 2017;
Eurostat
1.02 Regional Statistical Yearbook of Slovakia 2017;
OpenStreetMap
1.03 OECD
1.04 Statistical Office of the Slovak Republic;
Hungarian Central Statistical Office;
Państwowa Komisja Wyborcza;
Statistical Yearbook of Prague 2014;
Municipalities and regions in the Republic of Serbia 2017;
Kleine Berlin Statistik 2017 (in English)
1.05 Štatistická ročenka hlavného mesta SR Bratislavy 2017
1.06 Numbeo, www.numbeo.com
1.07 Územný generel dopravy hl. mesta SR Bratislavy
1.08 Eurostat

Prague

2.01 Statistical Yearbook of Prague 2017;
Eurostat
2.02 Statistical Yearbook of Prague 2017;
OpenStreetMap
2.03 Population projections of the Republic of Serbia 2011–2041;
Eurostat
2.04 Eurostat;
Municipalities and regions in the Republic of Serbia 2017
2.05 Statistical Yearbook of Prague 2017
2.06 Numbeo, www.numbeo.com
2.07 Prague Transportation Yearbook 2016
2.08 Eurostat

Berlin

3.01 Berlin. Statistisches Jahrbuch 2017;
Eurostat
3.02 Kleine Berlin Statistik 2017 (in English);
OpenStreetMap

3.03 The Cultural and Creative Cities Monitor
3.04 Statistical Office of the Republic of Serbia;
Berlin. Statistisches Jahrbuch 2017;
Štatistická ročenka hlavného mesta SR Bratislavy 2017;
Hungarian Central Statistical Office;
Statistical Office in Katowice;
Statistical Yearbook of Prague 2017;
Statistical Yearbook of Warsaw 2017;
Municipalities and regions in the Republic of Serbia 2017
3.05 Berlin. Statistisches Jahrbuch 2017
3.06 Numbeo, www.numbeo.com
3.07 Berlin. Statistisches Jahrbuch 2017
3.08 Eurostat

Belgrade

4.01 Municipalities and regions in the Republic of Serbia 2017;
Statistical Yearbook of the Republic of Serbia 2017
4.02 Municipalities and regions in the Republic of Serbia 2017;
OpenStreetMap
4.03 Tabellenbericht zum Forschungsprojekt „Mobilität in Städten – SrV 2013" in Berlin;
Balázs Mór Plan 2014–2030, Budapest Mobility Plan, Volume I: Objectives and Measures;
TEMS – The EPOMM Modal Split Tool;
Územný generel dopravy hl. mesta SR Bratislavy;
Wieloletni plan rozwoju zintegrowanego systemu transportowego miasta Katowice 2015;
Warszawskie Badanie Ruchu 2015;
Prague Transportation Yearbook 2016
4.04 Numbeo, www.numbeo.com
4.05 Municipalities and regions in the Republic of Serbia 2017
4.06 Numbeo, www.numbeo.com
4.07 Municipalities and regions in the Republic of Serbia 2017
4.08 Statistical Yearbook of Belgrade 2016

Katowice

5.01 Statistical Office in Katowice;
Eurostat
5.02 Statistical Office in Katowice;
OpenStreetMap
5.03 Municipalities and regions in the Republic of Serbia 2017;
Eurostat
5.04 Municipalities and regions in the Republic of Serbia 2017;
Berlin. Statistisches Jahrbuch 2017;
Štatistická ročenka hlavného mesta SR Bratislavy 2017;
Hungarian Central Statistical Office;
Statistical Yearbook of Prague 2017;
Statistical Office in Katowice;
Statistical Office in Warsaw
5.05 Statistical Office in Katowice
5.06 Numbeo, www.numbeo.com
5.07 Statistical Office in Katowice
5.08 Eurostat

Budapest

6.01 Hungarian Central Statistical Office;
Eurostat
6.02 Hungarian Central Statistical Office;
OpenStreetMap
6.03 Statistical Yearbook of Budapest 2015;
Statistical Office of the Republic of Serbia;
Berlin. Statistisches Jahrbuch 2017;
Štatistická ročenka hlavného mesta SR Bratislavy 2017;
Statistical Yearbook of Warsaw 2017;
Database of cultural facilities, IPR Prague;
Katowice City Hall, Department of Culture
6.04 Statistical Yearbook of the Republic of Serbia 2017
6.05 Hungarian Central Statistical Offilce
6.06 Numbeo, www.numbeo.com
6.07 Hungarian Central Statistical Office
6.08 Eurostat

Warsaw

7.01 Statistical Yearbook of Warsaw 2017;
Eurostat
7.02 Statistical Yearbook of Warsaw 2017;
OpenStreetMap
7.03 Statistical Yearbook of Belgrade 2016;
Kleine Berlin Statistik 2017 (in English);
Štatistická ročenka hlavného mesta SR Bratislavy 2017;
Hungarian Central Statistical Office;
Statistical Office in Katowice;
Statistical Yearbook of Prague 2017;
Statistical Office in Warsaw
7.04 OECD
7.05 Statistical Office in Warsaw
7.06 Numbeo, www.numbeo.com
7.07 Statistical Yearbook of Warsaw 2017
7.08 Eurostat

Olja Triaška Stefanović 48–59, 66–71, 75, 90–101, 136–145, 164–173, 204–213, 232–241, 261–263, 266–275
Academy of Fine Arts and Design in Bratislava 66–71
Faculty of Architecture of the Czech Technical University in Prague 67
2021 Architects (CC BY-NC-SA 3.0) 76–79
Goethe-Institut/Petra Hajská 106
ifau Berlin 106–107
reSITE 111, 112
Lydia Karagiannaki 113
Anastasia Eggers and Ottonie von Roeder 114–115
raumlaborberlin 149
Markus Ambach 150–151
Konrad Braun 150–151
Nabil Sami 151
KUNSTrePUBLIK 152
umschichten 153
Čuvari parka 180–181
Medialab Katowice (CC BY 4.0) 217–223
Hungarian Contemporary Architecture Centre – KÉK 245–253

The *Shared Cities Atlas. Post-Socialist Cities and Active Citizenship in Central Europe* is the final result of the *Shared Cities: Creative Momentum* project taking place in Belgrade, Berlin, Bratislava, Budapest, Katowice, Prague, and Warsaw.

Shared Cities: Creative Momentum (SCCM) is a European cultural platform addressing the contemporary urban challenges of European cities. SCCM is a joint project of Goethe-Institut (DE), Czech Centres (CZ), reSITE (CZ), Academy of Fine Arts and Design in Bratislava (SK), Association of Belgrade Architects (RS), Hungarian Contemporary Architecture Centre – KÉK (HU), Katowice City of Gardens (PL), KUNSTrePUBLIK (DE), Mindspace (HU), Old Market Hall Alliance (SK), Res Publica – Cities Magazine (PL). Co-funded by the Creative Europe Programme of the European Union.

www.sharedcities.eu
#SharedCities, #SCCM2020

Co-funded by the
Creative Europe Programme
of the European Union

Edited by Helena Doudová
Data Research Karol Piekarski
Data Design Paulina Urbańska, Waldemar Węgrzyn
Research Assistant (Data Stories) Milota Sidorová
Editorial Assistant Elizabet Kovačeva
Photography Olja Triaška Stefanović
Publication Coordination Stefanie Heublein, Kamil Pavelka

Copy Editing Leo Reijnen (Taal & Teken)
Design SJG/Joost Grootens, Dimitri Jeannottat
Printing Unicum
Publisher Eelco van Welie, nai010 publishers, Rotterdam

Printed and bound in the Netherlands

ISBN 978-94-6208-521-3
NUR 648, 758
BISAC ARC010000, SOC026030

nai010 publishers is an internationally orientated publisher specialized in developing, producing and distributing books in the fields of architecture, urbanism, art and design. www.nai010.com

nai010 books are available internationally at selected bookstores and from the following distribution partners:
North, Central and South America: Artbook | D.A.P., New York, USA, dap@dapinc.com
Rest of the world: Idea Books, Amsterdam, the Netherlands, idea@ideabooks.nl
For general questions, please contact nai010 publishers directly at sales@nai010.com or visit our website www.nai010.com for further information.